PENGUIN BOOKS

BERMONDSEY BOY

After a short spell in the merchant navy, Tommy Steele rose to fame in 1956 as Britain's first home-grown rock 'n' roll star. He went on to have a long career in stage and film musicals, starring in *Half A Sixpence*, *Hans Andersen*, *Singin' in the Rain* and *Finian's Rainbow* to name but a few, and most recently in *Scrooge* at the London Palladium. He lives in South London.

Bermondsey Boy

Memories of a Forgotten World

TOMMY STEELE

PENGUIN BOOKS

PENGUIN BOOKS

Published by the Penguin Group
Penguin Books Ltd, 80 Strand, London WC2R 0RL, England
Penguin Group (USA) Inc., 375 Hudson Street, New York, New York 10014, USA
Penguin Group (Canada), 90 Eglinton Avenue East, Suite 700, Toronto, Ontario, Canada M4P 2Y3
(a division of Pearson Penguin Canada Inc.)
Penguin Ireland, 25 St Stephen's Green, Dublin 2, Ireland
(a division of Penguin Books Ltd)
Penguin Group (Australia), 250 Camberwell Road, Camberwell, Victoria 3124, Australia
(a division of Pearson Australia Group Pty Ltd)
Penguin Books India Pvt Ltd, 11 Community Centre, Panchsheel Park, New Delhi – 110 017, India
Penguin Group (NZ), 67 Apollo Drive, Mairangi Bay, Auckland 1310, New Zealand
(a division of Pearson New Zealand Ltd)
Penguin Books (South Africa) (Pty) Ltd, 24 Sturdee Avenue, Rosebank, Johannesburg 2196, South Africa

Penguin Books Ltd, Registered Offices: 80 Strand, London WC2R 0RL, England

www.penguin.com

First published by Michael Joseph 2006
Published in Penguin Books 2007

1

Copyright © Tommy Steele, 2006
All rights reserved

The Acknowledgements on p. 309 constitute an extension of this copyright page.

The moral right of the author has been asserted

Typeset by Rowland Phototypesetting Ltd, Bury St Edmunds, Suffolk
Printed in England by Clays Ltd, St Ives plc

ISBN: 978-0-141-02802-6

for Darbo

Foreword

After I had celebrated the fiftieth year of rock and roll at the *Royal Variety Performance*, I was quizzed at the press conference on my beginnings in showbusiness.

According to theatrical record, I gave my first public perform-ance at the Empire Theatre, Sunderland, in the winter of 1956. On the other hand, the *History of Rock* has my début during the summer of that year, in the basement of the Two I's coffee bar, Soho, London. Yet again there is a fleet of merchant seamen who would swear on a gallon of grog that it took place on the after deck of the *Queen of Bermuda* in the spring of 1954. All wrong, I'm afraid. The truth is I played my first part on a steam train heading for Goodwood in 1946. My stage was a clattering corridor, my audience an elderly ticket collector with a Hitler moustache and suspicious eyes. At that moment I felt the thrill of the theatre for the first time. It never left me.

Tommy Steele
London Palladium
2006

The summer of 1946 was a full year after the end of the Second World War, and for me as a nine-year-old nothing much had changed in London. Rationing was the constant excuse for just about everything and, in spite of the Luftwaffe's best efforts, school was still open. I lived by the docks in Bermondsey, a place that even in August stayed grey and solemn. It lies to the south-east of London, built close to the Thames, and nowadays it boasts modern houses, flats and high-tech workshops, a transformation that has equalled the magic of a fairy godmother.

In medieval times this vast area, combined with Southwark, was the domain of the bishops of Winchester. They ruled it like a private kingdom, but it was not a realm of pride or honour 'but a pisse pot 'neath the arse of the City'. In other words, if the great City didn't want something, it got chucked over the Thames into 'the stews' of Southwark. Bear-baiters, cock-fighters, brothel-keepers and actors, all dragged themselves before the bishops and paid the going rate to set up shop in safety. Through centuries of bad press Bermondsey has gazed over the Thames like an innocent bystander, watching alleged traitors enter the gates of the Tower, seeing the smoke and flames of the Great Fire, then the rise of a brave new city.

Somehow even now, as you look across at Wren's immaculate spires and the work of New Age architects, you may wonder whether Bermondsey was forgotten during the shaping of things. Apart from the welcome modernization of the docks, the place is still pretty well stuck in the nineteenth century. It was a busy borough, this Bermondsey, and a happy place, the place of my birth and my father's before me.

★

Thomas Walter Hicks, also known as Darbo, was born in 1901. The family lived in Pits Head, a cul-de-sac off the notorious Pages Walk, an alley close to the Old Kent Road. Pits Head was always dark, its early-Georgian two-storeyed terraced houses had moved so close, with the soft ground, that the upper-floor windows almost touched those on the other side of the cobbled street. A stable at the end of the dwellings held the two magnificent horses that pulled my grandfather around the area, delivering coal. The house next to the stable's dung-heap was the family home, two rooms on each floor plus an outside lavatory. My grandparents and their fifteen kids slept in three rooms; the fourth, the scullery, was used for cooking, eating, washing and congregating.

In Victorian times Pages Walk was the equivalent of one of today's no-go areas: strangers, borough officials and police were not welcome there. On the rare occasions when a couple of coppers (they always walked in pairs) ventured into 'The Walk' they were grabbed, stripped and allowed to leave, suitably reminded not to come back. It was rough and tough and it was my grandmother Martha's pitch. She was a bookie's runner. In those times, off-course betting on dogs and horses was against the law. The only way a punter could get a bet on was either to go to the races or to seek out the illegal runner. It was a simple ritual: write your selection on a slip of paper, wrap up your stake money in it, go down Pages Walk and put the package into Martha's hand. Then at two p.m., before the racing started, she would take her handbag full of wagers and give it to the bookmaker in the Prince Tec pub. For this she received a bit of silver and, according to Darbo, spent the lot on snuff and Guinness.

Darbo didn't like his mother, but his young sister Mary was the light of his life. When he was eleven he protected her, fed her and clothed her. It was a well-known joke in The Walk that when the Jewish traders in the nearby market yelled, '*Gonif, gonif!*' Mary Hicks was about to get a new dress. Anything that Darbo could do for her, he did.

On one occasion just before the First World War, officialdom got through to The Walk. Martha was ordered to send all her children below the age of thirteen to school – by law. She told Darbo and Mary, grudgingly, to turn up at Webb Street School. 'So's I don't get no bleedin' trouble,' Martha told them, caring less about the education of her kids than about her position in the neighbourhood.

The sudden shock of being in a school was nothing like the embarrassment Darbo and Mary suffered on their first day: the whole place laughed at them because they had no shoes. It was nothing unusual for the Hicks kids to be barefoot, but to anybody else, especially children, it was a funny sight. Darbo and his sister were taunted and tormented – but only on that first day. Darbo wouldn't let it happen again. The next morning he crept into the Bermondsey market-place. The traders were gathered round their barrows, sorting their wares for the deals of the day. He crawled under the wheels and slowly made his way to the shoe stall. There he sat, listening to the traders talking in Yiddish, waiting for his chance to lift two pairs without discovery. Eventually the voices faded down the road. Darbo rose from the depths and grabbed what he wanted, but before the leather had cleared the pile, the cry came, '*Gonif, gonif!*' Darbo, though, was swift and determined. He reached The Walk safely ahead of his yelling pursuers, who daren't chase any further.

When he slowed to catch his breath he saw a team of urchins playing cards on the pavement. That day Mary went on to school in her new shoes while Darbo sold his for twopence and joined the card players. He did so well that within a week he was running the game and earning a living. He never went to school again. And, because officialdom wasn't welcome in The Walk, nobody complained – not even Martha, who was too busy taking bets to care.

As a little boy I had strict orders from my dad that I must never pass Gran without giving her a kiss. As she sat outside her little hovel in Dockhead she was always dressed from head to toe in black. She terrified me. Well into her eighties, she glared at any-one who came within striking distance. Brown lines of snuff ran from her nose towards her upper lip, her teeth were alternate gaps

and her left hand, gnarled with arthritis, gripped her purse while
the right played with a dark brown handkerchief that had once
been white.

'Allo, Gran.'

'Why?'

'Cos you're my gran.'

'Who are you?'

'I'm Darbo's boy.'

'Darbo?'

'Yes.'

'You little bastard, leavin' me here with all these bleedin' kids.'

She thought I was Darbo her husband.

'No, I'm Tommy.'

'Tommy? Come closer.'

I went as close as I dared. She peered at me like she was searching
my very soul. 'So you're Tommy.'

'Yes.'

Pause.

'You little bastard, leavin' me here with all these kids!'

Then she did what she always did: she wiped her nose with the
hankie, poked her fingers into her purse and pushed a silver sixpence into my hand. 'Go get me a Guinness,' she would mumble,
and as I dashed across the road towards the Ship Aground I'd hear
her usual cackle. 'And don't piss off wiv me tanner.'

I would return dutifully with her drink and the change. Then
she would dangle a penny in front of me. ''Ow about a kiss, then?'
she would murmur, and I knew I'd have to deliver. My lips were
going to have to touch that creased face. Her cheekbones poked
out at me like spears, threatening to cut my throat if I came any
closer. But I went closer, cos she was my gran and I had my dad's
orders.

So there she sat, day after day, year after year, Guinness after
Guinness. I never saw her stand. The only sign of life in her vicinity
was the shadowy figure of a thin, sinewy man with a gaunt face
and peppery hair, who shifted slowly in and out of her ever-open
door without word or eye-contact. Unmarried and unhurried, he

lived with the old girl without exchanging so much as a by-your-leave. The only sign of his involvement with anything of import seemed to be the brown-paper parcel that was always under his arm. On the odd occasion when I came face to face with him in the street or a shop, he would hold his parcel tight into his ribs and touch his lips as if we shared a secret. One day my curiosity found its tongue.

'Who's that, Gran?'

'Who's who?'

'That man in your passage.'

'That's my 'Arry.'

'What does he do?'

She paused for thought and sprinkled a pinch of snuff on to the back of her hand. Then, betwixt the sniff and the sneeze, she dragged my ear close to her lips and whispered, 'He knows where they lay!'

Dad was next on my list.

'Nobody knows!' He grinned. ''E's just our 'Arry.'

'But the parcel, Dad, it must be somethin'?'

'Like what?'

'Like something . . . laying!' I cried.

'Exactly.' He returned to his newspaper. In fact, Harry was my father's older brother, my uncle.

One summer day, listening to *Family Favourites* on the radio, my mum was knitting with my cousin Rosie, who lived with my aunt Mary in the flat above my gran. I decided that maybe she knew what 'Arry knew was 'laying about' somewhere. 'Sovereigns!' she whispered. 'Rumour tells that the old girl gave 'Arry a queen's ransom of golden sovereigns to keep safe for the family to share when she pops her clogs.'

Back to Darbo.

'What's "pop your clogs", Dad?'

''Ovis!' he exclaimed. 'Brown bread! Dead!'

'So it's all laying in that parcel, then?' I ventured. 'A queen's ransom of gold, to share with the family. How much do you reckon we'll get, Dad?'

'I'll tell you what,' he said, 'if you can leave me alone for five bleedin' minutes, you can 'ave my share, all right?'

So that was where the secret lay, until our 'Arry popped his 'Ovis one wet winter day. Mum was given the job of unwrapping the parcel. She made it last for ever, but it was more out of respect for 'Arry than to annoy the family standing in a ring round her. Finally the treasure was revealed. But it wasn't gold, it was silver. A faded silver frame, holding the photograph of a young girl with a lovely smile and long dark hair. Nobody recognized her. Even so, Mum placed the picture in Harry's coffin with the pressed flower that was hidden behind the frame.

It was in 1957, at the age of ninety-six, that Gran went for that great Guinness in the sky. That day, as I stood at the bottom of her bed, she looked like a wax dummy with her arms crossed in front of her.

'She looks like she's holding a baby.' A neighbour sighed.

'Well, she never held me,' Aunt Mary murmured.

'Me neither,' Darbo said, 'unless it was by the throat.'

When it came time for the funeral Mum took Darbo to one side and laid down the law. 'With our Tommy's success and everything,' she insisted, 'we can afford to pay for the funeral and the tea, and the cars and the stone and everything. It's only right.'

'How about the sovereigns laying about?' I asked, still wide-eyed after all the years of waiting.

'There's no sovereigns!' Mum laughed.

'Maybe a few bent coppers,' Dad cracked. 'If there's anything there they can 'ave it, with my compliments.'

But at Martha's funeral he was cracking on the other side of his wallet. During the tea, a nosy cousin found a box in the back of Gran's undies drawer: four hundred pounds' worth of gold sovereigns came to light, sending Mum into fits of laughter, and Darbo to the pub with envy in his heart and Hovis on his mind.

In the summer of '46 we were living at 52 Frean Street, and horseracing, the sport of kings, was at last returning to its glory days. The survivors of the war were flocking to the racecourses

Me and my gran (aged ninety-three) at the family home in Frean Street.

and, as a racing man, my dad was coming into his own – hence a request that came as a surprise to me and as an earth-shattering shock to my mother. 'But why do you want him to go to Good-wood Races all of a sudden?' she asked suspiciously.

My father gave his usual answer to questions he didn't welcome: a rub of the hands and a twinkle in his dancin' eyes. That was exactly what they did: they danced mischievously, especially when he was 'caught previous'. Previous to what, I never did discover but, knowing my dad, 'caught' was the operative word and 'not to be' his motto. I forget the excuse he made to get me out of the

house that Saturday morning but it took me on to the smoke-filled
concourse of Victoria station. This was the first time I had been
allowed to go on such an adventure. I was his eldest son, bound
for the races, and about to perform in public for the first time.

The Victoria station of my youth was that of the old black-and-
white movies: jam-packed with civilians and military, the high
cathedral roof filled with ever-descending smoke, and the station
announcer's voice echoing destinations in Swahili. Dad led me in
and out of the crowds. 'Do as you're told, don't ask questions, and
don't tell your mother,' he growled.

'Tell her what?'

'Anyfin'!'

Bouncing along on the tips of his toes, he moved gracefully in
spite of his size. At forty-five, he was short, fat and prematurely
bald, not unlike an athletic Churchill. He was so light on his feet
that when he danced at parties people stopped to watch, and he
sang with the same gusto.

Once across the concourse we came to the station buffet. There,
huddled in the far corner, stood three enormous men who, in spite
of the summer, were wearing heavy overcoats. 'They're your
uncles.' Dad smiled. 'Garlic, Nibbler and Lumps.'

The three giants beamed and gave me a combination of hair-
ruffles, handshakes, and friendly pats that felt like going the distance
with Joe Louis. From whatever side of the family these 'uncles'
came, they were strangers to me. They joked with each other
constantly, and when one wasn't pinching my cheek, another was
draping a gigantic arm round my neck. But it was their names that
intrigued me: Garlic, Nibbler, Lumps – it seemed that every man
known to my dad had a nickname, including Dad himself. God
knows how many times I'd asked him why he was called Darbo.
He always gave the same explanation. 'Cos I'm Tommy Hicks,
and my dad was Tommy Hicks, and so was his dad, and we was
all called Darbo.'

'But I'm Tommy Hicks so why ain't I Darbo?'

'Cos you ain't.'

And that was Darbo, never a great conversationalist. His life was

My dear dad Darbo.

like the Dark Ages: things happened to him, but whatever they were, they were between him and the Venerable Bede.

That Saturday in the buffet on Victoria station, he and the uncles were making their arrangements. They talked in a mixture of the King's English and rhyming slang. The slang has been part of Cockney folklore since the eighteenth century. Local footpads and burglars, ever wary of thief-takers, made it up as a code. Like all mysteries it was simple, once you knew the answer. For instance, if you want to say 'wife', you give the word a rhyme, '*trouble and strife*', then take away the rhyming word '*strife*' and you're left with '*trouble*'. Simple, isn't it?

Meanwhile, back at the buffet . . .

'On account of us being boracic,' Darbo said, 'we're going to have to work the oracle. It's a big rattler so there's bound to be a couple of khazis. So, on account of the saucepan, once we're on, it's going to have to be Waafcap.'

They all grinned at me as we walked out on to the concourse. Garlic bought five platform tickets at a penny each, which allowed us on to the platform of the Goodwood train but not on to the train. There we spread out, mingling with the host of other travellers until the guard blew his whistle and waved his flag. At that moment we jumped on to the moving train as it puffed out of the station. Swinging and swaying along the corridor we arrived at the first khazi.

'Waafcap,' Nibbler muttered.

Garlic pulled a Women's Auxiliary Air Force cap out of his pocket and stuffed it into my hands. 'Keep hold of that and dwell here outside the rory,' Darbo said, giving me a reassuring smile. Then he and the uncles dived into the khazi, slamming the door behind them. The sign above the lock snapped to 'Engaged'.

Silence.

I swayed for about ten minutes until the ticket collector arrived. 'Tickets, please,' he sang.

But I didn't have a ticket, just a Waaf's cap. He stopped for a second, studying me, then the cap, then the engaged sign on the door. Then, having put three and three together, he walked on by. As far as he was concerned, the Waaf in the loo had the tickets and he wasn't about to hang around waiting for her to finish. No sooner had he vanished into the next corridor than Darbo, me and the uncles were legging it towards the other end of the rattler and safety.

When we arrived at Goodwood station the boys went into the 'he's got it' routine, which was to get us off the platform. With the crowd of other passengers, we bundled our way past the mesmerized ticket collector at the end of the barrier, each uncle referring to an imaginary friend behind, saying, 'He's got it!' And even if the poor bloke rumbled the trick, it was too late. We were out of the station and following the throng to the races. The uncles strode out flushed with pride at their success, tracked by me, soaked with sweat and breathless as I fought to catch up.

Once they were on the racecourse the lads separated to go about their various tasks. Nibbler was a tic-tac man (he made arm signals used by bookmakers to transfer wagers). Lumps was a bookie's clerk, Garlic was a dip (pickpocket) and Darbo was a tipster, which meant he worked the crowds hoping to find a toby who would pay for inside information: this was a punter who believed that my dad knew something about the next race that nobody else did, and was daft enough to pay him for the privilege. It was called giving the fanny. Take, for example, a lone farmer head deep in his race card, pencil in his mouth, walking aimlessly in all directions, finally coming to rest by a Tote window waiting for divine intervention. Up comes Darbo.

Darbo: 'Did you back the winner in the last race?'

Farmer: ''Fraid not.'

Darbo: 'I did. I got it at seven to two.'

Farmer: 'It came in at two to one.'

Darbo: 'I backed it antepost, as soon as I got the information.'

Farmer: 'Information?'

Darbo: 'Yeah, I've got another horse for this race – then I'm off home.'

Farmer: 'But there's a full day's racing yet.'

Darbo: 'Not for me. I only bet on what I'm told. After the race I'm off.'

Pause. Darbo stood there studying his card, waiting for one of two reactions from the farmer: if he walked away, all was lost – but should he stay . . .

Farmer: 'What do you fancy, then?'

Darbo looked around carefully before confiding.

Darbo: 'It's not what I fancy it's what I *know* – give me your card.'

The farmer would hand it over gratefully. Darbo would 'mark his card' by ticking the name of the selected horse, then return it to the man's hands.

Darbo: 'I don't want anything from you for this – but if you like you can put a bit of silver on it for me.'

Away the farmer would go, heading for the Tote window to place his bet on a horse that Darbo only *hoped* might win – because if it did, then not only would he collect his winnings from a grateful punter but he would stay for the rest of the meeting under the pretence that more information had come his way. And if Lady Luck was still lurking, he might even pick another winner for the farmer with more than just a bit of silver on it – this time mebbe a couple of quid.

That was the happy end to the story.

The sad end was to be nobbled by the course stewards and ordered off the premises or even arrested for illegal touting. But there were more happy endings than sad: those boys were seasoned professionals, always on their guard, watching for stewards and farmers, safe because there were more of the latter every time.

When we reached the course, Darbo and the uncles parted company – they never hunted in packs. Garlic handed Dad a small carrier-bag, the three gave my hair a mass ruffle, then disappeared into the crowd.

Whatever money Dad had in his pocket got us through the public entrance, but that was not where he wanted to be: his eyes were on Shangri-La, the paddock. That clipped green carpet of elegance was no more than a hundred yards from where we stood but, owing to our financial circumstances, it might as well have been a million miles away. Darbo meant to get there, though, in spite of the hazards of which there were three: the Silver Ring, Tattersalls, and the members' grandstand, leading to the paddock. We had to pass into and out of each area undetected.

First from the public area into the Silver Ring: to achieve this we ducked under the rail between the enclosure and the racetrack, then followed the rail to the Silver Ring, which we entered without any trouble. Next, from the Silver Ring to Tattersalls – this would be harder: sharp-eyed stewards allowed entrance only when they saw the badges on lapels of legitimate holders. They were ever-watchful sentries, except when a race was running. Then the entrance was vulnerable – but just during the last thirty seconds to the finish. During this exciting moment only a cold fish could have ignored the thrilling climax; the mob yelling, jockeys with hands and heels pushing their magnificent steeds to the line, whips cracking, silks flapping. That was our chance, when the sentries' eyes were away to where the action *wasn't*. The time came and, like a flash, we were past the gate into Tattersalls and the members' grandstand. Only the paddock to crack now, and that was a walk-over. Beneath the impressive structure of the stand there was a four-foot-high open section. Only the thick iron stanchions buried in the concrete foundations barred our way. I passed them with no trouble. Darbo's short fat frame made hard work of it. We stopped a few times while he got his breath and dried a gallon of sweat off his red face. But eventually we reached the paddock end of the hazard. And there, hidden from view, we stayed for one more race. During this time the task of the day was explained to me.

'I've got a bit of business,' Darbo began, 'and I want you to do something for me.' He unpacked the carrier-bag and took out a pair of riding breeches, a hacking jacket and peaked cap. He bade me change into the outfit. 'There's an ice waiting for me,' he went on, 'and I've told him I may have some information on a horse as I have a connection with its stable. Now, just in case he doesn't believe the story, I've got a meet with him just before the big race in the paddock.' He studied my face for some sign of understanding – my eyes must have been bigger than saucers as I waited for him to explain *my* part in this adventure. 'So there we are,' he continued. 'Me and him are watching the runners saddling up, when all of a sudden I get a signal from the stable lad with the toffs around the favourite – you!'

Me! The heat started at my toes and hit the top of my head before I could draw breath.

'You don't have to do it if you don't want to,' he cautioned, 'but if you do I'd be obliged.'

I couldn't get the clothes on quick enough. The sheer excitement of this game was unbelievable. 'Once you get in the paddock, you don't say a dickie to anybody,' he went on, 'and if a toff comes up and asks who you are, tell him you're lost. Then they'll show you the way out and that'll be that, but if you're in the clear just stand by the horse and keep your minces open for me in the crowd. I'll wave to you, then all you do is touch your titfer and give me the thumbs-up. That's all – OK?'

Fifteen minutes before the start of the race we saw people moving towards the paddock and joined them. Two racehorses came from the direction of the stables; a steward at the entrance ticked off their numbers on a clipboard. Darbo gave me his mischievous smile and I was away, walking in with the animals, just an extra lad, there was no challenge. I was in. Within a few strides I was off the gravel and on to the manicured lawns of the centre circle.

It was slowly filling with all those connected to the next race. Horses, owners, trainers, head lads, friends, jockeys receiving final instructions – and me. My hands were trembling but I wasn't scared. I was excited. I prayed I wouldn't be challenged, and the longer I stayed there, the bigger the thrill of being someone I wasn't. For this one wonderful moment I was a real stable lad. I convinced myself I could ride a horse and one day I would be a jockey. I'd win the Derby and the Grand National on the same afternoon. And all those people watching from the paddock rail would know – 'Look at that lad,' they'd say. 'I wish I was him.' Well into my day-dream, I gazed at the host of faces watching from the paddock rail.

Then I saw Darbo, standing there with a man. He waved to me, as arranged, expecting my return signal. But his instructions seemed too easy, too quick. I wanted my part to be bigger than just a touched cap and thumbs-up. I needed a bit more to perfect my part – a horse!

And there it was, as if by order, right next to me, surrounded by well-wishers, the jockey mounting. I sauntered over to the animal's head where the real stable lad was holding its halter. He watched me in amazement as I held on to the other side of the bridle. I saw Darbo wave again in desperation. And now with my extra prop I was ready: I raised my cap and gave an enormous wave. Startled, the horse jerked its head and reared, tossing the jockey into the air, to land in the arms of the surrounding puzzled group.

Now came a chase in the true tradition of Mack Sennett. The horse was cantering over the lawn, scattering people in all directions, with the stable lad holding on to the bridle for dear life. The jockey followed, his little legs galloping in mid-air with owners and trainers in hot pursuit. But not only did *my* horse bolt, so did most of the other nags. There were horses everywhere, and people dashing about all over the place.

I had to get away.

Dad. I had to find Dad.

Thankfully he was still in the crowd. As I ran towards him I could see his face fixed like a white mask, the man beside him likewise. But even in my haste to escape, I remembered my part, and as I scampered past them I yelled, 'It's all right, Dad. It'll still win – honest.'

I left the disaster area without a caution, and even on the train home, Darbo didn't seem to mind. Apparently, in spite of the events of the day, our horse won by six lengths and we were going home with 'a bit of silver' in our pockets. I can still hear Nibbler, Garlic and Lumps laughing their heads off.

They were minor villains but they performed their misdemeanours with panache. On the odd occasions when they had their collars felt, they always smiled and went quietly. For me their tricks will always be a source of laughter – hilarious memories of unrelated uncles and beloved infidels.

We arrived back at Victoria in the early evening. Darbo hailed a taxi. It swung around in a dramatic U-turn and settled beside us like an ancient chariot. As it waited there the steady rattle of its engine clarified a mystery that had always been in the back of my mind. As a small child I had heard that sound in my dreams. Every now and again, late at night, I would be in my bed when that rattle came, like a siren call, in my subconscious. It was always followed by the street door opening and the sound of my mum and dad talking in excited whispers. Then I would hear Mum's wardrobe door opening and the rustle of clothes, the kindly voice of Mrs Martin from next door, the creak of the floorboards by my bed, followed by a warm motherly kiss on my forehead. Then the rattle would fade into the dark. But Mum was always there to wake me in the morning. So I knew that whatever had happened the night before was no threat to my happiness – but what *had* happened?

Now I had the answer: a taxi! It was Darbo's way to celebrate. 'Frean Street, Bermondsey,' he said.

The driver touched his cap, and my heart jumped with pride. The gears engaged, the rattle became a purr.

Now, as I winged homeward with Darbo in my taxi, I remembered that it was still Saturday. So much had happened, and it wasn't even dark yet. Eventually the chariot pulled into Frean Street. Its rattle drew most of the neighbours to their windows. The conquering heroes were home and Mum was at the door.

She waited until we were in the kitchen before she began the inquisition. 'Where? When? Why?' But all she got was what she had expected. Darbo and son had had a lucky day and the taxi was still waiting in the street to take them 'over the water' if she fancied it. Her excitement was like a breath of warm air. 'Can Tommy come?'

'"O" course.' Darbo grinned.

She ran next door to Mrs Martin, the babysitter. I heard them laughing in the street. Then she came back, grabbed my hand and dragged me playfully into the front room, the posh part of the house. It contained the upright joanna, the three-piece suite and a set of high-backed chairs with my dad's and my Sunday best shirts, neatly pressed and always at the ready for special occasions – weddings, funerals and the odd cabbage – then upstairs to her wardrobe. She took out my best suit and laid it on her bed, alongside her one good dress. 'Go wash your face and brush your hair,' she said.

A few minutes later I watched her and Darbo get ready. He gave a loud wolf-whistle every time she added something to the beautiful picture she made – lipstick (whistle), mascara (whistle), stockings (long, loud whistle, ending with a deep breath). She scolded him for that, and flushed. Eventually she was ready. She stood in the half-light of the bedside lamp like a real lady.

'D'you reckon that's it, then?' Darbo asked her, eyes full of mischief. Her hair was long and dark brown, falling in curls round her face, enhancing her strong, determined mouth and the vital blue-grey eyes that turned ice blue when she was tired – which, in my youth, was often. Like Darbo, she possessed a dazzling smile, and honesty shone out of her. She had the patience of an angel and the strength of a tank regiment.

Back in the taxi, I felt cocooned in luxury. At every red traffic-light I hoped a bus or tram would stagger to a halt alongside us so I could catch the eye of a passenger and pretend I was a millionaire on his way to the Palladium.

The Palladium!

That, above all else, was my ambition: one day I would go to the place to which, so far, only my imagination had taken me. But the Palladium was 'over the water' in the West End, and to go there involved a bus ride and crossing the Thames. To me, that was much the same as visiting a foreign country. 'Over the water' was over *there*, where St Paul's was, and the Houses of Parliament, the King and all kinds of pleasures and palaces. But I knew that one day, if I could ever get there, I'd make for that palace of all palaces: the Palladium.

The thrill of that journey was eclipsed when we drove past the Liberty store and round the corner into Argyll Street. In my wildest dreams I could not have pictured my great theatre in that pocket of a place – it sat tight among a host of shops and pubs. Vehicles crammed against each other in the narrow road, barely able to stay off the pavement, with hundreds of people spilling on to the thoroughfare, moving towards the oasis of light that was the Palladium. We left the taxi and joined a jovial mob of theatregoers. All around me were smiles and words of encouragement.

'Hope you get in, son.'

'Lovely night for a laugh, lad.'

My parents joined in the patter as if they knew everyone there. We moved onward, an inch at a time, towards the entrance. All of a sudden I was on the marble steps leading to the polished wood and shining brass. Then came the uniforms of the theatre staff, bright buttons, white gloves, their smiles of welcome, the box office and, finally, the auditorium. My shoes sank into the thick pile of the carpet – above me, chandeliers, and below, the live orchestra. Never had I seen such instruments – solid gold! There was a long roll from the big drums and the blood-red curtain flew up to reveal the blinding lights of the stage – and then the gods themselves.

That was my first evening at the theatre. Until that night I had lived between the pages of books and the sound of the radio, but now in the theatre it was all before me, live and in colour. All I had to do was watch and believe and dream of being on that stage! But how could I enter the world on the other side of the footlights? Wasn't it true that you had to be born backstage in a trunk to be a performer? When you could toddle, you walked on stage for the first time to a standing ovation, and when you were twelve you became Mickey Rooney.

But I hadn't been born in a trunk, and I wasn't Mickey Rooney. I was Tommy Hicks, eldest son of the two people sitting on either side of me, and just for a split second of a split minute, in the London Palladium on that Saturday night, I wished I wasn't.

2

The London Palladium! The theatre had become an obsession with me one Saturday soon after VE Day.

There was a bombsite on the corner of Tower Bridge Road. It had been there for years, ignored like all the other scars of the blitz, but that day there was a hive of activity around it. I sat on a nearby parapet and watched as a huge structure went up: it was a frame to hold a billboard, and once the banging had stopped they pasted on to it an enormous multi-coloured poster announcing, *The London Palladium Ace Variety Theatre of the World* and topping the bill was . . . *Tommy Trinder*, a legendary comedian with the catchphrase 'you lucky people'. But I'd never heard of the other acts like 'The Great Pollini – he fills the stage with flags!' or 'Igor Gridneff, the ladder man' or 'Elizabeth and Collins, Death on a Tightrope!' From then on, every Saturday morning I sat at the corner, waiting for the poster to be changed and imagining what the acts would do on the stage. But Saturday, 'my best day', had begun much earlier.

My first chore was to book the nine a.m. 'washing spot' at the Bermondsey Baths for my mum. It was the most popular time. Every wife in every household had their eye on it. To be in the washing hall at that hour meant that the family wash was finished in time for her to do the weekend shopping, the housework and cook the Saturday meal. To achieve this, I had to be one of the first in the line outside the huge tiled building that dominated Grange Road by six a.m. At five thirty on any given Saturday, Mum would be getting ready to go cleaning in the City, and I'd join her in the kitchen for the ritual of the mornin' cuppa. I can still taste it – the tannin bashing into the back of my dry morning throat, the aroma easing the sleep from my eyes, Mum fussing over bread cut like doorsteps that bulged with whatever was left in the outside larder box. Then, at the tram stop, her final order as she chased the 'iron maiden' down the hill. 'And don't let no one push in front!'

So, there I stood in the booking line, come rain, sleet or snow, anchored to the pavement, sandwiches in hand and a motto emblazoned on my brain: 'They shall not pass.' No matter if the line pushed, pulled, shoved or shifted – not even if a pregnant woman yelled for air – there I stood. That nine o'clock booking meant a lot and I wasn't budging. By five past eight I had the ticket clenched in my fist.

Then it was time for fun. First to Sampson's Tobacco, where they sold cigarettes by the single, to Mick's café for a mug of coffee, a fag and the *Champion*. It was the weekend boys' magazine, with the adventures of Johnny Fleetfoot, the Red Indian outside right, and Rockfist Rogan, the two-fisted fighter ace who always managed to win a boxing match just after shooting down a Doodlebug over London.

Soon Mum would appear for her ticket and I would follow her with the laundry to the washing hall at the baths. It took up the whole ground floor, and women in rag scarves moved like soldier ants in what looked like a film about Sing Sing Prison.

There was water everywhere. The walls ran with wet, the floors were a sea of puddles and the ceiling dripped like the trees in a rainforest. Before I could fill the steaming tub with clothes, Mum was like a wet flannel, and by the time she'd run the wringer, roasted at the drying rack and ironed it all, she could have swum home. But I never saw the end of the task: I was upstairs in another queue, waiting to enter the Street of a Thousand Bathtubs.

We had no bath at home, just the zinc Bismarck that hung on the kitchen door. But I wasn't a child any more, so sitting on the kitchen table to wash my privates wasn't on for 'my eldest', Mum said. So there I sat, towel in hand and pine needles (bath salts guaranteed to give out the scent of the South Seas, and at a penny extra, so they should) at the ready . . .

A buzzer jumped into life. The waterman appeared, a small chap with no hair – not even eyebrows. He wore a leather apron that started at his neck and finished at his ankles. He peered at you through huge glasses that were always misted over. They called him the Turtle.

'Number nine,' he would mutter, as you followed him into one of twenty tiny rooms with a bath, a cracked mirror and a nail on the door.

The door slammed shut. You locked it. You stripped. You stepped into the bath, which was already half full of clean warm water. You lay back and made an assessment. Then, having come to a decision, you yelled at the top of your voice, 'A drop more hot in number nine.'

Then you waited, sometimes a second, sometimes longer, depending on how many other orders were echoing round the walls.

'Drop o' cold in number two.'

'Bit of both in twelve.'

Outside the door you heard the clank of the Turtle's key in the water valve. Then the sudden gush of hot water, Poseidon's pee, and your privates took the shock. The pain passed. In went the pine needles, which melted, and the Saturday dreams began. Paradise!

Afterwards it was off for the poster ritual, then the walk up Tower Bridge Road to Joyce's Pie Shop for pie-and-mash, a real Cockney concoction of meat pie, mashed potato and a thick parsley sauce, called liquor. On to Edward's Bakery, for fresh doughnuts cooked as you watched, sizzling in the pan, then doused with a ton of caster sugar. Then it was time for the Saturday kids' matinée at the Trocette cinema which always began with the club sing-along: '*We come along on Saturday mornin', Greeting everybody with a smile . . .*'

For threepence, me and a thousand other kids piled into the picture-house for three hours of booing villains, galloping up and down the aisles and pelting Uncle Charlie on the Wurlitzer organ with empty ice-cream cartons as he disappeared into the depths of the orchestra pit – selections from Rimsky-Korsakov did not endear him to us. There was a mass charge for the exits, and home to tea – Camp coffee, cheese and tomato sandwiches and the radio, the box of wonder that had us transfixed till bedtime, just me and my mum.

She was born Elizabeth Ellen Bennett, in London in 1912, but always known as Betty. Her mother, Ellen, had died in childbirth and her father James looked after her, his only child, until he went to war in 1914. He returned home in 1917, badly injured, not from a bullet or a blast but from a kick in the head by a horse. My mum remembered his depressions, how he would sit alone in dark rooms, smoking his pipe. There were violent times too: Betty's gran and her aunt on Ellen's side were determined to take her away from him. As far as they were concerned, the man was not only sick, he was mad, staying indoors all the time, never giving them a welcome when they called, always disappearing into his damn room with his evil-smelling tobacco, stopping the child visiting them. Somehow they were going to get her away from him.

So they came round unannounced, with stern-faced official ladies in big feathered hats, who stood with them on the porch and waited for an answer to their knocking. Betty and her father would hide behind the wardrobe and wait for them to give up and leave. Eventually things caught up with them: James was presented with a summons. He had to prove he was a fit parent to raise a seven-year-old child, and began to despair. Then, during an interview with officialdom and his meddlesome in-laws, something was said: 'Course, if you could find a woman to marry you we wouldn't 'ave to worry, but she'd 'ave to be madder than you!'

The following spring he met and married Dorothea, a widow with two sons older than Betty. Mum's step-siblings were nowhere near as bad as the Ugly Sisters, but they resented their new father and avoided the little girl. Their mother, however, paid her more attention: she ordered her about and chastised her constantly. Betty's father was unable to interfere, still in his dark depression.

For my mother, the cleaning and general work she had to do was not as bad as combing her step-mother's hair. On those nights little Betty dreaded the summons to the parlour, where the 'witch' sat in front of a huge Victorian mirror in her dressing-gown, face washed and shining, a red ribbon in her long white hair. Standing on tiptoe, Betty would comb the tangled locks while the gramophone played grand opera. These summonses only came when the 'witch' was angry with Betty's father, and Betty knew that for every little knot she found and tugged, she would get a slap to her face.

Whenever my mother told this story she never showed any anger or sadness. She related it as if it were about someone else. 'You must have hated the old cow,' I said once, when I was much older.

'I suppose I did,' she said, 'but I didn't dare think about it, in case she suspected and made things worse, like telling my father I was a bad girl, which she did anyway.' After her father had been subjected to Dorothea's complaints, he would take his daughter aside and beg her not to upset the woman: she was making a home for a little girl and a sick man.

Before she was twelve he died. With her father gone, Betty stopped talking and sobbed all the time. She was offered no help until one night when she was lying on her bed thinking the thoughts that brought the tears. The door opened and two men in army uniforms came in. They smiled at her and indicated the window at the end of the room. Her father was standing there. He held out his arms to her. She went to him, no fear in her, just a child's need for a father's comfort.

'You're breaking my heart with all your crying, Betty,' he whispered, 'so I've come here to promise you that this unhappiness will not last. One day you will marry and you will have lovely children, a wonderful life and a loving husband, but first you must stop crying. To make things better, I'm going to send you a little friend.' Then he and the two soldiers left the room.

After that, there were no more tears. At the time she didn't tell a soul about his visit, but she took strength from it, and was determined to wait for her father to keep his promise.

She always told me the story at night, always by the fire and always when we were alone. And whenever she reached the point at which the ghostly soldiers would appear, I would snuggle close to her, watching the windows for my grandfather to come again. It wasn't a chilling thought and she never told the tale to scare me. It was something that had happened to her, and she shared it with a great pride. Sometimes I would mention the friend that my grandfather had said he would send. Then Mum's voice would change . . .

Every Sunday the witch took her two boys on their weekly visit to relatives. Betty was never included – nor did she want to be: they weren't her family, and besides with the others out for the day, she had a break from punishment – although she still had work to do. Sunday's chores were to blacken the grate and whiten the front step. Mum could never make up her mind in which order to do them. If she blackened first, she always had to scrub her hands so that the grate polish didn't mark the white step, and vice versa. Whichever way she approached the problem, she always ended up having to scrub her fingers till they stung. There seemed no way out of her dilemma – until Carrie came. 'That was the day I knew my father had kept his promise,' Mum whispered. 'He said he would send me a friend and there she was.'

She was peeping over the fence at the end of the garden, her hair soaked from a sudden downpour. The witch and the boys were still in the house putting their coats on. Betty watched the little girl for a time and gave her a shy wave, but she didn't wave back. Then she had to go to the front door to lock it behind the family. When she got back, the girl was gone. 'I thought that mebbe she was just a dream, there because I wanted her to be,' Mum said. 'Seeing her looking for me made me feel important. It was as if a special person had made a visit just for me.'

Mum could hardly wait for the next Sunday in case she saw her again.

At long last it arrived. The two boys dressed and prepared to leave the house. The witch sat at the mirror, glaring at Betty as she fought with the tangles in her hair. Eventually she gave an impatient sigh, snatched the comb out of her hand and sent her to the corner. If any of the children made her angry, she sent them there – to stand, with their backs to the room, in silence until they were told to move.

It was on that Sunday Mum saw Carrie again. From the corner where she was standing, she had a view of the back garden, and there at the fence she saw blonde pigtails bobbing up and down as the little girl tried to see over the top. The witch moved out of her chair and went towards the window. Mum closed her eyes and willed the little girl to go away in case she was discovered. When she opened them, the child had vanished. Then the witch was gone too, with the boys.

Betty went out into the garden and called to the visitor. But there was no answer – and time was flying. She still had her jobs to do, the step and the grate.

A few minutes later, the doorbell rang. And there she was, much smaller than my mum, with a serious chalk-white face. 'I'm Carrie,' she said, 'and as it's not raining today, perhaps I could whiten your step.' Every Sunday for the rest of Betty's childhood, the two girls met. And the witch never discovered their friendship.

By the time Betty was nearing her eighteenth birthday, she was working at a tin-box factory in Southwark. She was still living at home with the witch and the two boys, and she was becoming anxious about her future.

One Sunday Carrie mentioned a Mrs Stubbs, a strange woman in Streatham who, according to local rumour, was an amazing fortune-teller and not expensive. The only drawback was that they had to make an appointment to see her. There was no telephone, and no hope of an answer to a letter: all prospective clients had to call at her house, and wait in a small room next to another room with a large bed in it. In the bed was Mrs Stubbs, who slept constantly. However, now and again she would wake and yell, at the top of her voice, 'Send one in.' In some cases, the wait for that yell took days.

But when Carrie took Betty to the house, luck was with them: they had been waiting for less than an hour when the yell came, and my mother was ushered into Mrs Stubbs's den.

The old lady lay back on her pillows and studied the girl standing by the bed. 'Shuffle and lay the tarots on my eiderdown,' she
ordered.

Betty obeyed. The ancient cards revealed an array of frightening
images. Mrs Stubbs gazed into them. Then she took Betty's hand.
'Standing here today you will not believe the life you have before
you,' she began. 'It will be a life full of such wonderful things that
I could easily change places with you – except that I couldn't bear
the heartache that comes with it.' Then she fell back on to her
pillows, asleep. Betty crept towards the door. As she touched the
knob, Mrs Stubbs woke again and yelled, 'You'll marry in six
weeks.'

The possibility of meeting, falling in love with and marrying
someone who was still a complete stranger was so remote that
Carrie and Betty didn't pay much heed to the rest of Mrs Stubbs's
prediction. In six weeks? *A marriage?* Daft! It was intriguing,
though. Could such a thing happen so quickly because an old girl
in Streatham had said so? Where would this husband come from?
And how would he find his way to Betty? And even if he did,
would she like him enough to fall in love with and marry him?
And so fast?

Impossible! But it was fun to talk about in the tram going home.

Two weeks later, the prediction took shape.

Darbo had been invited to a party by two pub performers – Frankie
and Barry. Frankie was a superb pianist – 'He could syncopate
better'n anyone,' Darbo enthused – and Barry was the vocalist,
but one night, at a pub called the Gregorian Arms, Darbo invited
himself on to the podium to sing, *'Ain't misbehavin', I'm savin' my
love for you . . .'*

Frankie loved the phrasing Darbo gave to the song so he and
Barry took him to a cabbage in Peckham to sing it again.

Darbo told me about his first sight of Betty: 'She was sitting in
a corner with her mate. I knew I liked her – and I knew she was
listening. But when I finished the number, she carried on talking
and ignored me. I made a few inquiries anyway – she was so lovely.

But all anybody knew about her was that she was a tin basher at the Feavers Box Factory.

'I was boracic at the time, but I waited a couple of weeks till I had a few bob, then I stood outside the factory till she came out. When I saw her, I went up and said, "I've been waiting," and she said, "So have I." We got married two weeks later, on her eighteenth birthday.'

So, the Stubbs prediction had miraculously come to pass. Mum met Dad and her future had begun with the love and hope she had dreamed of. But the heartache was yet to come. It began two years later, in 1932, with the birth of her first child, Colin.

Their home was a flat in Mason Street, which is a tributary of the Old Kent Road. It had two rooms, and in the tiny bedroom, Betty gave birth to her son. He was a bonny boy, who had beautiful white hair, but at six months old he caught double pneumonia and whooping-cough. 'A mother can take most things when a child is suffering,' she told me, 'but that cough – that constant cough. I can still hear his exhausted cries as he tried to breathe between the convulsions. In the end his little lungs gave up – bless his heart.'

My parents were sad, but resigned to losing him. In the early thirties infant death was common, much more so than it is today. Diphtheria was rampant, with measles and polio, and when a child was lost – tragic as it was – it was more a matter of bad luck than of bad medicine.

I was born on 17 December 1936. Like my brother before me, I was full of bounce and blessed with the same mop of white hair. While Mum continued her part-time job at Feavers, Darbo was working in Soho, then a seedy part of London's West End. He was a minder at a nightclub called the Nest, the gathering centre for black entertainers.

When I was a week old, Darbo invited a crowd to the flat to celebrate, including the cast of *Blackbirds of '36*, an American revue, with the Nicholas Brothers and Cyril Lagey, the crazy percussionist from the comedy act the Nitwits. 'They was all your godfathers,' Darbo told me. 'Somethin' must 'ave rubbed off.'

When I was three my sister was born and named Betty after our

Me and my mum. Aren't I looking smart!

mother. She had chubby red cheeks, big blue eyes and that trade-mark of the Hicks children, a thatch of snow-white hair. Now we were four, Mason Street was no longer big enough. Luckily, most of Dad's family lived on the Dickens Estate and somebody knew somebody who knew somebody else, and we got moved to Nickleby House, Dockhead. In the passage at the new flat Mum now had that luxury of luxuries, a carriage perambulator, not to be confused with the usual 'prams' of the area. This vehicle was high, wide and handsome, polished to perfection and balanced on four wheels perfect for a a brace of princes. Betty lay at one end, resplendent on her down pillows, while I sat at the other admiring her. The pram was so well sprung that we bounced along with our white locks flowing, our proud mother at the helm, relishing her brood and accepting the hundred and one compliments that came with every shopping trip. Until that day in Borough High Street.

Mum was just about to go into Woolworths when an old lady opened the door for the pram. She stopped to admire little Betty and me. 'Such lovely hair,' she remarked, as she patted our heads. She hesitated over my sister, then parted her hair and studied the top of her forehead. 'This one's only lent to you,' she said to Mum, and walked away.

After her father's ghostly visit and Mrs Stubbs's predictions, my mum took this comment to heart. 'Lent? What did she mean, lent?'

'The old girl was probably mad or drunk or both,' Darbo counselled. 'Anyway, it's all a load of codswallop.'

But Mum couldn't leave it there: she'd already gone through the hell of losing one child and the prospect of parting with another was too terrible to contemplate. She took Betty to the Evelina Children's Hospital for an examination.

'What are her symptoms?' the doctor asked.

'There aren't any.'

'Then why is she here?'

'Just in case . . .'

She took the child home, relieved, but the dark thought

remained at the back of her mind, a nagging voice telling her that mebbe disaster was on the way. Or perhaps not: she discovered she was pregnant again – so mebbe the future was brighter than she'd feared.

A week later the Second World War started. *'The Germans are coming!'* Now things were changing fast.

3

Darbo saw his job in Soho fade away. Somehow, during that period called the phoney war, the night life that was our bread and butter died out: the Nest lost most of its American clientele. 'The Yanks just stopped coming,' he said. 'All the foreign stars in the big shows didn't want to risk being caught in the fighting so they stayed at home.' But during the phoney war there was little fighting – the antagonists faced each other, like kids in a playground, looked threatening but not much more – until Dunkirk. Now the balloon had gone up, and soon all the posters and radio warnings about air-raids and blackouts were fulfilled. The Germans were coming and we had to be ready.

Notices went up in the streets with huge arrows pointing to the air raid shelters. Gas masks were issued in adult and child sizes, and there was a terrible contraption for babies, which my mother flatly refused to use with my little sister. 'Looks like a bleedin' coffin,' she snapped, and threw the thing into the bottom of the wardrobe. 'If they bomb, they bomb, but I'll keep my kids in my arms.'

In midsummer they came. Total war, no quarter, the London blitz. Not a night went by without we were woken by the air-raid siren. Like the scream of a banshee, it was, warning of the coming Armageddon. Then the distant crump! crump! of early bombs, searchlights stabbing the dark sky, then deafening guns – and the flares of the Nazi pathfinders as they lit up the targets. Bombs fell on *our* streets, on *our* homes – killing *our* people.

Darbo would take baby Betty and the suitcase with the 'essentials', while Mum, heavily pregnant again, pulled me out of their warm bed and joined him in the panic of the streets. There was no time to dress before the rush to the public shelter at the end of the road.

> *Run bugger run*
> *Shout me mum*
> *Show your bum and hide your eyes*
> *Who's gonna look when house is shook*
> *And bombs is dropping from the skies . . .*

I dreaded those nightly runs, not for the death and destruction but because I was stark naked. It wasn't until we were safe in the shelter that Mum got me dressed. Then we would huddle with our neighbours, listening to the thumps and crunches outside. Every time a bomb fell close, a cloud of dust would fall on us from above. Everyone around us would try to guess which street had taken that particular hit, and whose house would now be rubble. Then, in the half-light, names were called.

'Are the Smiths here?' No answer.

'It sounded like Tabard Street.'

'The Smiths live there.'

'Well, they ain't here.'

'It was Tabard Street, no doubt about it.'

'And the Smiths definitely ain't here.'

Pause.

'Poor sods.'

The long night continued until the all-clear sounded.

Then we went up into the smoke-filled city, with dust-covered firemen standing on mountains of hot rubble, playing their brass spouts of gushing water on to the burning embers, and the air-raid wardens called out the names of the streets that were no more, warning us to watch out for craters in the roads, escaping gas and unexploded bombs. When daylight came, the children went to school, the parents went to work and the chaos of the night before was dealt with by the exhausted firemen, the ambulances and others who tried to put some dignity back into what had once been someone's home. Night after night the blitz raged; day after day there were sad tales to tell.

Until the day our luck ran out.

On a Monday in late summer, the afternoon was approaching

evening but the skies were clear. Mum, little Betty and I were shopping in the Old Kent Road. Suddenly the air-raid siren sounded. We left the shop and ran into the street, everywhere getting dark, just people running in silence, the wail of the siren and the coming enemy. We were crossing the street towards the shelter in Walworth Road when a speeding truck came out of nowhere. It just missed me, but hit my mum and the pram. They flew into the air like feathers as the bangs and flashes of the bombs lit the street. I stood by the battered pram, looking at my sister sleeping in a pool of blood on the pavement. A policeman and a warden were cradling my mum in their arms and all around the bombs were falling, but all I could hear was Mum's screams. The old lady had been right: Betty was only lent.

Once more there was sadness in our house, but compared to the sadness everyone else was feeling, we had one saving grace: Mum's pregnancy was intact despite the accident and she was now in her eighth month. Soon there would be something to cuddle. But with the continuing carnage of the blitz and Darbo's difficulty in making a living, it was decided that Mum and I would leave London and go somewhere safe for her to have her new baby.

'Cornwall's lovely,' Darbo enthused, 'and once you've had the saucepan you can come home. The war might be over by then.'

Well, Cornwall *was* lovely, but hardly friendly. It was February. The cottage we had to live in was in the middle of nowhere, a bleak part of the world, with nothing but hills, small paths through the odd clump of trees and the nearest neighbour a long walk into the mist. We arrived by horse and cart from the little village station late at night. There was no electricity and no heating, which didn't help. Then we discovered there was no mains water. Mum sat in the half-light of a candle, shaking and unwell.

'Are you 'aving it?' I asked.

'No, I just need some water.' She smiled.

But there wasn't any. The jugs in the kitchen were empty and outside in the yard there were just empty buckets, no water tap.

However, we could see light from a distant cottage. 'Could you go over there,' Mum said weakly, 'and ask for some water?'

I ran over craggy stones and wet marshland. By the time I reached the neighbour's house I was soaked to the knees. I knocked at the door. A woman opened it, her face lit by an oil lamp. 'I'm from next door,' I puffed. 'Can I borrow some water?'

The woman turned back into the dark. 'You'd better come in,' she murmured. Her West Country burr came to me like a foreign language. I followed her into a room where five people sat at a table playing cards. They stopped and stared at me.

'The boy wants water,' the woman said.

'We haven't got any,' a voice rasped from the table.

'But my mum ain't well,' I said.

A long pause, then the voice again: 'We have to walk for our water here.'

'My mum's gonna have a baby, and she's shaking and she wants a cuppa tea.'

Silence.

Then the woman who had brought me in pushed a milk bottle half full of water into my hand and led me back to the front door. 'Don't ask again,' she rapped. 'There's a path over there that leads to a well two miles away. You gets your water same as us.' With that she closed the door behind me.

I was six.

At first light the next morning Mum and I carried a tin bath the two miles to the well. The journey back was painful but funny. We made the mistake of filling it to the brim, so we could hardly make any headway and the water slopped over the edge, soaking our feet. We made it back to the cottage with a quarter of the original contents, but we were in fits of laughter. From then on, every time we went to the well, we used half of the water in splash fighting each time we stopped for a rest.

The time Mum and I spent in the cottage we filled with lots of laughter and games. She was only twenty-six, and had had three children but lost two before they were three. She was resilient, determined and strong.

While we were waiting for the baby to come, the war was still raging but we were away from it. Every Saturday we would go to the village, five miles in the opposite direction from the well, on the once-daily local bus. Mum would keep her appointment with the district nurse at the clinic next to the post office. We had a cup of milky Camp coffee and Spam 'n' chips in the tiny café, then went to the telephone box in the post office to make the long-distance call to the Bricklayers Arms for the chat with my dad in Bermondsey. She always called at one o'clock sharp when Darbo was guaranteed to be there, and I would listen to her telling him she missed him and wanted to come home. But the bombs were still falling, Dad wasn't making much money and, besides, the Cornwall cottage was cheap and safer than London. So we stayed on.

The weather in that part of the world can be harsh but there were lovely days too. On one spring morning Mum took the washing out and I held the pegs. Afterwards she sat by the porch. The sun was sharp and the sky clear. She fell asleep, and I looked at High Tor in the distance. To me it was a mountain, but it was probably no more than a hill. It was standing there, daring me to climb it. It had done that to me before, but the time hadn't been right. Now I was ready. This was the day.

I knew it would be a huge task so I decided not to tell Mum but I needed provisions for the trek. There was a biscuit in the kitchen and a can of water, so I was prepared. Mum was still asleep, so I took my opportunity and dashed for the hedges, then through a copse, across a field and into woodland. I went over the stream and up the bank, through the brambles, then on to the dusty beginnings of the tor. A glance back at the cottage: no sign of Mum waving or shouting for me, so I decided to have a rest before I made for the summit. The biscuit and the water vanished, then I made tracks. Eventually, fingers caked with dust, knees scratched and shoes scuffed to smithereens, I reached the top of the tor. The view was lovely: a winding river, dense trees, more tors, and I was above them all – a champion! In my mind I could hear bands playing and crowds cheering.

Then came the drone of an engine. I wasn't imagining that. I knew the sound – every boy did. The skies were filling with the power of the Merlin, the fastest aero-engine in the world, invented by Rolls-Royce and attached to the Spitfire.

Then it came – first a whistle, then a whine and then the plane zoomed over my head. It passed so close that I saw the pilot clearly. He had blond hair and a red face, no flying jacket, just his RAF tunic – I could even see the wings. He *waved* at me and smiled – and then, to top it all, he flipped over into a victory roll and revved his engine. Baroom! I strained my eyes as the fighter plane disappeared into a dot.

That night Mum sat by my bed and listened while I told and retold my tale. She believed me, but no one else ever did.

Pretty soon after my Spitfire, Mum went into labour. One night she woke me gently and pushed my hair back from my eyes – she always did that when I wasn't well. But this was different: *she* was in pain and unable to move too far. 'I'm going to need the district nurse,' she said.

'The one in the village?' I asked. She nodded, helping me to pull on my sweater.

'Are you 'aving it?' I blurted, expecting a newborn baby to appear as if by magic.

'There's that cottage you went to for the water,' she said. 'Go there, see if they can phone.' In spite of her outward calm, I could see my mother was in pain: she was very pale and doubled up. I dashed into the night. 'You be careful now,' I heard, as I turned from the gate and made for the 'cruel cottage'.

It was a strange night, not cold or rainy, just a weird wind blowing ominously in a low hum like a billion bees angry as hell and waiting to take vengeance. As I neared the neighbours', I could feel the wind following me, humming in my ears, trying to make me turn and run home. But Mum was 'aving it so I had to go on.

Then the cottage was before me, dark and unfriendly. I re-membered the woman and the card players and somehow I couldn't go the last few yards to the door. I knew they would tell me to go away, and it was late – they might hit me or worse. No, I wouldn't wake them, I decided. I'd go to the village. I took the path that led to the road with the bus stop. That wind was in my face now – I felt it was trying to stop me getting help for my mum. What with the noise and my fear, I became confused, couldn't get my bearings – where was the bus stop? The fact that there wouldn't be a bus at that time of night didn't occur to me. I crossed a field, climbed a small wall and I was deep in no man's land, with nothing but the dark and the wind, until at last I saw the bus stop, standing in silhouette like a gibbet.

I ran towards it and something grabbed me from behind, stopping me in my tracks. I wanted to scream but my voice wouldn't work – I just stood stiff, waiting for whatever would come next. Then, high above me, I saw the tall tree, its branches bending with the wind, creaking with each gust. The demon that had me by the neck was a branch. I tore myself free, the bus stop and the village forgotten. I wanted my mum!

I climbed up on to the slate wall and searched for the lights of our cottage. It was there, to the left, in the dark shadow of the High Tor. I ran towards it for what seemed like an age. But when I got there, the front door was wide open. I dashed into the little parlour. The fire was out and Mum's shawl was lying in the hearth. The front door was banging, and the wind was blowing into every corner.

Then, from upstairs, I heard a crash. I raced up – 'Mum! Mum!' I yelled. I went into the bedroom, but it was empty. A window was swinging on its hinges, but my mum was gone. I ran into every other room, all empty.

Where was she?

I went back out into the night. 'Mum! Mum!' I started to cry, more from frustration than fear. I had to find her. But which way should I go? Everywhere I looked had bending trees. The village, I decided, that's where she'll be. Once more I went into the wind, making for the road to the village, everything still dark.

Then I saw a figure. But it wasn't Mum: it was tall and huge and bounding towards me. I turned in panic and fled for my life.

Soon I felt heavy breathing on the back of my head. I stopped. An arm went round my shoulders. I fell back exhausted and gazed up into a man's face. 'It's all right, lad,' he said. 'I've been looking all over the place for you.' It was one of the card players from the 'cruel cottage'. 'We've got Mum back home.' He smiled. 'She's quite safe, and you've got a little brother.'

When we got there, our neighbours were fussing around kindly, and my little brother was safe and snug. He was named Colin, after the one who had died.

Soon afterwards we went back to London. Within a month me, my parents and baby Colin were blasted out of the flat in Nickleby House. We had to move into 'sheltered accommodation', which consisted of bunks or mattresses in church and drill halls around the borough. Eventually we went back to Nickleby House at Dockhead. Dockhead! Its name tells its story.

Our abode was at the head of the London docks so we were slap-bang in the centre of what the Germans were bombing. Once again I was making the naked runs to the shelter. While Darbo led the way with the new baby, Mum dragged me along behind. It was as if I was caught inside a huge firework, smoke and sparks making my eyes smart. There was the sudden crash of an explosion, then the musical ricochets of shrapnel clanging and whistling round the buildings that were still standing, and a heavy thud as the local ack-ack guns fired salvos at the silhouettes of Nazi bombers.

On one occasion I saw this often futile action make a kill. It was the night when the great church at the corner of Dockhead got a direct hit. The blast shattered every window in a half-mile radius, including those of Nickleby House. Mum came to my bed and told me not to move while she and Dad removed the mass of glass splinters from the blanket covering me. Outside the raid was in full swing.

'Out! Out!' Dad yelled, with Colin under his arm. And, once more, we were off into the firework.

The skies flickered an ever-changing orange. We came to the rubble that used to be the church – flames, firemen, police, parishioners, wardens. A great landmark had been destroyed. It was also the site of a public shelter, now surrounded by ambulances and distraught onlookers. Everyone knew that there was little the services could do: a direct hit of that magnitude left nothing to save or salvage.

'Bastards!' Dad growled. 'We'll have to go to Hays Wharf.'

That was the nearest shelter. It was well towards the river and the main battle, but it was our only chance. Across Jamaica Road we ran, down past the tea-houses and into the Hays. Above us, enemy parachutes hovered with flaming flares to guide the pilots to their targets – the whistle of a falling bomb, the drone of a plane pulling away, then the beam of a searchlight stabbing into it. Trapped! More lights joined the first. Now the plane seemed to be at the centre of a kaleidoscope.

Ack-ack-ack!

A flash of flame belched from its fuselage and its engine spluttered. It had been hit.

Mum, Dad and I stopped running. We watched the searchlight follow the stricken bomber down towards the Thames – I didn't hear the rest of the raid: my every sense was focused on the enemy getting back what it had been giving.

Suddenly the plane vanished behind the buildings. An ear-splitting crash was followed by a mushroom of high-explosive and petrol flames.

Darbo ran to the river's edge and yelled, 'And that's for bombin' our fuckin' chip shop!'

I was now nearly seven and there was an added inconvenience to the business of war. At the cinema I was always engrossed in the plot of whatever film we were watching, but also dreading the warning that would flash on the screen. It always came. 'There is an air-raid in progress.' Patrons could either continue to watch the film, or leave for somewhere safer. My parents always opted to leave.

No matter how much I moaned and no matter how close the film was to the end, we left. We went out into the street in search of a shelter, away from the magic of the movie into the reality of fire-engine bells, the whistles of the wardens and the *crump! crump!* of destruction.

We were doing the wise thing but I was a child – surely the last ten minutes of *Robin Hood* were better than this? But my folks were frightened that the cinema would be hit. They were right, of course – but not when Errol Flynn was about to dispatch Basil Rathbone in the final sword fight!

On my seventh birthday Mum took me to meet Carrie for the first time. We went on the bus to Deptford, and walked a dozen streets before we got to hers, with its tiny terraced Georgian houses. As I knew the Carrie story, I was a bit disappointed: I was more prepared for a tree-house, and when the front door opened I expected to see a little girl with blonde pigtails, but she was just like my mum. There was no mystery about her. She was warm and cuddly and giggled a lot. She had children, two girls, and a lovely big Old English Sheepdog. It was going to have puppies and she promised I could have one.

One Sunday, when the dog had had its litter, Mum took me to collect the promise. During the bus trip to Deptford I kept looking down at my empty hands and imagining a puppy in them. The long walk to Carrie's house felt like for ever, but at last we came to the final corner that would lead us into her street. I tore my hand away from Mum's and ran round it – to find that the line of terraced houses was gone. All that was left was a long, high pile of smoking rubble with firemen walking over it like ants. The street had received a direct hit during an air raid last night.

'No survivors,' a warden told Mum. 'They didn't know what hit them.' As he read out the names of the dead, I walked over to a heap of mangled sheets. On top of them lay the dead puppies and their mother.

My mum cried all the way home.

'But Carrie's a magic person,' I reasoned. 'She can't be dead. She wasn't on the sheets with the puppies.'

We revisited Carrie's bombed terrace on a few more Sundays, until Mum grasped the reality of her loss. Eventually a Sunday came when we didn't go. We searched through a box of photographs instead. When Mum found what she was looking for – a fading snapshot of three soldiers – she said, 'That's your grandfather,' and pointed to the handsome man in the middle. 'The other two were his best friends, both killed at the Somme. The last time I saw them together was the night my father came to my room, when he told me to stop crying and promised me a best friend.'

'Carrie,' I blurted out.

'No, it wasn't Carrie.' She smiled. 'It was you.'

The cuddle that followed those words will stay with me for ever.

Then I got sick.

4

I don't remember the symptoms, just the experience of being in a hospital. I had pneumonia and pleurisy. All my mum could think about was her dead babies, Colin and Betty, Mrs Stubbs's prophecy of heartache, and that old lady at Woolworths – 'just lent'.

Mum took me, a bundle of half-breaths, to St Olave's Hospital opposite the Rotherhithe Tunnel. It must have been frightening for her. It was for me.

It was night and strange faces looked down at me as I lay wrapped tight in blankets, flat on a trolley. Then I was moving along as if I was suspended on a great cushion of air. Long corridors, overhead lights flashing past, then a big wooden room with doors of clanging iron, like a prison. A mechanical whine and the room rising, like the great cranes in the docks, high into the sky. The room shuddered to a halt, the clanking iron doors opened, sucking in a waft of air that smelt of iodine and floor polish. All quiet now, just the squeak of trolley wheels with a man in uniform pushing it, talking to my mum in whispers.

Still quiet.

Now dark.

Just a hooded light, and a lady in a white bonnet tied with a big bow at her throat. She smiled down at me. More whispers. Now I was moving again, then lifted on to a bed. More whispers, more bonnets, more smiles.

Then they wrapped me in Cellophane – I felt very frightened, as if I might cry, scream even, but I couldn't breathe. Then a cool mist blew into the transparent tent and I could breathe – better, better. Now I could have screamed if I'd wanted to, but I didn't want to. I felt like I used to, everything normal, Mum looking through the Cellophane and I was breathing.

When I woke up the next morning Dad had replaced Mum in

the chair by the bed. He waved to me and gave a thumbs-up. He didn't think I could hear him through the oxygen tent. He stayed for ages – his arms must have been falling off with all the signalling he did to me – until Mum came back. The tent was taken away and I was sitting up. For the first time I saw the ward. It was a long, long room, with a line of beds along each high wall. There were men and boys of all ages and ailments in the beds. In the middle of the room there was a clear expanse of polished linoleum along which the nurses walked at the double, their starched skirts snapping and their shining shoes squeaking with efficiency.

And such kindness. Always a tuck of the sheets and a gentle chat as we waited for the thermometer to work. And at night, 'How would you like a nice cup of Ovaltine to send you off?' Oh, those nightly Ovaltines! I would sit up under the little reading light – everyone else asleep, snoring and coughing, the nurse with the big bow at her desk – and drink it while I read my book. The first the nurse brought me was *Kidnapped*. I had found my wonderworld.

As I was improving, my parents came only at the official visiting times, bearing gifts of rare sweets and comics but the most important of all was – an egg! Today it seems ridiculous that a single egg could cause so much fuss, but there was a war on and it was a precious commodity.

First it was unwrapped and shown to me like a long-lost jewel. 'It's *your* egg,' Mum said. 'Write your name on it with your pencil.' Ever mindful of the thin shell, I wrote 'T. Hicks'.

Matron was summoned. She was a battleaxe, the ideal person to look after the treasure. Mum said, 'One egg, Matron, with his name on it.'

Matron answered, 'One egg, name affixed.' She handled it with extreme care, arm outstretched with index finger and thumb of the right hand holding it with respect and reverence. She came to attention, gave a sharp half-turn, the starch in her skirts crackled and she was off in the direction of the kitchen and the cold room. There, a meal awaited the future pleasure of the kid in bed six with the books.

Those books – those wonderful books! *Treasure Island*, *Ship of the Line* and *Kidnapped* – I read them again and again. The fat doctor with hair in his ears told me that the stories were 'a bit old for you, Sonny Jim'. If he meant I couldn't understand them, he was probably half right. There were moments when a sentence needed a double reading, but I didn't need to be older to follow the action or get the gist of the dialogue. I mean, Blind Pugh was Blind Pugh, and the Black Spot meant death, and a midshipman was less than an officer and France had been our enemy once, just like Germany was now.

Anyway, by the time Mum came to take me home I was hooked. Now I could understand why she enjoyed reading those love stories when she had ten minutes to herself. She got them from the public lending library in Spa Road. It was a vast Victorian building with grand gables and tall thin windows that glared down, daring you to enter. I persuaded Mum to let me return her books so that I could browse the shelves in search of more adventure. 'I'd like something romantic for me mum,' I'd say, to the beanpole with the glasses. 'Cavaliers and Roundheads, if possible.'

And then, when she delivered a suggestion, I'd say, 'And do you have anything by C. S. Forester for me?'

She laughed, but I didn't see the joke. Over time, Miss Collins became my Chingachgook, guiding me to *The Last of the Mohicans* and other tales by James Fenimore Cooper.

After two more blastings, courtesy of the Germans, Nickleby House lost its charm and Dad decided we needed to move somewhere safer. So we did. About a hundred and fifty yards away, across Jamaica Road to Frean Street. With *Ginger Thompson*!

Ginger and me were inseparable. Together we smoked our first Woodbine, scrumped our first apple and smashed our first window. There were so many to choose from among all the bombed-out buildings that this last misdemeanour was enacted every time one of us gave the other a dare – 'I dare you to knock on that door or whistle at that girl.' Dares carried a certain amount of points based on the degree of difficulty. But the darest dare of all was the 'hopalong'.

In nearby Druid Street there was a big derelict warehouse. It was guarded by an old gaffer with a thick walrus moustache and a club foot. We called him Hopalong after our cowboy hero, Hopalong Cassidy. His lair was a sort of sentry-box by the entrance to the building, and as he was a big, fat man, barely able to get the whole of himself into his den, his club foot was always sticking out, which told me and Ginger that he was 'at home'. It was on these occasions that the dare went into action. The rules of engagement were: Ginger and me would load up with stones and present ourselves outside the warehouse, about fifty yards from Hopalong's box. Then we would pelt the building with the stones, aiming at the windows that weren't yet broken. This caused the watchman to heave himself out of his box and run towards us, yelling expletives through his moustache. Me and Ginger had to stand our ground, still pelting, until the last possible second before capture. Then, and only then, we ran for it. The winner was the last one to scarper. Needless to say, we got caught more often than not, and I don't believe there's a chastisement in Christendom to match a clip round the ear and a club foot up your arse.

Boys get up to macabre things sometimes. Especially when they hunt in pairs, and more especially when they're blood-brothers like we were, Ginger and me.

We were in his mother's kitchen one evening – we'd had our tea and were contemplating the next couple of hours before a wash and bed. 'They did it with tomahawks,' I said, referring to a ritual I'd read about the night before.

Ginger's eyes were fair bursting out of their sockets. 'And then what?' he asked.

I explained: 'The Indian brave and the white-eye slashed down into their veins and, as the blood spurted out, they joined hands, both cuts running red together.' Ginger was now as red as his barnet, but not yet convinced he should join the club.

I decided to press him with a quote from the book: 'And there, so every warrior could see, they held aloft their arms – no one could break this bond – now they were true friends – now they were one.'

Ginger had gulped a mouthful of Oxo and near choked it back into the mug. 'Can you die from it?' he asked.

'Nah!'

'How d'ya know?'

'Well, they didn't in the book.'

He pushed a slab of bread round his plate, deep in thought. 'I ain't doin' it if I die,' he mumbled. 'My mum'll kill me.'

I had to think of something to convince both of us. 'They had a *medicine man*,' I remembered, 'just in case.'

'In case of what?'

'In case you need one.'

Pause for more thought. Then, 'What's a medicine man?'

'A sort of chemist.'

This last jolt of information appeared to settle him. 'Well, I ain't usin' no tommy-'awk,' he growled. 'A cut is a cut. I ain't choppin' me fingers off – and, anyway, you can get lockjaw from cuts.'

By the time Ginger was satisfied with the arrangements, we had agreed that pricking our thumbs with a pin was better than using his dad's fretsaw, and in case we got lockjaw we waited for the local chemist in Jamaica Road to close and did it in the doorway. Later that night, we celebrated our blood bond by going to the Last Chance Saloon, my mum's kitchen, leaning against the drain-ing-board with our feet up on two buckets, smoking a Woodbine of peace, and swigging vinegar from egg-cups. Don't try it – the urine burns for days!

There is a wonderful camaraderie between boys – girls, I'm sure, have a togetherness of their own – a mutual understanding, a desire to do things together, share dares and dreams. As Jane Austen moved her characters across the pages, so too did Mark Twain. And Ginger and me were Tom and Huckleberry.

The streets were our Okefenokee, the Thames our Mississippi. The stories were always in my mind, if a bit jumbled up:

'One day I'm goin' up there,' Huck said. 'I'm goin' up the Mississippi.'

'And what'll you find?' Tom asked.

'A whole mess of friends, just like you, Tom Sawyer.'

'But they won't *be* me,' Tom cried.

'Well, you best better come too,' Huck said.

And so it came to pass.

Ginger Thompson and Tommy Hicks, blood-brothers of Bermondsey, vowed one day that they, too, would brave their big river and sail away to seek that far-off land called Fortune.

And for us that, too, came to pass. I joined the Merchant Navy, and he went into the Royal Navy. He was killed in a submarine accident off Gibraltar in 1958.

5

Number fifty-two Frean Street was in a line of terraced houses in a tiny street opposite St James's Church with backyards that lay flush with the railway arches. The house consisted of three small rooms on the ground floor and three above, with a backyard that spent most of the day in a cloud of smoke from the passing steam engines. It was a friendly street: big men came and went with the stature of kings, their women leaning at their front doors after tea, arms folded, full of conversation, the little kids playing round their aprons, the older ones sitting on the kerbs telling jokes and swapping fag cards.

At fifty-two, our lavatory was outside in the yard and, with only half a door, afforded little privacy: your head and ankles were open to the elements. The other drawback was that it was vulnerable to the wind and the acrid smoke pouring out of the ever-puffin' engines, as they clanked across the Druid Street arches to all points anywhere. On such days you had the choice to run back indoors half empty, or hold your breath and close your eyes until the smoke cleared and your eyes stopped smarting.

The seasons, too, came and went, with the call of the pony traders. In summer, on a Sunday, when the shouts of 'Get your ripe tomatoes, hearty lettuce' came, the street would fill with all the neighbourhood ladies flocking round the salad cart, poking inspecting fingers into the fruit and vegetables. The kids chucked gob-stoppers and liquorice allsorts into the pony's mouth – he refused nothing.

Then there was the cart for all seasons. 'Any old iron?' came the shout. The rag-and-bone man always stood tall, towering over a nag that was barely able to stand, having to drag around a couple of tons of metal all day. But with a handful of old clothes, and the odd broken bike, a family could get through a couple of slap-up Sundays with no trouble.

Signing autographs on the doorstep of 52 Frean Street.

The most dramatic calls were those that came during heavy winters. First you heard the shrill of the police whistles, then distant shouts coming closer and closer until you could just make out the words: 'One down, one down.'

The street doors would fly open and the men would rush out, bare arms cold white with the sleet or snow, faces fixed solemn for what was waiting on the brow of Dockhead Rise. Then their women came, followed by us kids, able to run faster, but holding back so that we didn't get to the 'down site' first. The scene waiting for us would need the courage of an Achilles to handle, which we didn't have.

So, my memory of those moments is of fascination tinged with sadness that I associated with the death of Goliath. But the scene I witnessed did not take place in the Bible but on an ice-coated road with a mob of concerned men looking down at the great body of a shire horse lying prostrate where the slippery cobbles had sent him crashing to the ground. His great legs would shake down to his enormous hoofs, as he lay tangled with the shafts of the laden cart he was dragging from the docks. But it was his huge dark eyes pleading for help that brought a sigh from me. He was a giant, with the strength of Goliath, but now he gave a soft, helpless neigh.

The carter, his driver, presented the mob with three long lines of thick rope, which he carried for such times. One went to the mane, one to the girth and one to the belly above the hind legs. The cart came off the shafts and was moved alongside the horse. Half of the men, holding the ends of the ropes, got into the cart, while the others kept them in place round the horse. The local bobby called for them to take the strain. Then, he blew his whistle and everybody heaved, muscles tense, grunting. The animal seemed to know that it was for his own good and kicked out, trying to get a grip, then whinnied encouragement. The men carried on, their strength fading by the second. They knew that if the animal wasn't back on his feet with one last mass attempt then it would be too late.

He would die there in the white.

When that happened the women took the places of the men, who retired to the pub. Just softness now. Whispers from the women, as they administered long, gentle strokes that always seemed to calm the beast. Until the bloke with the death bolt turned up. Then us kids left – we knew that Goliath was about to die. We didn't need to watch the whole sad scene to the bitter end. Satisfied with a gentle kiss for the horse, I went home thinking of great warriors past and allowed the sadness to pass.

By 1943 London had returned to some sort of normality. Long queues and rationing prevailed but things were better – for me especially. I could sit through a whole evening at the pictures without being bombed out of the plot and, best of all, the children who had been evacuated to safer places were now returning to the open arms of their parents. The still-standing streets were refilling with kids looking for a game of football or a sly fag in the alley. The thoroughfares that separated one neighbourhood from the next now rang with bikes and skates and, rarest of all, the homemade 'scooter', consisting of one vertical plank (five inches wide, two feet high) stuck to a horizontal one (same size) with a ball-bearing wheel at each end. The rarity of the machine related to the ball-bearing – there was still a war on! Somehow, sometimes, someone somewhere 'found' one – but the real knack was in 'finding' two. Once found – wow! They were noisy, cumbersome velocipedes, but with his right foot on the horizontal and his left foot pushing against the pavement a boy could get up enough speed to match Fangio. Once more the world was wonderful.

But then, as suddenly as they had come, all the kids were gone again.

That summer everything seemed to have changed back. I couldn't understand it. One day I had a load of mates, the next it was like during the blitz. Hardly anyone around. Every street I went to in search of a lark was the same as the next – empty, like ghost towns in the cowboy pictures.

What could have spirited them away?

Mum told me. 'Hops,' she said. 'They've all gone hopping in
Kent.'

'What's "hopping"?'

'It's like farming. Every summer most Cockneys like to go and
pick the hops.'

'Why?'

'Cos they earn money and cos hops make beer.'

'The kind Dad likes?'

'Exactly.'

'But why can't the farmers do the picking?'

'Cos there's a lot of hops!'

'Why?'

'Cos your dad likes his beer.'

Another pause, while I reflected. Then I asked, 'Why don't *we*
go hopping?'

'Cos boys come back with fleas, girls come back with babies,
your fingers are numb for a month 'n' everything you put in your
mouth tastes bitter!'

'But Ginger Thompson goes and his mum don't mind.'

'Well, *your* mum does. Do you want to spend the summer living
in a wooden shack running alive with rats?'

Now I pause for deeper thought – numb fingers, bitter tastes,
rats, fleas and my best mate Ginger Thompson. 'Yes,' I said.

But it didn't make any difference. I didn't go.

So, for two whole months I suffered the slings and arrows of an
empty street until, early one Sunday, the sound of carts and barrows
rattling over the cobbles announced the return of the pickers –
and Ginger.

I ran to his flat and rapped on the front door. His mother opened
it.

'Is Ginger coming out?' I asked.

'His name ain't Ginger, it's Alfred.'

'Is Alfred coming out, then?'

'No, he's washing his hair.'

Ginger Alfred Thompson was at the sink, pouring gallons and
gallons of boiling water over his red hair. But not enough. Not

even the bars of carbolic would kill the army of fleas that had taken over his head, biting into his brain.

'Can he come out later, then?'

'No, he's having his dinner.'

I could see that too: Ginger's dinner, sitting on the plate with the poor sod not able to tell the Spam from the chips on account of the bitter taste in his mouth.

Then Ginger Alfred Thompson came to the door. ''Allo, Tom,' he said.

''Allo, Ginge – Alf . . . *Alfred*! Yer mum says you can't come out.'

He said to his mum, 'How about tomorrow, then?'

She shrugged.

I asked, 'What's happening tomorrow?'

'We're playing football in Tabard Street. D'you want to?'

Did I want to? Not half! Eight weeks I'd been waiting, and now at last with the coming of the morrow I'd be rushing down the wing, heading towards the goal, with Ginger Thompson standing betwixt the coats, knees bent, arms outstretched, preparing to save my shot.

Some chance, I thought. Not with numb fingers, he won't!

So the summer cooled into autumn, and Mum was pregnant again.

6

By the spring my own particular war had quietened down. The blitz was long over, the Battle of Britain won and the speeches of Winston Churchill had gone from the rousing 'fight on the beaches' to the victorious 'so much owed by so many to so few'. Now we had been lulled by the soft song of President Roosevelt: 'a day of infamy' was his angry reference to the surprise Japanese attack on Pearl Harbor in late 1941 that had caused America to declare war on Japan. Hitler, surprisingly, declared war on America by return, bringing hope to our weary hearts and the Yanks back to London.

Within weeks, with their fine uniforms and finance, they were 'drum-drumming everywhere' and Soho was buzzing once more. Dad was in his element and there was silver in our pockets. The Yanks called him 'Winnie' because of his remarkable likeness to the British leader, but he didn't like it much. 'Me name's Darbo,' he insisted, but the boys from 'over there' were adamant: 'Winnie' he looked, so 'Winnie' he was. Eventually Dad appeared to relent: whenever he was addressed as the great man, he would give the two-fingered victory salute − 'only I give it backwards. They *thought* it was hello, but I *knew* it was . . . bollocks.' So everything was great − almost!

Dad was still working at the Nest club in Soho, but the family needed more cash. Mum had an office-cleaning job in the City, but she was a part-timer, just mornings. Besides, she had a saucepan on the way and two on the floor, so Darbo decided to return to the racetrack. He'd been making a good living 'going away' before the war but, what with one thing and another, he'd felt he should be 'on the doorstep'. Now, though, he felt he'd have to work the courses *and* the clubs, leaving Mum to take it a bit easier and prepare for the new arrival.

His return to racing was not difficult. There were many jobs he could do. He could tic-tac, he could tout, sell and distribute lists of the runners to the bookies, and he could clerk. 'Clerking' is perhaps the most difficult and most admired job on a racecourse. The next time you see a bookmaker at his hod, waving his ticket-filled hands, shouting the odds, look to his left, just back a bit – out of the limelight. The bloke sitting there with his head buried deep in a ledger is the clerk. He listens to the bookie taking the bets: 'Happy Dancer at five to four – a score to one seventy-six.' The clerk notes in his ledger that the horse Happy Dancer is laid at five to four and the punter has placed twenty pounds on it, receiving ticket 176 as his receipt. This continues until minutes before the race is run. Then the clerk collates all of the wagers on all of the nags in that particular contest, and works out what 'danger' the bookmaker is facing. For example, horse one has two hundred pounds laid at five to four, horse two, five hundred at seven to two, horse three, four hundred at a hundred to thirty, plus any place bets at quarter odds. So there he sits, adding, subtracting, dividing in his head, until eventually he has to advise which bets to keep and which to 'lay off'. The bookmaker takes the final decision and then the race is run without too much risk (if any) to the firm. This is called 'making a book'. Hence . . . bookmaker.

When you consider the schooling my father never had, it was a mystery how he managed it. 'Orf the top of me 'ead,' he would say. 'It's only numbers, ain't it?'

Darbo was at Kempton Park during the spring meeting when, at the end of racing, he had a visit from one of the course stewards, ordering him to attend the office of the clerk of the course. 'On the way over to the grandstand, I was racking me brains trying to work out what had occurred,' he said. 'You don't get pulled up to the top toffs unless you're in a bit of bother.'

Darbo sat in the waiting room for some time. Eventually the door to the inner sanctum opened and the clerk of the course, a retired colonel, smiled and invited him in. 'Hicks, isn't it?' he asked, knowing the answer.

'Yus, sir,' faltered Darbo.

'My God, you really do . . .'

'Whassat, sir?'

'Look like him!'

'Who, sir?'

'Never mind. Had a decent day?'

'The last favourite done me, sir.'

'They usually do.'

'Yus, sir.'

'Care for a sherry?'

'Don't mind if I do, sir.'

There they sat sipping, the colonel thoughtful, Darbo still await-ing the reason for the summons. The colonel broke the silence. 'The war looks like ending, don't you think?'

'Yus, sir.'

'We're going to win, y'know.'

'Yus, sir.'

'And when that occurs, racing will take on a new lease of life, and we in the fraternity will have new ideas to prepare for the peace, together with the Jockey Club. I propose to form a standing committee to discuss the future of the sport.'

Darbo squirmed, glancing behind him in the hope that the colonel was talking to somebody else, but he wasn't.

'I'd like you to join us,' the colonel told him. 'I'm giving a small dinner party at the Savoy Grill this coming Wednesday. Perhaps I could telephone you to arrange to send my car.'

'I ain't got a phone,' Darbo spluttered, his vest sticking to his boiling back.

'Well, you have a home, don't you?' the colonel snapped.

'Yus. I got one of them.'

'And you do have a dark suit and tie?'

'Yus, sir.'

'A bow-tie would be preferred. It is, after all, the Grill.'

'Yus, sir.'

'Very well. Leave your address with my secretary and I'll call for you at . . . shall we say seven?'

'Yus, let's.'

Darbo made to scamper out of the web.

'Oh, and let's keep this to ourselves,' the colonel said. 'Standing committees need to be somewhat secret . . . if you follow?'

'I do,' Darbo agreed, and dashed out into the fresh air to revive himself.

'Well, I don't know, I'm sure,' Mum said at home that night. 'If you don't know what they're talking about, how can you sit down to dinner with them? You'll look a right berk!'

'I've gotta go.' Darbo sighed. 'I can't give him the needle, I could get warned off!'

'Mebbe you missed something he said,' Mum suggested.

'I didn't miss nuffin'. He said what he said, and I 'eard every word.'

No matter how many times they went over the permutations, my parents came to the conclusion that Darbo was going to dinner that coming Wednesday at seven o'clock to join a committee of top toffs and discuss matters a thousand miles from his comprehension. If that was a puzzle, the scenario that followed was Chinese in the extreme.

That Wednesday a car arrived with a liveried chauffeur. Dad, in his Sunday-best suit and tie, kissed Mum a fond farewell and entered the back of the vehicle to find the colonel sitting in the half-light.

'Capital, Hicks, capital!' He beamed. 'Have a cigar. You do smoke, don't you?'

'Yus, sir, I don't mind if I do,' Darbo said. He accepted one, lit it and puffed tentatively, then felt an enormous cough building up.

Half an hour later they cruised to an elegant halt outside the Savoy Hotel. A matching pair of doormen greeted them, and Darbo and the colonel were ushered into the foyer of the famous Grill. The head waiter led them into the grand room, softly lit by candlelight. As they waltzed between the tables Darbo felt the eyes of every diner on him. 'I nigh shit meself,' he said. 'I just kept going by pulling harder and harder on me cigar. I must have looked like the *Flying Scot*.'

Eventually they arrived at the table that held the rest of the committee, placed judiciously in an alcove. They stood for formal introductions. There were four of them, two men in dinner suits and two in uniform, an air-vice-marshal and an American admiral.

'I don't remember what I ate,' Darbo told Mum later. 'A sort of soup and chicken. But they was nice, especially the Yank. He wasn't posh like the others, so I talked to him mostly. He was from Kentucky. I asked him if the grass was really blue there and how many Kentucky Derbys he had seen. Funny thing was, he hadn't seen any! I thought, Strange, him being on a racin' committee 'n' all.'

The meal drifted into brandy and cigars, the colonel declared the meeting over, the committee rose as one and left the Grill in tandem. As the car made for Frean Street, the colonel beamed. 'I thought you did rather well tonight, Hicks,' he remarked, 'and may I say how much my colleagues and I are looking forward to our next meeting? How do you feel about that?'

'Pat and Mick, to be honest, sir.'

'Capital. Capital!' the Colonel exclaimed, and pressed something into his hand. 'For expenses incurred,' he whispered.

'It was a jacks!' Darbo laid the five-pound note on the kitchen table so that Mum could admire it. 'I don't know much about this committee game, love, but if I'm getting fed and bunged at the same time, who's complainin'?'

'Well, you just keep quiet about it, like the colonel says,' Mum counselled. 'You don't want anyone else gettin' in on it.'

And no one else did.

Throughout the rest of the war, from 1943 to 1945, Darbo attended the committee five more times. The colonel was always present, the venue was always the Grill, but the committee changed each time. There were always military men among their number but they never came to a decision. It seemed that, as far as they were concerned, racing could find its own future.

One day, at the end of the war, Darbo got a telegram from the colonel inviting him and Mum to dinner at the Grill (suitably dressed) the following week. Remembering past evenings at the Savoy Darbo was determined that his wife would 'look the business' and she did. Then he in his hired dinner suit, with her on his arm, floated into the waiting car and set off for the Grill. They entered with the pomp and circumstance that Dad had come to expect, but at the table in the alcove, all their expectations flew out of the window.

'There was this colonel,' Mum said, 'and three Winston Churchills! We all stood there starin' at each other. Then this colonel starts laughing, and the Churchills. Then I see it all too. I see your dad, and them, and I see what he sees is so funny – *he was a Churchill, too!*'

During the evening it was revealed that British Intelligence had devised a plan called 'Doppel' (short for doppelgänger, the German for double). 'So, if Hitler had a rumour that Winnie was meeting Stalin somewhere in the Baltic,' the colonel explained, 'his fifth column would refer to the dinner being held that same night, in the Grill, with one of *our* Churchills! Confusing, eh!'

'I'll say,' Darbo agreed. 'Wiv bleedin' knobs on.'

Mum decided to have the new baby at home. I don't know whether it was the experience of Cornwall or that she had little Colin running all over the place. Anyway, she made up her mind and 52 Frean Street was prepared. She gave up the office-cleaning job a few weeks before the expected arrival, and spent the rest of the time drilling Dad on what was expected of him.

Item One. If in the pub when labour begins, must leave pub and *not* stay for one more round to celebrate.

Item Two. During labour to attend midwife – prepare constant hot water. Do not swear in her presence, do not go to the pub for *anything*, including medicinal purposes.

Item Three. Prepare meals and clean clothes for the kids, offer the midwife a cup of tea at regular intervals. Do not swear in her presence. Do *not* invite her to the pub for a drink.

Item Four. Stay away from the pub!

Roy was born in the late afternoon betwixt the time the pubs

closed after lunch and opened again for the evening, putting Dad
for ever in his debt. But could I ever forget the turmoil of that
birth?

I sat at the foot of the wardrobe and watched, fascinated by the
performance on the bed and amused by Darbo running round like
a scared cat. It seemed that every time he attempted to follow an
instruction he messed it up.

The midwife called, 'More water over here.'

Darbo repeated, 'More water over there.'

Midwife annoyed: 'Not *there* – here.'

A stub of a toe, a trip, a crash followed by a splash, followed by
. . . 'Fuck it!'

> *'My Gawd,' he cried, 'I could have died,*
> *When I took me chance and peep'd inside*
> *I couldn't see the missus there.*
> *She was sort of hidden by the towels on the chair,*
> *The doctor was washin' his hands by the bed,*
> *The midwife was shoutin' kinda losin' her head,*
> *She called my Mabel a "lazy mare",*
> *And told her to push and pull here an' there.*
>
> *'And what with that and the kids downstairs*
> *And the neighbours next door playing musical chairs*
> *And the boiling water all over the floor*
> *And the gas goin' out when they wanted some more,*
>
> *'I'll tell you this much, mate – straight and plain*
> *I'll never go through a childbirth again.'*

My brother Roy was five minutes old when the room settled
down. The midwife was in the kitchen having her hundredth
cuppa. Little Colin was sitting at the foot of the bed, and I was in
charge of cleaning the new baby's hands. Dad sat at the top bathing
Mum's sweating forehead. 'Are ye thirsty, love?' he whispered
lovingly.

Big brother Tommy with (from right to left) Roy, Colin and Mum, on the beach in Ramsgate.

Mum nodded tiredly. He kissed her lips. And dragged a crate of light ale from under the bed.

So there we were, the Hicks family: Mum, Darbo and their three sons. The only thing missing from our total joy was money. Whenever I talked about this period with my mother I would suggest we were poor. It would always bring a black flash to her lovely eyes, her neck would stiffen and she'd go into her impenetrable defence. 'Never poor – a little short sometimes, but we never wanted for nothin'.'

Then I would press her gently: 'Yeah! But surely . . .'

'And we never borrowed neither,' she'd snap. 'If you kids needed somethin', you got it, in time, but we never had luxury we couldn't afford – and no tallyman knocked at our door. I couldn't have took the shame.'

The tallyman was the area debt collector. The modern name is hire-purchase or 'the never-never', but take away the names and the process is the same: you get now, but you pay later. This my mother would not accept.

She contributed to a Christmas Club (sixpence a week) and a local clothing club (a shilling a month). Anything else she desired, like a three-piece suite or a holiday, she talked about enthusiastically and whatever small change was available went into a cake tin in the coal-hole. Then at long intervals we would dig out the box, sit in the kitchen and empty its contents on to the table. The collection of half-crowns, florins, shillings and sixpences would sparkle like buried treasure. When she had counted it, Mum would announce how close our particular target was – this was followed by a cheer or a groan – then put back the box to be covered with coal until the next deposit.

So, there was financial order in the household.

But it was a growing household. How did they make ends meet? With a rota system.

Dad was still working at the races during the day and in Soho at night. When baby Roy was settled, Mum went back to the early-morning office-cleaning job so their timetable ran thus. Dad returned from the Nest at four in the morning and woke Mum, who left for the City. He watched the kids till Mum returned at seven thirty, then he slept and she fed the kids. I went to junior school and Colin to the infants'. Dad left for the races at noon and got back at about eight p.m. Mum worked the day shift at Peek Freans biscuit factory and got home in time to cook and serve dinner, Dad slept till eleven, then went to Soho. Mum slept till he returned at four a.m., and so it went on.

On Sunday we were all at home and the only blot on the landscape was getting Dad out of the pub for Sunday lunch. Somehow, when they were planning this sequence of events, he'd got Mum to release him for a couple of hours to have a drink. 'You be back at one o'clock,' she'd say firmly.

He always answered with a whistled tune as he ambled out *en route* to the Ship Aground, but as sure as roast beef follows Yorkshire pudding, come the witching hour there would be no sign of him and there was Mum in the kitchen, watching the boiling cabbage, the bubbling gravy, the rising Yorkshires. 'Tommy, go and get him,' she'd yell.

That was my cue to run to the pub and shout through the public bar, 'Dad, it's on the table.'

He would wave from the smoke-filled room and bring me out

a glass of lemonade. 'I won't be long,' he'd say, then smile and go back into the bar.

I'd drink the lemonade in a couple of gasps and follow him. 'She says right now, Dad, or she's coming round herself.'

The crowd would laugh – so did Dad. He'd drain his drink and I joined him on the unsteady walk home.

Then – the entrance of the gladiators.

We both stood in the passage at home. Ahead of us, in the kitchen, Mum sat, glaring, at the table.

Dad rubbed his hands together, eyes dancing. 'What's occurred?'

Mum's glare crept into a half-smile. The meal began and Dad had won again. It really was like a fencing match between them. Mum would thrust, Dad would parry.

Whenever he deserved it, she would scold because it was expected. He, realizing she was marking her territory, would accept the reprimand but, with that mischievous way of his, the situation, no matter how hot, would cool within the glint of a smile and the crack of a line.

7

In the winter of 1944, I felt pain for the first time. It wasn't the sting of a slap or a grazed knee, it was that time in everyone's life when *real* pain hits. The unforgettable moment when you know your body means it. Mine came in the middle of playtime at St Joseph's. It was like an eruption in the pit of my stomach, so acute, so strong, that I still remember falling to my knees and trying to tell someone I was dying. They laid me on the podium in assembly, and put a flannel on my forehead. The pain passed and they sent me home.

'Wind,' Dad said. 'If you get it again, try farting.'

That night I did get it again. And the more I tried to pass wind the worse it got. It hurt so much that I cried – I tried not to, you don't cry with wind, Ginger Thompson wouldn't. But now I was feverish – sweat and shakes.

Mum took me to St Olave's Hospital.

The same ritual: the rising room, the smell, the bonnets and bows. I lay on a bed for ages while people pushed and prodded me. But still that awful nagging gnawing bite in the pit of my tummy. Lots more bonnets, white coats, stethoscopes, fingers pushing, hands pressing, one day, two days. The pain was as constant as the uncertainty. Possible peritonitis was demoted to possible appendicitis, demoted again to chronic constipation, perhaps acute constipation.

Two weeks later came my introduction to torture. There is no other word for it. I was about to meet an invention of the devil. It looked like a relic from the Inquisition and to me, the poor sod receiving it, it felt like it.

It was my eighth birthday.

Once more I was in the throes of the pain. I lay in the ward literally crying out – I couldn't help myself. Any bravery had gone.

Now I hurt worse than ever and I wanted everyone to know in case one of them could stop it.

'Enema,' someone suggested. 'It's in the bowel, so let's give him an enema.'

Everyone, except Mum, left the bedside.

She kept smiling at me, pushed my hair back from my forehead and kissed me, but I sensed her confusion. I knew we were both lost.

Then it came: a tin tumbrel rattling along the lino, a trolley with a huge steaming jug on it with a big black funnel and a long piece of red rubber hosepipe. It clanked to a stop at the foot of the bed. The crowd returned, armed with awful-smelling rubber blankets, which they lifted me on to face down.

'You needn't stay, Mother,' I heard Matron whisper.

I felt a kiss on my shoulder.

The screens came round and a nurse whispered, into my ear, 'I want you to listen carefully, young man. What we are about to do is going to be a little uncomfortable, but it will take away the pain. Do you understand?'

My head was deep in the pillow so I muttered something affirmative. I wanted to tell her that the smell of the rubber blankets coupled with my pain was about to make me sick – but what happened next took my mind off all that.

Someone was putting something greasy into my rectum: the hose – the red rubber snake from the trolley. I flinched with surprise and embarrassment. The voice of the nurse came again: 'It is very important that you do not move. Soon you will feel something warm going into you. You will want to pass it. Don't!'

Pass it? What did she mean, pass it?

Then it came – that never-to-be-forgotten sensation. That alien thing, like a serpent spitting hot venom into my bum, into my colon and now my bowel, building up into some animal about to bust out of me. I wanted to let it go – but my little muscles were told to hold on. Do *not* pass it! My toes were wriggling a thousand to the second, anything to hold on to the serpent. *I mustn't let it go*. But that stuff was still going in – the torture wasn't over. I wanted to tell the nurse I'd give in – tell the Gestapo everything – but no more hot oil. Please, please, let me *pass* it!

Suddenly the pouring stopped.

'Hold it,' the nurse encouraged me.

The hose came away roughly from my throbbing rectum. I heard the metallic clank of the bedpan and I was dragged up into a sitting position on to it. I let my knees go, and my thighs and my tight bum, and away from me went the worst moment of my life. I was swaying from the sheer experience. My head swam. The tips of my fingers dug into the rubber blankets to steady me. The stench from the pan engulfed me, adding to the threatening faint.

But after they'd cleared everything away I lay in that bed knowing that the pain *hadn't* gone. It was still there, nagging like before.

'Feel better, darlin'?' Mum asked. She looked guilty – she'd done nothing to stop them doing what they'd done.

'Much better, Mum,' I lied. I couldn't tell her the truth – I was terrified they might torture me again.

But by that night I was in agony. The next morning I woke to the sound of the tin tumbrel rattling down the ward. The beast was back.

I was given an enema each day for God knows how long. It did absolutely nothing for me. Then they decided to concentrate on easing the pain, not attacking it. This they did by preparing a huge wad of cotton wool, almost like a pillow. Whenever the pain came, the wad was placed in an oven until it was hot. Then, with me on my back, they would lay it on my stomach. God, it was wonderful, that warm cuddle of a cure. The pain would subside and all would be calm – until the next time and the next.

Then at long last . . .

During the second month of this desperate search, everything about my illness was a mystery – except the pain. Then came the discovery. Eureka!

'He has purpura,' the specialist told my folks. 'A type of spotted fever, internal bleeding due to bacterial poisoning of the capillaries. His platelets are possibly infected too, this plus the bleeding into the intestine . . .'

'He's not well, then?' Darbo suggested.

I ended up in a convalescent home in Carshalton on a long course of rest and vitamin C. It was my first introduction to an institution and it was a cross between Wormwood Scrubs and *One Flew Over the Cuckoo's Nest*. However, like all the other medical facilities I was placed in, I always had the feeling that, in spite of the methods, the staff cared. That was a safety valve in my young, confused state, whether I was having to wash my own undies, or my teeth were being filled without anaesthetic. We wore a uniform and there were strict rules. Certain parts of the grounds were out of bounds and we were allowed one visit per week, on Sunday. It also had a library boasting Jack London, Joseph Conrad and an illustrated copy of Malory's *Le Morte D'Arthur*. As the months went by, I delved into Conan Doyle, the Crowborough edition. This was treasure indeed – the complete works. *Rodney Stone* was the first, then *The Adventures of Gerard* and, much later, the brilliant *Sherlock*.

Still the months went by – almost a year.

Then I found a book that told true stories. Trevelyan's *History of England*. It took a lot of getting into, but once I taught myself not to look at the dates and not to dwell on the footnotes, I found my heritage. It was a proud read.

8

Two victories came in 1945: we beat Hitler and I beat purpura.

The war ended in Europe on 8 May 1945, and before the shrapnel had cooled we had parades, street parties and the King on his Buckingham Palace balcony waving victoriously to the multitudes. Ginger Thompson went with his uncle that day and saw an 'uncle' of mine arguing with two policemen in front of the Victoria monument. It was Garlic, the dip, and Darbo soon realized that the silly sod had been doing a bit of business in the crowd and had had his collar felt.

By mid-June all thoughts of war had disappeared. There was an air of calm: people went to work, kids went to school and the cargo ships still crawled alongside the hungry grey wharves. But now the great nets that had once brought our life's blood from the crammed holds pulled clear with no urgency. Instead of guns – tea; in place of tanks – sugar cane; in place of bullets – bananas!

Me and Ginger could hardly say the name, but if the rumour was true, the one boat we had dreamed about had docked. The banana boat! We two and every able-bodied tearaway in the area made our way to Hays Wharf. When we got there it was like a scene from a western: a mass of kids, silent and suspicious, like every Apache should be, stood on piles of empty crates and heaps of peeling pallets, gazing down from the hills to the canyon below that held the dream boat. Into her gaping hold the probing nets went. Each time they came out, they bulged with what we knew was the treasure of the West Indies. The yellow fruit! We had heard many times of this delicacy. Our elders had thrilled us with stories of its golden skin and sweet flesh. It was written that the gods had given it to the world and taken it back at the start of war, but with the death of Adolf they had returned it to us.

That day every docker who swarmed round the area knew he

was being watched by us hawks. Every man jack of them knew that one mistake, one slip of the grappling hook, and a crate would crash open on to the dock floor sending the produce into the clutches of the natives waiting above.

Sure enough it happened – as if on cue!

The holding net was a full fifteen feet above the ground when the crane shuddered and a crate hit the concrete.

Splat! The bananas spewed out like a batch of boomerangs.

We were poised to charge down from our hills, but we watched for the sign – the all-important sign from the white-eyes below.

Then it came. The dock foreman stood tall and, with a flourish of his flat cap, invited us to feed. Down we rushed, laughing, shouting, screaming with the thrill of the coming food fest.

Me and Ginger examined our first banana with excitement and disappointment. We both agreed it felt new and mysterious, but somehow it didn't cry out to be devoured. It sat in my hand like a bright green culinary . . . cosh! Worst of all, where had the yellow gone?

I knew nothing of ripe or unripe – an apple was an apple, a pear was a pear, but this blinkin' thing was beyond me.

Ginger wasn't going to do anything with his, so I pushed mine into my mouth and bit into it. The combination of skin and sponge stuck to my teeth like an old school rubber and tasted about the same. Undaunted, I attempted to swallow – but whatever was forcing itself down my gullet wasn't nice. All around me I saw the same reactions as, one by one, my fellow braves chucked half-bitten erasers at the feet of the laughing dockers and threw up *en masse* into the Thames.

We learned an eternal truth that day: a banana wasn't worth the chew and the gods were full of crap!

Then came the dreaded day that Mum mentioned school. 'Bacon's,' she enthused.

Dad nodded in agreement. 'A good gaff,' he said, remembering his childhood.

Bacon's School for Boys was right next door to Pages Walk, the notorious dwelling of his misspent youth. He had always passed it on his way to some devilment – but locally Bacon's was admired.

'And they wear uniforms,' Mum said, impressed, so off I went at eleven years old, with hardly any primary schooling, to face my first elementary test.

Mr R. H. Binger, the headmaster, was a bespectacled little man, with skin as rough as the hides that were tanned a few hundred yards down the road. He sat at his desk and looked across at me, with Mum by my side, and then he studied the entry exam paper I had just tried to complete. 'You have no maths,' he said sternly.

'What's that, then?' Mum inquired.

'He has no figures, Mrs Hicks – no arithmetic. He can't add, subtract, divide. He has no idea of fractions – he doesn't even know his tables.'

My mother glared at me as if I'd just smashed a window.

Mr Binger went further: 'His geography is very weak for a boy of his age – and I'm afraid –'

'I've never done it,' I interjected.

'But you're eleven,' he growled.

'He's been away a lot, sir,' Mum pleaded. 'Hospitals, convalescent homes, the war an' all.'

The headmaster sat there studying me. Mebbe he saw how much I needed to go to his school, to wear his uniform, to be back in an institutional harness. 'History,' he said, casting me a last lifeline. 'Do you know any history?'

'What family?' I asked.

Mr Binger leaned forward, his hands under his chin. 'I ask "History?" and you answer, "What family?" Can you explain that?'

I understood the question, but it was a wide one. I struggled for words. 'I mean like Tudor, sir, or Stuart – y'know, *families*.'

'I'm sure I don't know what he's up to,' Mum said. 'He's not like this at home.'

But Mr Binger was on the scent. He stood up and opened the door for my mother to leave the room. 'Mrs Hicks, would you be kind enough, just for a few minutes?'

Mum left in confusion.

Mr Binger stayed at the door and said gently, 'Let's start with the family Stuart.'

'James the First of England,' I began, 'took the throne cos Elizabeth Tudor didn't have any kids . . .' And so I continued.

After a few more examples he gave me a sheet of paper. 'Write down the books you read,' he said.

Later that day he told Mum that, in his experience of schooling, he had never encountered another young boy with such a yen for history and that, plus my English, would be enough for me to enter the school. 'The rest will come in the fullness of time,' he said, as he shook her hand and pinched my cheek.

For the next four years this man was my guide. Through him, I wrote my first play, my first essays, cried at Dickens and laughed with Betjeman. In that sense school was a mine of discovery.

In another it was like the Third World War.

As I was eleven I was expected to study for grammar-school entrance, but I was also expected to protect myself, like all Bermondsey boys. My initiation in this came during my first playtime at the school.

The playground was not unlike that portrayed in films about Alcatraz. It was a yard with pockets of boys perched at intervals along a large wall that had white goalposts painted on it. They seemed to be guarding it: every time some lad ventured to pass them, they surrounded him and knocked him about with a combination of slaps and kicks. I stood at the beginning of the wall, knowing that to get to the games at the other end, I would have to run a sort of gauntlet. Did I have the guts to do it?

Someone tugged at my sleeve. He was a little bloke, his hair shorn so short that he looked bald. His face was marked with cuts and plasters but his eyes were sharp and full of humour. They darted left and right like a pigeon risking an offered crumb. He spoke in short, sharp sentences. 'Can you fight?'

'Dunno – can you?'

'Yeah. How old are you?'

'Eleven.'

'So am I.' Then he looked along the line of boys who were watching me, working out who I was and what they might do to me. 'D'you fancy it, then?' he asked.

'What?'

'Gettin' bashed up.'

'No, I don't.'

'Sod ya, then.' He smiled, and walked the wall.

He had no fear – he went from one group to the next, taking a slap or a punch without offering one in return and then, once past the parade, he waved to me. 'Fuck 'em,' he shouted. 'Me name's Billy Larkin – I'm adopted.'

'It means he doesn't have a mum and dad,' Mum told me. 'Well, not real ones.'

'Is that why he gets bashed up?' I asked.

This brought Dad into the conversation. 'Bashed up? Who gets bashed up?'

'Billy Larkin does – every playtime.'

'Who bashes him? Not you, I 'ope,' Mum put in.

'No, the gangs do it along the wall.'

'Well, long as they don't bash you,' Dad said, returning to the racing page of the *Daily Express*.

But, pretty soon, it *was* me getting bashed. It was my third day and I *had* to pass that bloody wall. I asked Larkie how best to survive.

'Just don't care,' he said. 'I don't – I'm adopted.'

So I followed him into the groups. First I got pushed, with the question, 'What's your fuckin' game?' Then I was punched – 'Fancy yer chances, do ya?' Next I got kicked, with the threat of more to come.

I was not only terrified, I was ashamed.

At night I couldn't sleep. And Larkie's advice was no solution. I *did* care: mebbe it was because I wasn't adopted – or was I? Larkie had told me about his eleventh birthday. After his parents had given him his present, they'd said they had something important to tell him. They explained his adoption: they'd had him since he was two months old and decided to keep it from him until now. As he told me this, he became very agitated – and clenched his fists.

'What did you say?' I asked, eyes wide with shock.

'Nuffin',' he said, glaring at me. 'D'ya wanna make somethin' of it?'

One night, soon after Larkie's explanation, I lay in bed *knowing* I, too, was adopted. It was obvious – I could remember Colin's birth, and Betty's and Roy's, but not my own. If I can't remember being born mebbe . . . and I was eleven, just like Larkie was when they told him. I tried to fight back the sadness. In my mind's eye I could see my adoptive family sitting in a warm group of love, looking at me with the same pity I felt for Billy Larkin . . . 'Happy birthday, son. You're adopted.'

I wanted to ask my mum, but I was too frightened of the answer – mebbe Dad. Then I remembered my aunt Mary. I rushed round to her flat and rapped on the door. She opened it with her usual smile.

'Am I adopted?' I gasped. 'Cos I'm eleven and I ought to know. I thought you might tell me as I might have to make arrangements.'

It was a very serious little lad standing at her door that day, a young man full of dread and a little too much imagination – but I well recall my 'arrangements'.

If the worst came to the worst and my fears were well placed, I was away to the wharves, there to find a ship that was about to sail, board her and find the darkness of a covered lifeboat. Then the wait, the long hungry wait, till her engine began to purr, her screws to turn, and I would be away to the deep sevens when I would reveal myself to the crew, and throw my future into their weatherbeaten hands. Messrs Conrad and Co. had a lot to answer for.

Aunt Mary laughed. Then, over a thick lump of bread and Marmite, she told me about my birth – watching me arrive from my mum's tummy and my dad getting pissed from sheer joy, my first bootees and the big furry bunny rabbit she gave me that I've never forgotten.

My sea adventure would have to wait. I skipped home to my family – one more worry out of the way.

There was only that damn wall now.

I knew I had to pass it again soon and, slowly but surely, fear was overcome by shame. I took the plunge on a Wednesday. I told Larkie I'd do it at the eleven o'clock break. Pretty soon the bell rang and boys spewed out of packed classrooms into the corridors, ran down the staircases, through the assembly hall, and out on to the playground. The wall was soon occupied, each group talking among themselves and ignoring the others. As they were all seasoned street fighters, they rarely fought each other. Instead they focused their hunting eyes on where I was standing with Billy Larkin.

'C'mon, then.' He grinned, with split lips. We set off towards the trouble.

But I didn't follow. Somehow I couldn't make my legs move in the direction of a bashing. There didn't seem any sense in it. Surely it was more sensible not to go looking for trouble than to do the opposite. So, I stayed where I was and watched Larkie walk the wall on his own.

That night I sat in our kitchen feeling more depressed than ever. I was still in the throes of missing the convalescent home, my family were still 'on probation', and I was facing a dilemma I could not come to terms with. Where does common sense end and shame begin?

Then Mum said to me, 'Anything wrong, love?'

'No, I'm all right.'

'You sure?'

'Yeah, 'cept that . . .'

''Cept that what?' She rubbed her wet hands on her apron, and sat opposite me at the table.

'Well, there's these boys at school and they stand at this wall and . . .' I told her the whole story, during which she nodded or shook her head but she didn't interrupt or make a comment, except to say, 'Your dad's late home tonight – don't worry.'

The next morning he woke me up for school. Usually he would

joke and fuss about, but not now. He was strangely silent. I was on my way up the passage to go out to school, when Mum arrived back from the office-cleaning job. She saw the troubled look in my eyes. 'Have you talked to him?' she called to my dad.

He came out of the kitchen sheepishly. 'No, I 'aven't.'

Mum double-checked with me. ' 'E 'asn't talked to you, then?' I affirmed with a nod.

'Well, someone 'ad better talk to someone 'ere,' she yelled, and stormed into the front room, slamming the door, leaving Dad and me in the passage.

He began tentatively: 'Look, son, Mum says you're 'aving trouble.'

I nodded.

'And she says I should 'elp you wiv it.'

My pulse leaped. Mebbe he was coming to school with me? That would be great – my dad walking the wall with me. Then he dashed my hopes. 'Well, I can't.'

Disappointed, I turned away from him, back up the passage towards the front door. He came too and stopped me before I got into the street. 'I can't 'elp you, cos I can't be there all the time,' he said – more firmly but still tentative. 'And, anyway, you should be 'elping yourself.'

God! I thought. He's my dad and he doesn't understand what's happening. I blurted out, 'But they're a gang, Dad, and they're tough, and all they have to do is bash people up and I think it's terrible cos they don't have any reason for it.'

He smiled grimly. 'But they *'ave* got a reason. They're daft. They're growing up thinking that if they're hard and tough no one will notice they're thick as two short planks – like me.'

That came as a shock. My dad – thick?

'What's the worst thing they can do to you?' he said. His eyes were getting darker and his face was taut.

I shrugged.

He answered himself: 'The worst thing is that they might hit you like this.' He slapped me hard across the face. 'Or like this.' He slapped me again.

I leaned against the door in confusion – he had never struck me before. Whenever there was any chastising to do in the family, Mum did it – but not like this, not cold and not so hard. Then he said, 'You either give it or you take it, son. Give it and you're known for giving it. In time they'll leave you alone. But if you take it, you'll take it for ever. Like this.' And he slapped me again.

'Now hit me back,' he growled. But I couldn't. He was my dad.

'C'mon, son, you've got a reason now. Hit me back or I'll hit you again.'

His face was right up against mine and all of a sudden I knew that he'd meant what he'd said – so I slapped him back.

My fingers rang with the impact of it on his face.

That passage was boiling with emotion. There we stood, glaring at each other, hot, sweating.

Then, he continued, as if our duel hadn't happened: 'These boys, and this bleedin' wall, tell me about them.'

'There's a lot of them, Dad, and they –'

'It don't matter how many, son. Who's the leader?'

'Georgie Morris – and he's big and –'

'Don't matter how big, as long as you can reach his nose. Can you do that? Can you reach his nose?'

I pictured Morris and considered the question. 'Yes, I think so.'

'Well, you don't think, son, you *do* it. You go up to this wall and you sort out this Georgie Porgie and you ask, "Are you the Hard One?" Don't forget to say *Hard One*! Then, before he talks, punch him right on his fuckin' 'ooter and watch.'

'Watch what, Dad?'

'His blood. If you hit hard and on target the little bastard will bleed. Then, chances are, you won't get any more trouble – and even if he hits you back, he'll 'ave to kill you to match what you did to him. And that won't 'appen, will it?'

'No, Dad,' I said hopefully.

Then he opened the door and let me out into the street. 'See ya, son.' He grinned. The way he said 'son' made me so proud. I was his son, his eldest, and my father had just given me advice, and I was taking it like a son should.

That thought lasted me about ten minutes.

Then school approached, and playtime. The pit of my stomach filled with negatives . . .

The bell rang.

I walked along the corridors, down the stairs, through the assembly hall, and went into the playground.

The wall was waiting.

Georgie Morris was in his group, holding court. I stood watching him, transfixed, my head full of jumbled-up half-rehearsed words of defiance – but still no will to use them. Suddenly our eyes met. Twenty yards from each other we were eyeballing. Then, somewhere in my shaking soul, I stopped shaking. I started to walk towards my adversary. The group around me seemed to sense an occurrence. They turned to look too. Somehow I didn't feel scared as I usually did: I felt strong. The other groups were staring at me, too, and I felt stronger still. Then I was there, facing Morris. 'Are you the Hard One?' I said, cool as a cucumber.

Morris was half-way between a nod and a threat when I punched him.

His nose seemed to collapse into the surprise on his face – and, miracle of miracles, the blood flowed just like Dad said it would.

I didn't get hit back, and I didn't get killed, and I was the talk of the school for a week and, if truth be told, that last accolade meant more to me than anything else.

Nowadays right-thinking people would view the event as animalistic. As with all things viewed in retrospect, look at the time and place. Social workers, Citizens Advice Bureaux and the Law were not around – or not that you'd notice! Any problem between individuals or families had to be sorted out between themselves. Theft was rare – burglars worked away from home. If you burgled a neighbour and got caught, you were punished very firmly. Suffice to say, the culprit never did it again.

Arguments – between unhappy neighbours, over money-lending, death-bed wills – were all settled in front rooms or, if that failed, in the streets. Such confrontations were quickly over and done, with good compromise. Sometimes there was a family feud, but not often.

One fight I witnessed, between the Smiths and Longs, took place in Southwark Park in midsummer. What it was about, nobody now knows, but it was considered serious enough for the two complete families to meet face to face. From all over London they came, and more than a hundred men and women fought each other for at least an hour. When it ended, come dusk, the Longs had the moral victory as they had more women fighting than men and the Smiths had cheated by importing two visiting cousins from Australia!

The Hicks family had mini-feuds, and one in particular happened that summer. One early evening in the area called the Bull Ring of the estate, a sort of communal playground, a fight broke out between my brother Colin and a girl called Brenda Johnson. She was twelve and much bigger than him. It wasn't really a fight – Brenda hit Colin and he ran to my mum, crying. She led him back to Brenda. 'Now you hit her,' she told him. Which he did. End of episode? No!

An hour later there was a rap at our door and there they stood – the Johnson family: mother, father, uncle, aunt, three sons and two daughters.

To my mum Mrs Johnson snarled, 'What's all this about you 'itting my Brenda?'

'I didn't hit your Brenda, my Colin did.'

'That's not what I 'eard,' Mr Johnson growled.

'Well, you've got shit in your ears,' Mum gritted, and hit him on the chin.

Now the Johnsons bunched up and prepared for battle. I went to my mum's side and kicked Mr Johnson's legs. Mrs Johnson dragged me away and pretty soon the pushing and hitting turned into verbals, and away they went, with Mum very upset and me trying to settle her down.

That night when my dad came home I was in bed. I heard them

talking in the kitchen. Then his voice rose and I heard Mum upset again. The street door opened and he walked out.

I got up and stood with my mum at the door. We watched him stride into the middle of the Bull Ring. It was pitch-black night – every one of the flats surrounding him was in darkness, all asleep.

Then he shouted, his voice directed up to the top floors where the Johnsons lived.

'Johnson!' he yelled. *'Johnson!'*

One by one the tiny windows of the surrounding dwellings lit up. Then, as my dad yelled, the long parapets started to fill with people coming out to witness what was up. Only the two Johnson flats stayed dark. My dad called again: 'If anyone wants to give me trouble, wait till I get home – like now!'

He stood there until, slowly, the parapets cleared of onlookers and all the lights went out. Then he came in and told my mum off for not controlling the kids. That was the only occasion I saw him involved in inter-family quarrels.

The main reason for this was my mum. Many times she would have an argument, over us kids mostly, but she would always handle it herself. I wasn't to tell Dad, she'd say. He was left in reserve – like the Seventh Cavalry. But, as the eldest son, it was my duty to protect my brothers and put up a strong account of myself.

I hated it.

I dreaded coming home from school and seeing the street empty of my brothers, and my mum peeping from behind the curtains, waiting for me. Then the hurried talk in the passage before I put my books down: 'It's the Wilson boys. They kicked baby Roy and set on Colin when he interfered.'

'Where are they?'

'In their flat.'

Over to the Wilsons, or whoever, I'd go, with no anger – and no desire to fight, yet I knew I had to. I knew, too, that my mum was breaking her heart watching me from behind those curtains. We both knew I had to do what I was about to do. I would rap

on the Wilsons' door. The two boys inside were about my age so
it would be a fair fight – but they had parents in there too and
anything might happen. I would rap again and again, until at last
the door opened.

I would stare at Bill Wilson – still not angry. I liked him really
– he liked me too.

'What's bin goin' on?' I'd say, hoping Bill would tell me to fuck
off or mind my own business, anything to get me going. But he'd
just look at me. I couldn't weaken – someone had hit my brothers
and I had to make it known that it wasn't going to be ignored.
Now Bill's older brother Vic was at the door, moving between
me and Bill. I knew I'd got a fight on now because Vic was the
eldest and he, too, had to protect.

'What d'you want?' he said.

But I still hadn't the anger I needed to strike.

'None of your business,' I replied – knowing that it *was* his
business and might draw a rousing riposte.

Then it came.

'Who says so?' Vic sneered.

That was enough – nearly. I tried one more joust.

'I do,' I growled.

'Oh, yeah?' Vic sneered again.

And that was it. I threw the first punch and the second, and had
the same back. Then I was roughing it into their passage, giving
and getting until an adult stopped us.

'All right, all right,' said Bill and Vic's mum. 'That's enough.'

And it was – by tea-time the next day the episode was forgotten.
The point had been made and my dad wasn't involved – much to
Mum's relief.

Some wonderful additions came to Frean Street. We had a dog,
Bob, a small Welsh collie, and Bimbo the rabbit, bought to boost
a coming Christmas dinner but he outgrew five hutches.

So, all in all, we had no complaints. The war was over and, apart
from rationing, we wanted for little, except perhaps a sister, and
with Mum about to give birth the odds on having one were good.

'You'd get four to one easy if you 'ad a bet,' Dad told us. 'You stand on me, boys,' he explained. 'This time it's a girl, I can feel it in me water.'

My brother Rodney arrived on schedule and wore pink for the first year of his life. After that he left my mum's bedroom and moved into mine, his cot next to my bed. He was a smashing kid – he always giggled at the top of his little voice and loved to play jokes. His big trick was to throw a rubber ball at my head in the middle of the night. Whack! 'Ouch!' Little giggle. I tried to keep the missile away from him last thing at night, but he was a clever little sod. He just wouldn't go to sleep without it – he'd yell and shout until he had it in his hand. When he got it he'd lie down on his pillow, catch my eye and then give me a sly smile, as if to say, 'See you at about two in the morning, bruv.'

The best thing about our relationship was that Mum trusted me with him. When she returned to her early-morning cleaning job and Dad was sleeping after his night work in Soho, it was left to me to get the kids up. Colin always gave me trouble but got on eventually. Roy was never one to cause upset, but Rodney needed attention and care, and over time we became closer than we were with our other siblings. I think the lad's main attraction was his sense of humour – young as he was, he could cause or recognize something funny. He knew when things were comic – a dropped cup, a chucked rusk. He was no fool, our Rodney, but – in line with Mrs Stubbs's predictions – he was destined not to amuse for long.

The tragedy occurred soon after I had joined the CUM – the Cambridge University Mission. This was a boys' club put together and financed by young theologians from the university. They were wonderful blokes: they supplied the club, the table tennis, football all for free and all for us Bermondsey boys. The only catch was that at the end of the evening we had to sit down for the epilogue: the bloke would tell us how God had made the club possible and how thankful we were, then a short song of praise and home. It was bloody boring and those of us who weren't quick enough to get out just before the bell had to sit and watch the hopeful young clergy rehearse. But they got the message through to some of us.

My particular apostle was a Mr Law – I suppose he was about twenty-two. He was great at sport, didn't keep reminding us that we shouldn't swear, a teller of tales and his epilogues were much more interesting than the others'. So it followed that in due course me and a couple of others would forgo football to listen to the stories. Eventually he and I discussed Jesus and His absence in my heart, how I should consider asking Him to come into it so that I might have everlasting life. This idea, with its promises and good-will to all men, came to me as a revelation. A world war had just ended. Stories of the death camps and the cruelty of my fellow man were constant reminders of a godless time. And there in the CUM I was given a key to the Holy Kingdom.

I well remember that prayer, on my knees with Mr Law, eyes tight shut, knuckles white in anticipation. *Please, God, come into my heart*. 'Is that all?' I asked, as we got back on to our feet.

'The rest is up to you,' Mr Law said.

That night I bounded home. I felt so pure – so clean. God was in my heart and I was so happy.

Then came my brother's agony. There were no more rubber balls. Instead Rodney would cry out in the night and I would see him clutching his tiny genitals and kicking out his little legs just as I had with the purpura. My mum would try to nurse him to sleep. 'I don't know what to do,' she said to me. 'I can't see nuthin' wrong in him, except I know he's in pain.'

The doctor came.

I prayed that Rodney would get better.

More pain.

The doctor again.

More prayer – a little desperate now.

The doctor again, twice a day now.

This pain was louder – my little brother was in infant turmoil.

So was my heart. 'Come on, God, he's only a nipper. Stop the hurt, please.'

But God and the doctor were just not up to it. Pretty soon Rodney had to go to hospital.

Mum never took us brothers with her to visit, but the gaunt

look on her face every time she returned was enough to tell me that things were no better. 'Is he still hurting?' I ventured one afternoon.

Mum burst into tears. Then Dad told me that my little brother had cancer of the bladder, and that Mum was very tired and that he and Borough Council had arranged for me and Colin to go on holiday so Mum could have some rest.

'Will Rodney get better?' I asked.

'O' course he will.' Dad smiled. 'Soon.'

'Soon?' I cried. 'What about *now*? What about his pain?'

Mum's crying gave me the answer.

I ran upstairs and sat on my bed, looking at my little brother's empty cot. In my imagination I could see him twisting in pain – and pain was something I knew well. Once more I prayed: 'Oh, God, please, please, he's done no harm to anyone. He's just a little kid – stop the hurt, please, please.'

The next day me and Colin were taken to Bournemouth by train. It was summer and we counted the cows in the fleeting fields – only the black and whites because they were the racing colours of Lord Derby, a man much admired by our dad. The two women accompanying us were like twin sisters: they wore flowered hats and twinsets, and spoke with a very posh, clipped accent. They sat with their backs stiff and straight, hands clasped in their laps. I had seen stiff sisters like this in my books. They amused me, for a while, but by the time Colin and I had unpacked our vests and socks, I knew we had been betrayed. This could not possibly be a holiday.

Not here – not House Beautiful.

That was the name of the holiday home – *House Beautiful*! The post-war equivalent of Dotheboys Hall.

9

To this point I had enjoyed the discipline of an institutional life, but this place was like what a workhouse must have been. The house was full of underprivileged children. There were all sorts – kids from broken homes, kids from families below the poverty line and kids like me and my brother, there to give our folks a rest because they couldn't afford to send us to Southend. The staff, like the sisters on the train, were stiff and tough. Their regime was based on what you didn't do – 'You don't do this, you don't do that.' I made friends with a little fat kid called Trevor Binns. He had already been there for a week and, the same age as me (twelve), was old enough to know that this wasn't a place for a holiday.

From the moment we awoke – at six a.m. to the clang of a loud gong – we were ushered about in groups, six at a time. Six kids, six washes, six cornflakes, six teas, six bread and marmalade, six prayers of thanks, six sit down in the playroom – do not move from designated games and speak quietly. Next six in, please – quiet now! Eventually the playroom was full and the weather was stifling hot.

'When do we see the sea?' I asked Fat Trev.

He shrugged. 'Bin 'ere a week – ain't seen it yet.'

'Please, Miss,' I called across the playroom to Stiff Sister Grim, 'when will we see the sea?'

'When you deserve it,' she snapped.

I looked at Fat Trev in amazement. 'What are we doing *not* to deserve it?' I whispered.

'I dunno.'

By the third day I was close to despair. We were still stuck indoors and it was still boiling hot outside.

Colin wasn't taking this holiday too well. He missed Mum, and because so far he hadn't been sick, he hadn't experienced hospital so he didn't know how to handle being away from home. But I was an old hand. I knew what it was like. But here, in this place, there were no bonnets and bows – or books. Just games that kept kids sitting down – Snakes and Ladders, Tiddlywinks – and those little chairs with straight backs and us kids sitting facing each other, never daring to move without permission.

Fat Trev came to me on the fourth night.

'I'm goin' 'ome,' he whispered. 'I've 'ad enough – I bin 'ere a week and I still ain't seen the sea. D'you fancy runnin' away with me?'

But I couldn't do that: I had my brother Colin to think of and he was far too young to leave. So I begged Trev to stay. 'Let's give it another day,' I suggested.

The next morning after breakfast it was announced that ten kids would be taken to the beach, me, Colin and Fat Trev among them. All was forgiven.

We walked in close twos while the stiff sisters bobbed along in front, unsmiling as usual. We walked in silence for twenty minutes until at last we could hear the seagulls, smell the sea and taste the salt.

Then we saw it – the beach, the sand and the waves breaking over it, people laughing and playing. I grabbed Colin's hand and made to rush for the fun – but I was dragged back and cuffed round the ear. 'Stay,' Stiff Sister Grim snapped. She led us away from the other kids to a line of huts with chairs outside. 'Sit,' she cracked, pointing to the sand at her feet.

So I sat with Colin between my legs. Stiff Sister Smug took the others to the edge of the water. There I watched the kids remove their shoes and socks and stand there on the spot, coats still on, sun belting down on them. The only part of their young bodies they were allowed to move was their toes in the water.

I was worse off. Me and Colin were still stuck between Stiff Sister Grim's legs. She clumped me across the face every time she looked down.

Then she fell asleep.

The journey back to the house was in complete silence, but

once we were inside Stiff Sister Grim lowered the boom. 'You can pack your things tonight, as you and Colin are going home tomorrow,' she snapped. And then, before I could cheer, 'Apparently your brother Rodney died,' she added, with a winning sneer.

That last night, lying in the dormitory, my mind was a mixture of emotions. On the one hand Colin and I were going home: that was joyful. On the other, we were going home to death. Once I started to think about Rodney, everything else seemed unimportant. Rodney – my best little mate, that laughing, joking bunch of cuddle – was dead, gone, no more. All his pain had been part of his going.

And where were my other mates, God and Jesus? Where were they when they were handing out trust? And what about suffer the little children?

Well, he'd 'come unto them' and I guess you can't argue that if God wants a child He gets it, but in taking my brother, why did He have to hurt him? Was it so important that that innocent kid had had to *suffer*? And why did this God bloke like kids to experience agony?

Well, fuck you, chum! I decided.

I went out into the deserted garden of the dreaded house and let go my anger and confusion. I swore, I kicked at an imaginary God in the bushes, I rolled on the night grass grappling with Jesus, ripping Him from my heart. 'Piss off out of it,' I cried. 'And anuvver fing . . .' I glared at the dark sky but I was too exhausted to go on.

Come morning, I said goodbye to Fat Trev Binns and, holding Colin's hand tight, I retreated from House Beautiful.

When we arrived in London Mum met us at the station in black. She looked so very beautiful. 'Roy's at home with Dad.' She smiled as she led us to the tram.

'Where's Rodney?' Colin asked, because I hadn't had the guts to tell him.

Mum replied gently, 'He's gone to heaven.'

I glanced up to the clouds and, just between God and me, shook my fist.

Over the next few months home was a place of sadness. My mum and dad moved around as if in constant thought, my dad unusually distant. Yet it was never really gloomy. We all knew of our loss and the void that hung over us, but my parents had a way of conveying happiness.

I became aware of the deep sadness only once. I was taken short in the middle of the night and crept downstairs to make for the outside lavatory, which meant going through the kitchen. As I made to open the door I could hear my mum crying on the other side. She was all alone in the dead of darkness.

I paused. What do I do? Open the door?

No.

As young as I was, I knew that this was my mum's time and I had no part in it – so I went back to my bedroom and relieved myself out of the window. I missed Rodney and still wondered about the Lord for whom I had lost respect and trust. Colin had to rely on Roy for company, which did not suit him, so there was friction: me ignoring Colin, Colin ignoring Roy, Roy holding on to Mum, Mum emotionally exhausted and Dad in another world looking for a lost son.

10

Gradually I drifted into another phase of my life. As well as my books I had now discovered radio, that small electric thingummy-bob in the middle of the sitting-room table. It was a magic box! It gave out comedy shows, like *ITMA* and *Charlie Chester*, and musical programmes, like *Variety Bandbox* and *Henry Hall's Guest Night*, all this and the plays. I loved it.

There were moments during those entertainments, during a solo song from Vera Lynn perhaps, when I would creep behind the radio and peep into the back, half expecting to see the famous vocalist standing in a shaft of light singing her heart out. I kept these investigations to myself, knowing that if I did catch them out I would have a whole cast of entertainers all to myself, no bigger than my thumb.

It was a time of my youth when I tended to keep things inside me, my ever-changing thoughts, just for me. I shared little. Partly because I wasn't sure that what I had was worth sharing, except perhaps *Dick Barton, Special Agent*. And that only with Ginger Thompson.

We spent every weekday evening bent over the radio for the spellbinding fifteen minutes of the exploits of Dick, Jock and Snowy. Cliffhanger after cliffhanger had us on the edge of our chairs. Then as the strains of 'Devil's Gallop', the theme music, died away we would drive our imaginary Wolseley Super Snipe cars down Frean Street into St James's Park and re-enact the episode.

Music plays mysterioso
DICK: OK, Jock, Snowy, help me force this door.
DICK/JOCK/SNOWY: *Grunts and puffs.*
DICK: C'mon, chaps, harder – harder.

Door creaks open.

JOCK: It's very dark in there, Mr Barton.

DICK: Yes, I'm afraid it is. Well, here goes.

SNOWY: Just a minute, Captain, you ain't finkin' of goin' in there on your own, are you?

DICK: There's nothing to worry about, chaps – you two stay here. If I need help I'll call.

JOCK, SNOWY: But, sir!

Door creaks again.

Footsteps echo.

DICK *(echo)*: Now, I'll just move into the dark and feel my way along this wall.

More footsteps.

Ah! Another door – mmm, *open* this time. I'll ease myself inside and light a match.

Match lights (echo). Distant male scream.

JOCK *(shouts)*: Mr Barton!!

SNOWY *(desperate)*: Captain Barton!!!

Cue theme music.

And, I suppose, like Dick Barton, our family came through its own personal cliffhanger. Eventually Mum came out of her thoughts and started to talk again. Dad, too, came back with his dancing eyes. It was as if someone had flicked a switch: we were happy again. Once more, Mum and I would spend special time in the sitting room, deep in our reading, listening to Ted Ray or Glenn Miller – and especially Paul Temple. At the first few bars of the 'Coronation Scot' she would rush out of the kitchen with tea and sandwiches, safe in the knowledge that the kids were abed and Dad in Soho, then snuggle up close to me as the great mysteries unfolded.

To add to all this she became pregnant again. She and Dad were determined to have that daughter! They would sit and chat about their little girl constantly. Dad would wax lyrical about her while Mum would knit and I would sit listening, sometimes holding the yarn while she rolled wool into balls. Her face was flushed with

Dad's talk about a daughter, so much so that I knew if another boy turned up it might break her heart. Everything in the house was pink again.

I decided to give God one more chance. I pointed out that I still didn't understand why He had done what He did to Rodney – and that I would bring the subject up again and again until He told me – so He owed me and my family a favour. If He fixed it for Mum to have a little girl, we could be friends again.

He accepted the suggestion.

My sister Sandra was born. White hair again, big eyes – and female!

This was not a baby to be bounced, I decided. This was not a sticks-and-snails-and-puppy-dog-tails baby. This was a little girl – and I was her slave. Like Rodney, she eventually went into the cot next to me. And it seemed that I was forever checking her breathing and tucking her in, washing her pretty little hands and slipping her the odd rusk at night just so I could hear her munching in contentment. I was also given the honour of taking her to the local kindergarten at Kintore Way each morning.

Mum now had a full-time job at the Peek Freans biscuit factory. She kept on the office-cleaning job so her mornings were stacked. But with me taking charge of Sandra, she and Dad could concentrate on the other kids and on their jobs.

School, too, was playing a great part in my life. It wasn't so much the learning – I still found maths and geography a chore – but the English and history lessons were exciting. I couldn't wait to put pen to paper: my composition book was full of short stories. I wrote my first play *The Bermondsey Gang* and directed it for the school prize-giving, then produced a novel and sent it to Enid Blyton for her comments. There were five murders in the first chapter, and she suggested that I might concentrate more on punctuation and a little less on pugilism.

But my stories and plays brought me listeners and watchers and I enjoyed the celebrity. I bathed in the laughter at a joke or Mum's gasp of surprise at a twist in a plot. I knew now that I liked being the centre of attention. I knew now how my dad felt when he sang at parties and people clapped. All this plus the coming of our

Relaxing at home in Frean Street with my little sister Sandra.

radiogram was the dawning of my fate: not only did it have a radio it had something new, something I had never seen. A turntable! And with it, that first Sunday afternoon, had come a record: 'Knock On Wood' by Danny Kaye.

Danny Kaye was my idol. His zany performance in those super-colour musicals coming out of post-war Hollywood was out-rageous when compared with the song-and-dance men of the day. Now, in my hands, I had a record of him singing and I could play it over and over again. Coincidentally around this time I saw two brothers in a film doing an act just as crazy as Kaye's – George and Bert Bernard. Their speciality was miming to records, but they didn't just mouth along with the sound, they added a performance of their own. It was a remarkably funny idea, especially when they were mimicking female opera singers. Their attitude and their daft costumes impressed me so much that I tried out the concept one quiet afternoon at home.

Radiogram switched on, record on turntable, me and the mirror. I must have played Danny's song a thousand times, but every time I discovered something new: when to breathe, when to react facially at a gag in the lyric, how to move when the band played solo, how to start and how to finish. Soon I had to find out if I was on the right track – was the idea funny? Would it amuse? Entertain, even? That evening the sitting room was packed to capacity. Mum sat with Sandra on her lap, Dad took charge of Roy, who was determined to be somewhere else, and Colin knelt on the floor with Bob the collie. I switched on the radiogram and we waited for it to warm up. A soft buzz came through the speakers. I lifted the stylus on to the black lacquer disc, and the orchestra – *my* orchestra – crashed out the opening bars of the number. I jumped from the radiogram and strutted, pranced, dipped and dived my way through the routine. Then came the finale: the big drums rolled, the saxophones soared, the brass section screamed as Danny and I sang:

> *Knock, knock, knock, honey*
> *Knock, knock, knock on wood*

Smash finish.

The family took it terrific. They laughed, they clapped, and within a few minutes of wallowing in the euphoria that only a performer feels when things go right, I knew I had found something – something so magical that I didn't want to let it go. Their smiling eyes, the laughs, the applause, the knowledge that this had been their true reaction.

Or had it?

Dad thought it was so good that Auntie Mary and my cousins, Rose, Billy and George Junior, should see it, so me, him and the record went over to the Neckinger Estate and presented ourselves at their door. Uncle George answered it. 'What's occurred?' he said, in half-welcome.

'My Tommy's got somethin' to show you,' Dad said, leading me into the flat.

Auntie Mary beamed from the stove.

'Everyone sit down,' Dad ordered, eyes dancing. The family sat. Dad waved at me. 'OK, son, hit it!'

I looked around. There was no radiogram, not even a gramophone. 'Hit what?'

'Blimey, ain't you got a gram?' Dad cried to Mary.

The family shook their heads in unison.

But he wasn't going to let the moment die. 'Who's got one, then?'

'They've got one in the Ship,' Uncle George muttered, confused.

'We'll go to the Ship, then.' Dad led us out of the flat and across to the pub.

The public bar was half full, a dozen or so standing at the counter, two crowded tables and a few people warming themselves by the open fire. Bing Crosby was crooning from the speakers of the gramophone at the end of the room. Dad ordered a round of drinks and had a quiet word with the publican. Bing was demoted and Danny Kaye went on the turntable. There was no introduction. I just went into the routine as rehearsed. No fear, no second-thoughts delay. I oozed with the confidence of innocence and sold it with all my might. The audience started with 'What's all this, then?' and ended with the same reaction I'd got at home, only it was louder – they whistled and cheered.

I was on my fifth lemonade and my fifth encore when Colin came to the door. 'Mum says she's goin' to bed,' he shouted.

'No, she ain't!' Dad roared. 'We're 'aving a whip round.' A hat was produced to collect donations for the party. Auntie Mary and Cousin Rose ran home to get bread, butter, cheese and tomatoes, and I tore round to Frean Street to warn Mum that a cabbage was about to begin. The front room was cleared – the radiogram pushed in, chairs arranged – and all that night Frean Street rang with the best knees-up I'd ever had. It was my first opening-night party.

For months after, me and my records – I'd added 'Every Street's A Boulevard (In Old New York)' by Dean Martin and Jerry Lewis

– were invited to most parties in the area. Mum and Dad came too, and the pride in their faces each time I performed was like a standing ovation.

At fourteen, I was approaching the end of my schooling and preparing for what I would do when I reached fifteen and was let loose on the world. What I really wanted to be in my heart of hearts was a performer, but in spite of my act with the records and my dreams in front of the Palladium posters, I knew it could never be. So, what *would* I do?

Mum wanted me to go 'in the print', which meant the newspaper-printing business. 'From the print shop you can get into the news office,' she said. 'Then one day you might be a journalist on *The Times*.'

'Or a tipster on the *Sporting Life*,' Dad retorted.

I went to Fleet Street and, with the help of a relative, I got to walk on the print floor for a day, but instead of feeling excited by all the buzzing machinery, I could see only iron, grease and ink. 'I don't fancy it,' I told Mum.

'But you like words – you like writing,' she argued.

'It's just a factory,' I said, and she knew I would not relent. True, I didn't know *what* I wanted, but working from nine to five in a factory environment did not appeal.

At school, during that last year, we boys about to leave would go on 'tea trips', days out visiting local factories on a recruitment recce. I went to leather tanneries, vinegar factories, even Mum's old haunt Feavers, the tin-box makers. But for all the slap-up teas and the over-friendly foremen, I was determined not to give in. Then someone in a pub mentioned the Savoy Hotel. He knew the personnel manager, a Mr Toye: he was always looking for smart young people who wished to follow the catering trade. Mum took me over the water to meet him. Once again I was heading for that other world. We left the tram at Waterloo station and

walked across Waterloo Bridge. Mum said, 'You get a nice view
of the hotel from here.'

And we did.

As we walked the bridge, I looked out to my left and below me
the muddy grey Thames lapped along at its confident pace. Then
I saw the Savoy, standing above the trees along the Embankment
like a wedding cake, all white stone with a great clock. My heart
gave a leap. I could imagine having a job in such a place – *belonging*
to it. We walked along the Strand with its high-backed buses and
the great Lyceum Theatre perched on the corner. Then I saw the
Adelphi – I was entering hallowed ground now – and we turned
into the Savoy courtyard.

The first thing that struck me was the great effigy of Britannia
poised above the entrance guarding the splendour within and, on
the right, the Savoy Theatre – I had read a biography of W. S.
Gilbert that told its story. In order to present their operas in their
own way, Gilbert and Sullivan, with their friend the impresario
Richard D'Oyly Carte, had built the theatre, which, for the first
time in Britain, had electric lighting. I touched the brick of the
façade. My fingers tingled.

I wondered if Mum could tell what was going on in my heart
– I wondered whether she knew that if someone came out of this
showplace and offered me a job licking the floor I would only ask,
'How wet do you want it?'

But Mum was thinking elsewhere. She was looking across the
small drive at the entrance to the famous Grill. Two doormen,
solid chaps, moved sharply to every taxi and private car, snatching
open the doors to allow beautifully dressed patrons to glide over
the polished pavement into the eatery.

Mum's eyes flashed and she gripped her purse to her bosom.
'I bin in there,' she said proudly, 'an' not to clean it neiver.'

We braved the front entrance to meet Mr Toye. He was a small,
jovial man with thick horn-rimmed glasses. He met us in the grand
foyer. 'Perfect, perfect – you'll be absolutely perfect,' he chortled
to me.

I felt quite welcome.

He led the way past the reception area into the main public rooms, up in the lift and along the luxurious corridors where the suites were. We entered one. Huge windows looked over the Thames towards Bermondsey, whose distant roofs and smoky chimneys seemed a million miles away from the plush splendour of the room I was standing in, up to my knees in carpet. But I didn't feel comfortable – I didn't belong.

Mum kept saying, 'Well I never,' and 'Oooh, Tommy!'

Eventually we returned to Reception. 'Now, Tommy,' Mr Toye said kindly, 'when you start at the Savoy, it will be as a bell-boy, so let's watch the desk and observe what a bell-boy does.'

We sat and watched. Occasionally a bell would ring and a boy would spring out from behind a partition at the rear of the desk. Red pillbox hat and a jacket with gold buttons all over it, black trousers, highly polished shoes and white gloves neatly placed in the left gold-braid epaulette. He would receive his task from the receptionist and dash off into the hotel.

Then another bell. Another boy.

Then another.

Mr Toye took me behind the partition. It was a tight little alcove, like a rabbit hutch. There were two long benches packed with pillboxed bell-boys, all sitting with their heads buried in comics. No conversation. Above their heads was a big bell, which rang every now and then, causing the next boy in the line to stuff his comic up his jacket and rush round to the desk. I couldn't imagine spending my life sitting in line reacting to a bell.

I looked at my mum and she understood.

'I knew,' she said, on the tram home, 'soon as that bleedin' bell rang, I knew you wasn't 'aving any of it. Well, I don't blame you – but I don't know what you're goin' to do with yourself.'

'He's goin' racin',' Dad announced that night.

'No, he ain't,' Mum said, stirring her tea so fast that it lapped over the lip of the cup. 'Over my dead bleedin' body.'

But, as usual, Dad had his way and I was relieved. Racing wasn't exactly the future I'd had in mind, but the opportunity of being

From baby boy to cabin boy.

with the 'uncles' again and doing the Jack and Danny was not to be ignored.

But Darbo had other plans. 'You're going to learn a trade,' he said. 'You ain't goin' about doin' what I do cos it's a mug's game in the long run.'

'What am I going to do, then?' I asked.

'I'm givin' you to Dummy,' he said, with no further explanation. He went back to reading his paper, with Mum still stirring anxiously.

'Who or what is Dummy?' I asked her in a whisper.

She shrugged her shoulders. 'If your father says it's all right then it's all right. He only wants the best for you, son – trust him.'

'Do you?' I asked mischievously.

She merely grinned and sipped her tea.

As I was still at school I had to wait for Saturday to join Darbo at the races, but on the Friday night before the big day, he announced that he was taking me on a 'meet'.

'Who with?' Mum asked suspiciously.

'Dummy,' Darbo replied.

Later that night, in my Sunday-best suit, I got the tram with Darbo to London Bridge. We waited outside the station for a while, until Uncles Garlic and Nibbler swaggered round a corner, overcoat collars above their ears, trilby hats at an angle over one eye. They had obviously been on the piss. We stood there looking at each other, no one speaking, me and Dad staring, Garlic and Nibbler swaying happily with big grins on their faces. Then Darbo broke the silence. 'Well?' he said.

'Well what?' Garlic replied.

'Well, where is he?' Darbo asked impatiently.

Garlic and Nibbler looked behind them, then realized they were alone, staggered back to the corner and shouted to someone on the other side. 'Oi, Dummy – Dummy,' they cried, and then louder. 'Dummy, for Gawd's sake!' Nothing happened.

Then Garlic reached into his pocket and took out a handful of stones. He selected one, about the size of a conker, and threw it at something – or someone – on the other side of the road. 'C'mon, we're over here,' he cried. There was a slight pause, then it came into the light.

Now, the uncles were big. But the man who lurched towards us was gigantic. Six feet four and the same wide. He wore a fedora hat that resembled a Blenheim bomber, his shoes were shrimp boats and the material in his overcoat would have clothed a company of Cossacks. Everything he passed disappeared into shadow. He came to an uncertain halt in front of Darbo. Then, extending his huge arms, he took hold of him and lifted him five feet off the ground with an ear-splitting roar. 'DOAARB!!!'

Then he put Dad down and he turned to me. I was getting neckache just looking up at him. The great arms came down towards me like a couple of cranes. Then I, too, was hoisted with another great roar. 'OOAARH!'

Darbo wiped the sweat off his bald head and spoke to the giant. 'This is my boy, Tommy,' he said, mouthing the words big and slow. 'TOODEE!' the giant roared.

'Yus, that's it – Tommy.' Darbo grinned, patting him as if he was an elephant. Then he spoke to me: 'Say hello to Uncle Dummy.'

'Hello, Uncle Dummy.'

'OOAARHOOO,' Dummy bellowed, picked me up again and swung me around as if I was a piece of silk.

'Fancy a drink?' Garlic suggested, and began to walk back towards the corner.

Darbo and Nibbler followed, leaving Dummy with me, still in mid-air.

He put me down and, like the other uncles, ruffled my hair. He had a smile that came like a sunrise. His eyes were those of a gentle St Bernard – and now that he had greeted us he was calmer.

'DEBADOOM,' he said, and showed me a card that said he was deaf and dumb. Another 'conker' came from the corner and hit his back. He turned with a good-natured grin and acknowledged Uncle Garlic's summons. I followed him across the road to the pub. And there I sat, surrounded by the uncles and Darbo, listening to the jokes and the anecdotes. Dummy listened too, seeming to grasp every word, his kind eyes searching the mouths, working out the words. Occasionally he would thump the table with a giant fist and emit a sound. 'OOAHGOOGH!'

The rest of the table would either burst into laughter or nod in serious agreement with what only they could decipher.

Darbo told me later that they had all been together since they were children and Dummy could hold his own with any of them. ''E don't miss a bleedin' trick,' Darbo said. 'Ever since 'e was born 'e's bin like it. The only trouble we ever 'ad was gettin' his attention till someone thought of these.' He showed me a handful of stones like Garlic's. 'We all carry 'em just in case,' he said. He had seen the effect they had on me – I didn't like the way my father and his friends practised their aim on Dummy.

'Don't you worry about him,' he said. 'I told you, he don't miss a trick. He knows what goes on and he knows we're his mates – nuffin' we do together is out of order. You just listen to what he learns ya and you'll be fine.'

Before we parted that evening the giant took me to one side. 'OUDAHUDS,' he roared, pointing at me.

I'd no idea what he wanted.

'OUDAHUDS,' he roared again, pulling at my wrists.

He wanted me to hold out my hands. I did as he bade me. He took them gently in his own and touched my forehead with my right hand. 'Unnah!' he growled.

I stared at him. Then Darbo whispered in my ear: 'One,' he said. 'Say one.'

'One,' I said.

Dummy ruffled my hair. 'Unnah,' he roared. He was pleased. Then he and the uncles left.

Darbo and me walked to the tram – he had his arm round my shoulders. 'Well, son, tomorrow's the day.'

'When I start my trade?'

'That's right. Tomorrow you start – he likes you.'

'Who likes me?'

'Dummy does . . .'E just showed you 'ow to do a one.'

We jumped on to the tram. A thousand questions sat on my tongue. Darbo chuckled and pulled me close to him. 'He's the best in the world, our Dummy,' he said. 'You watch what he learns you and one day you'll be fine.'

It was the second time he'd said that but he didn't explain any more – we just sat huddled together till we got home.

Kempton Park Races did not seem as big as Goodwood but it still had the usual enclosures – Silver Ring, Tattersalls and the grandstand. Dummy met me and Darbo outside the grandstand gates. He gave me an enclosure ticket, which I tied to the lapel of my jacket. Then Darbo waved goodbye and left us.

I followed the giant into the grandstand and we walked up the steep wooden stairs to the top. Then he put on a pair of white gloves and, looking out at the expanse of bookmakers' stands through huge binoculars, he took a deep breath and gave a great roar: 'OOOAGHAA.'

Everyone around us jumped. He roared again, then began to wave his gloved hands in the air, touching his head and his shoulders in a series of fast signals. All was revealed. He was a tic-tac man. More than that, he was a champion. No one in the profession could see quicker or signal clearer than Dummy – no one else in the game had his concentration. When he was working he could shut out the whole world and talk with his hands to the faceless people out there in the betting areas hanging on his every movement.

After the first race he gave me a pair of gloves. 'POHDER-OON,' he said, indicating that I put them on.

Then he took me through the signals for one, two, three, four and five. By the end of the meeting I had a smattering of the betting signal system, but it was not until the end of the season, five months later, that he allowed me to send a message. I had to lay an eleven to ten-on favourite.

Because of my small size Dummy grabbed my hips and lifted me above the crowd. With a set of clear and concise signals, I sent the wager across the course towards a receiver in the Silver Ring.

Nothing happened, just a sea of heads going about their business.

Me and Dummy watched for an answer.

Suddenly, far over to the left, a flap of gloves hit the sky like a pair of white doves. The bet was accepted.

Dummy gave a shout to equal Pan himself. Then he dragged me down the grandstand steps and into the bar. 'DOOLA-BODAYS,' he ordered, thumping the counter.

Two lemonades were served and we toasted each other.

That night as we said goodbye, he stared into my face and murmured, 'Eefoguh!'

I had no idea what he meant until he pressed a handful of stones into my hand and lurched away.

But my future was still waiting in the mist . . .

'How about the Grenadier Guards?' Ginger suggested. 'They look after the King and live in Waterloo. You can go 'ome for tea every evening.'

'You'll have to get taller first,' Dad told me. I was just four feet eight inches.

'How long will that be?'

'When you're taller.'

For weeks I measured myself after every meal. The wall in my bedroom bore a series of dots where I had stood close and stubbed a pencil mark just above my head. But the upward movement of my frame was non-existent – so much so that when I joined the dots together one night with a red crayon all I saw was a straight horizontal line. I was in despair.

Then Ginger found the answer. He came round one evening as usual, just before *Dick Barton, Special Agent* on the radio, dragging two iron manhole covers that he'd 'borrowed' from the back of the post office and an ex-German parachute harness that his mum had found in a hopfield in Kent. Up in my bedroom, he tied one end of the harness to the outside knob of my door, and lifted me up in it on the other side, left me dangling and attached the manhole covers to my ankles. Now I knew what growing pains were! I hung there for an hour, until my dad came to see what we were up to. He looked at me. 'What's he doin' up there?'

'Growin',' Ginger replied.

Dad walked away without a word, came back with one of his old suits and laid it on my bed.

'You'll be needin' that for school in the mornin',' he said, and went back downstairs.

We tried the idea for two more days, but the dots still didn't rise so we gave up and concentrated on Dick Barton instead.

Until that terrible, terrible day.

An awesome occurrence made me believe that this year was to be full of disappointment.

Sir,
I still remember that dark night in the earliest of the fifties when, complete with my corned-beef sandwich and Bovril, I settled down to hold my breath for the fifteen-minute ritual *Dick Barton, Special Agent*. Huddled next to the radio, the sound turned to environmental hazard, I prepared to gasp with Mr Barton, argue with Jock and panic with Snowy, but it was not to be. 'Tonight,' the announcer said, 'we present *The Archers*, an everyday story of country folk.' Country folk? I sprinted next door to Ginger Thompson's set – curses! It had said the same. Together Ginger and I turned the knobs in search of our beloved hero – to no avail, just those monotonous Ambridge accents. It was then that I glared into the

speaker and uttered my curse. 'I wish,' I wailed, 'that TV makes you redundant. I wish that commercial radio steals your thunder and, worse, I wish upon you all manner of de Manios, Blackburns, Saviles and Youngs.'

But tonight, twenty years on, my beloved Barton is back. I hereby give notice to Auntie Beeb that all is forgiven. But I still reserve my rights on curses relating to other lost favourites: *Ray's a Laugh*, *Variety Bandbox* and the Voice of Frederick Ferrari.

Letter to *The Times*, 1972

In the late summer of 1951 my mum was given a new office-cleaning job in the City at a huge building in Leadenhall Street. She started work at five a.m. and by seven she was on the executive floor, admiring a collection of model ships in glass cases. When she got home she told me about them. 'They weren't with sails, they had them great funnels and port'oles all over the place, and not like them greasy tubs that come to the wharves! All polish they was, painted and clean.'

A couple of days later she came home with a set of postcards. They were in full colour, each featuring a different part of the world, a bay in the West Indies, the New York skyline, the Pyramids. In each picture there was a ship with huge decks and majestic smokestacks. 'Where are these boats?' I asked.

'Cunard House in Leadenhall Street.'

The idea that a fleet of luxury liners could be berthed in the middle of the City of London was pretty far-fetched, but if Mum said they were in Leadenhall Street, they were, and I was intrigued.

'If you get up early tomorrow, you can come and have a butcher's if you like.'

When I arrived at Cunard House the next morning the building was deserted, with just the odd light on in the offices that hadn't yet been cleaned. I met my mum at the side entrance. I'd never seen her in her work clothes before, with a turban on her head, her curls peeping out of the sides, a stained rubber apron over her dress, kneepads and some kind of material tied round her feet. She looked very tired. She took my hand and led me into the building, her fingers red raw and rough as sandpaper. As she took me through the polished corridors, I thought of all the years that she had looked like this, away from our eyes at home. I wanted to take hold of those tired hands and tell her she didn't have to do it ever again. Then we met a couple of her mates scrubbing a flight of stairs.

'This is Tommy, my eldest.'

'Coo, just like you, Betty, the bleedin' image!' They smiled.

They were a motley lot, those ladies. They cleaned and laughed and joked, and by the time Mum and me reached the executive floor I'd met even more of the workforce. I knew then that they did not share the feelings I had about their job. They were a group of independent women who did the work for simple reasons, to earn some money and enjoy the company of friends. Maybe home and its chores were deadly dull compared to the laughs in Leadenhall Street.

The model ships on the executive floor of Cunard House were unbelievable. The idea that vessels the size of the ones behind the glass could float was beyond me – and if they were just models, what was the real thing like? I could taste the adventure in them.

'I wouldn't risk it,' Dad warned in our kitchen. 'I knew a bloke called Titanic Ted, one of the few survivors 'e was, and once they got 'im 'ome 'e was so frightened of water that 'e never 'ad a wash for twelve months.'

It didn't make any difference. I had made up my mind. I was going to sea.

One early morning Mum was finishing on the executive floor when he came into Reception. About sixty, he was, a tall man in a blue naval uniform, sporting gold stripes across his sleeves and a cap with gold on its peak tucked under his arm. He wished Mum good morning and disappeared into a large office. ''E's the fleet commodore,' said Elsie Sparks, in answer to Mum's question. 'I ain't seen him for ages. 'E usually works out of Liverpool.'

'What does he do, then?' Mum pressed.

'Everyfing,' Elsie said, scrubbing down the stairs with Mum alongside.

'Where does he work? How do I meet him?'

Elsie stopped dead in her tracks. 'Meet who?'

'The commodore.'

'Betty Hicks! You, of all people, fancyin' a soddin' sailor!'

Mum blushed. 'I don't fancy 'im. I need 'im.'

'Flippin' 'ell, this is gettin' worse!'

'I need him to help my Tommy, you randy old cow. If I ask, he might put in a word, get him started, you know . . . sort of . . .'

'Push 'is boat out?' Elsie suggested.

'Yeah,' Mum said thoughtfully. 'First, I 'ave to meet him proper, though, y'know, businesslike.'

As the two women scrubbed their way to the bottom of the stairs, they discussed the various permutations of meeting the commodore. But no matter how many times they got excited about an idea, they were stopped in their tracks by the fact that the 'top tar' worked and lived in Liverpool, and only came to Leadenhall Street once in a blue moon.

'It will 'ave to be today, then,' Mum announced. 'He's upstairs now so all I 'ave to do is —'

'Wet yourself!' May Thomas said, washing her arms in the service sink. 'Cos that's what I'd do, standin' there in me kneepads, wavin' a scrubbin' brush in the bleedin' air. "'Scuse me, skipper, but my boy Tommy wants to be a sailor like you. Any chance of lendin' 'im yer boat?" No, I'd forget it, Betty, honest I would. You could get the sack!'

Mum wasn't giving in; she had an idea but needed help.

The offices opened for business at nine a.m., giving her half an hour to make herself decent. The clothes she'd come to work in were worn and colourless. Her mates came to the rescue. May had a sweet outfit, Sassy Coates had a freshly heeled pair of shoes and good old Elsie had a new hat and coat. 'But don't sit down in it. I only bought it yesterday for a funeral today and don't want it creased,' she pleaded.

They curled her hair with a couple of forks on a gas ring, the chipped and torn nails looked better after Dolly Walker's nail polish, and a vertical line drawn with Elsie's eyebrow pencil down the back of her legs gave the appearance of stockings. Mum was ready.

By the time she reached the executive floor a receptionist was at her desk. 'Can I help you, madam?'

'Yes, please. I'd like to see the commodore.'

'Name, please?'

'Hicks, Mrs Elizabeth Hicks.'

'You do have an appointment, Mrs Hicks?'

''Fraid not, but I thought maybe . . .'

'I'm very sorry but the commodore is only here for the day and is booked solid.'

'Not even a minute?'

'Sorry, no. Not even a minute.'

Mum was about to leave when a voice stopped her in her tracks. It was the commodore standing by his office door, his brain ticking over as he tried to place her. 'Haven't we met before?'

'Oh, yes,' Mum said craftily.

Downstairs in the cleaners' room, Elsie and the girls were watching the clock.

'Well, she ain't back yet.'

'That means she's in.'

'Or out! On 'er ear'ole!'

'Not in my new bleedin' coat.'

'She's got some cheek, I'll give her that.'

'Bottle!' Elsie exclaimed. 'She's got bottle.'

'Or the sack,' someone put in. The others nodded mournfully.

'So you have a son who wants to go to sea, eh?' the commodore said, sitting on the corner of his vast desk.

Mum nodded, holding tight to her handbag for dear life, sinking into the plush leather sofa cushions, dreading the state of Elsie's coat when she got up again – if she got up again.

'So, he's about to leave school at fifteen and wants to sail the oceans of the world with Cunard?'

'Yes, sir.'

'He's a mite young, Mrs H.'

'But he's so keen, sir. Can't you send him?'

'Send him? The days of the press-gang are gone, alas!' He smiled.

'He told me that last night.' Mum sighed.

'Told you what?'

'About press-gangs and Trafalgar Square and some geezer called Dick chasing this whale. Y'know, books, all the bleedin' time. Captain Hornblower and that Charles Laughton thing wiv Clark Gable.'

'*Mutiny on the Bounty*?' the commodore suggested.

Mum nodded and clutched her bag tighter.

'Well, there is one way that we might get him into the service – as a cabin boy. Let's have a cup of tea on it.'

The girls were getting worried.

'She's been arrested, charged for impersonating a lady.'

'She is a lady, you dozy cow.'

'Or raped – 'e could 'ave taken advantage of her! 'E's a sailor, don't forget.'

Upstairs in the commodore's office Mum was finishing her biscuit. 'Thank you for the tea.'

'It's not as good as the stuff you girls make downstairs.' He grinned and led her to the head of the stairs, ignoring her blushes.

The girls watched from below as Betty Hicks descended from Olympus, with Zeus waving a gold-braided arm in fond farewell.

'I've gotta hear about this,' May said, scandalized.

'Me too!' Elsie cried.

'But you got a funeral to go to.'

'Sod the funeral! If you think I'm goin' to miss one blinkin' word, you can think again.'

And everything that Mum told her mates she told me and my dad. All we had to do now was hope that the commodore kept his promise.

The letter arrived within days.

Dear Thomas Hicks,
We are pleased to inform you that you have been accepted by the National Sea Training School under the Cunard quota. Please send the fee of twenty-five pounds by return. This fee is non-refundable. The course begins on 7th January 1952.
    Yours . . .

Twenty-five pounds by return. I needed money quick! Impossible!

It was nearly Christmas and there was no way my folks could find such a sum. Me and Ginger kicked a brick around a bombsite and discussed it. He knew a relation of Tim Sackett, the fruiterer near Southwark Park, who was usually on the lookout for an errand boy; it was only for Saturdays but it paid five shillings. Then there was Bert the milkman: he was getting on a bit and always willing to pay for someone to hump heavy crates up tenement stairs. 'It's mornin's only before school,' Bert puffed, as he pushed his fully laden cart up Dockhead Rise. 'Monday to Friday, five bob.'

That plus Sackett's came to ten shillings a week. Not enough.

Then there came an extra bit of luck in the shape of Harry Meadows. 'Harry the Horse' had one solitary tooth in the middle of his upper gum, and spoke in a staccato lisp. He leaned against the corner of London Bridge and Southwark Cathedral selling evening newspapers in all weathers, his arthritic hand covered with a mangy old mitten. As each paper changed hands old Harry would spit on the coin offered, chuck it into his leather pouch and pull his mitten back to his wrist with a tug of his tooth. Rain, sleet or snow, there he stood, worn plimsolls digging into the pavement as he held on to his wares and yelled over the traffic, 'Shta, *News* a' *Standard* . . . Shta, *News* a' *Standard*.'

'Poor sod,' everyone said. 'No wonder 'e can never get any 'elp!' He was indeed a terrible advertisement for his job.

I figured if old Harry was desperate enough maybe we could make a deal, and he agreed. I was to work the papers Monday to

Friday, every evening after school, and he would give me a per-
centage on every quire I sold. I worked out that by January,
counting the papers and the other two jobs, I could save twelve
pounds. Still not enough.

It was time for an extraordinary general meeting. Mum began:
'Now, you do really want to go, don't you?'

I nodded.

'Cos it's so near Christmas and your birthday, and what with all
the expense –'

'I've got twelve quid,' I exploded, anxious for the meeting to
get off to a good start.

Mum darted a look at Dad, who shifted in his chair uncomfortably. 'What did you do? Rob a bank?' he quipped.

'Well, I ain't got it all now, but by January I will. I've got three
jobs.'

When they heard what I had been up to they must have been
betwixt telling me off and patting me on the back, but they did
neither. Mum continued, 'Anyway, we've got to 'ave twenty-five
pounds now. I've had a word with Auntie Mary and she and Uncle
George have nicely said we can borrow it.'

'Only don't drown yourself the first day!' Dad added.

Then they went into the kitchen chuckling and cuddling each
other.

I sat in my room upstairs with a combination of joy and concern.
My mum had actually borrowed money. It must have hurt her
dignity to make that decision – even if the debt was to Auntie
Mary. Perhaps I should go back downstairs and tell them I had
changed my mind. But I hadn't – I couldn't. I had to come to
terms with the fact that I was going to sea. No matter what.

In the meantime the only thing I could do was make sure that
the twelve quid I had promised was on the table when it was
needed – and, of course, pass out of the training school with the
proficiency badge Mum said the commodore had mentioned.
But certain happy happenstances before and after that coming
Christmas made the possible twelve pounds into a probable twenty.

★

My 'act' was still in demand. I had added to the programme 'Mule Train' by Frankie Laine, with a piece of cotton at the end of a pencil to mime the crack of the whip, and the duet 'When I'm Calling You' from *Rose Marie* by Jeanette MacDonald and Nelson Eddy. My performances now ran to more than ten minutes. I don't know whether my parents 'suggested' it, or whether their friends had heard about my quest for quids. But, strangely, when I turned up at parties now I was given the odd ten shillings here and there for performing. Imagine! I was fourteen, on my way to the thrill of the sea, saving money like mad to go to training school and now I was getting paid for doing what I really wanted to do but never could: the theatre. Confusing!

But the act was going terrific. With the laughter, the applause and mingling with the 'audience' afterwards, getting all those pats on the back and kind encouragement, it was no wonder that I always spent the day after a show walking round in a trance with a fixed smile. I would carry the milk crates for Bert Williams before school and sell the evening papers for Harry Meadows afterwards. It was midwinter: the early mornings were foggy and wet, and the evenings on London Bridge had the added ingredient of a high wind from the Thames: their jobs were nigh impossible to do, let alone enjoy. But with their humour and outlook on life, I made it to the weekends and the comparative quiet of Sackett's Fruiterers.

At last January dawned. I had left school, and to celebrate that great event, plus a rosy future, I took Mum and Dad to the Trocadero cinema at the Elephant and Castle for a live Sunday concert. Reg 'Confidentially' Dixon, the famous comedian, was the star, supported by the Tito Burns Quintet, and that night for the first time I saw and heard a guitar. Its sound rang through the packed theatre like a kiss. Unlike the other instruments it seemed able to change colour and mood with a mere shift of the player's fingers. It fascinated me.

Afterwards we walked from the Elephant up to the Bricklayers Arms. All I could talk about was the show, while Mum kept harking back to the fact that I was off to Gravesend the next morning. I didn't want to discuss it. I was feeling the strain a bit, going away from home, a new environment, new friends, when Dad started, 'Which one of us would you like to go wiv you tomorrow?'

'None of you.'

Then Mum put in her pennyworth. 'Don't be silly. You can't go to a new school without a parent.'

'It didn't say anyfing about parents going in the letter.'

'It didn't say we shouldn't either,' Dad said.

'I'd like to be on my own,' I said, as firmly as the eldest son dared.

'What you like and what you get ain't always the way, so which one?' Dad replied.

Mum drew the short straw.

The following day, at first light, she packed my brown-paper parcel, tied the string and left me and my dad together in my bedroom.

'There ain't nuffin' out there you can't 'andle,' he murmured.

I just nodded – my hands were trying not to shake.

'An' even if somethin' did occur, you've got me, ain't you?'

I nodded again. 'Just try and make yer mum proud, son – all right?' He held out his hand and for the first time we shook as two adults. I felt a warm half-crown move from his palm to mine. 'It's your fare 'ome – any time you wanna come.' He smiled.

In that short moment I knew that my going was not as impor-tant as my coming back . . . And I knew, too, that I could face Gravesend and anything else.

Dad waved from the front door as me and Mum went up to Jamaica Road to catch the bus to the station. I was still dead set against her coming, but she was determined to see me to the door of the school.

'What if there are other boys on the train?' I moaned.

'They'll 'ave their parents with them,' she said.

'But s'posin' they ain't – I'll look like a blinkin' baby.'

She pressed her purse to her bosom and strode out with me and my parcel in tow. There was nothing more to be said.

Eventually we pulled into Gravesend station and my knees went into freefall. We were here! I clasped my parcel, and Mum reached for me. Then as we stepped on to the platform, I saw a sign in the hand of a stern-looking officer.

NATIONAL SEA TRAINING SCHOOL
MUSTER HERE

Boys with baggage appeared from various parts of the crowd and walked towards the sign. I froze: boys, strangers, officers – they were all alone except me with my blinkin' mother. I turned to have a whimper at her but she was gone. I looked around anxiously, but she'd vanished. I gravitated towards the muster. The officer snapped at me: 'Name?'

'Hicks.'

'Sir!'

'Sir.'

He ticked off my name on his list and confirmed that we were all there. 'Follow me,' he ordered, and the line of chicks moved off behind him.

I glanced around one last time for my mum. Although my head was full of what lay ahead I missed her kiss goodbye. We went across the road in front of the station and put our belongings into the back of a truck with the Merchant Navy emblem. 'All aboard, sharpish now!' the officer rapped.

One by one we stepped into the vehicle with not a word to each other. The engine stuttered into life and, with a crunch of gears, we staggered forward. I took one last look at civilization as we pulled out of the station yard and saw my mum standing on the open platform, watching us leave. I think I missed her and Dad and the kids more in that moment than I ever have before or since. I watched her until she wasn't there any more and then, with the contentment of the love and understanding waiting for me at home, I sat back and prepared for whatever was waiting at the other end of my journey.

'Our task here,' the officer growled, 'is to make sure none of you little bastards ever get to sea.'

12

During the first week we, the 'new bastards', began to form into small cliques. I was in a gang with Jackie Pellew, a Londoner, nineteen. He'd spent two years on the railway, serving meals in the buffet car. He was looked upon as the Knowall. There wasn't one lesson taught that he hadn't done before. He got on your nerves sometimes, but he was great company. Clive Mower was from Somerset, seventeen. After leaving school he'd spent two years working on his dad's farm but, like the rest of us, he wanted to see the world. We called him Hayseed. At first he seemed a bit slow, but I came to learn it was mostly his accent. That, plus his gentle countenance, made him welcome with everyone. He never argued and always went along with any plans. Peter Barnes was from Norfolk, also seventeen. All he ever talked about was sea-faring explorers. If I'd thought I knew history, then this bloke knew his sailors: James Cook's exploration of the Pacific, Magellan, Columbus. He could take a map and trace their sea passages from memory. We called him Ben Gunn – that was my idea.

They called me the Show-off.

After lessons every evening, the gymnasium and the recreation area were packed with all those boys not 'going ashore', the most prized recreation of all. Unfortunately 'new bastards' never got to go for the first two weeks, and those fourteen nights of watching the lucky ones march out of the gates were filled with jealousy and need. By the middle of the second week me and the gang were sick of lessons.

Then on Monday evening of the third week, my name, along-side those of my mates, appeared on the bulletin board: 'Ratings for Shore Leave – Hicks, T., Pellew, J., Mower, C., and Barnes, P. We rushed to the bath-house and scrubbed ourselves. We hogged the mirrors, combing and recombing our hair. Then, with boots shined, we dressed ourselves proudly in our spanking new number-ones – boy, did we look the part!

Later we mustered outside the gates for inspection.

'During your leave at no time will you unbutton your jacket,' Chief Officer Lambert warned. 'Any rating seen like this, or minus his beret, will receive seven days CB.'

'What's CB?' Knowall whispered.

'Don't tell me you don't know that,' Ben Gunn whispered back.

'Well, I *don't* – so what does it mean?'

'Fucked if I know.'

'It means "confined to barracks",' someone said, behind us.

'I thought so,' Knowall exclaimed.

'And furthermore,' Chief Officer Lambert continued, 'fraternizing with the girls of Gravesend is punishable by being dismissed from the school and sent home in disgrace, without any rebate of monies received.'

The muster shuffled uncomfortably.

'All ratings back at nine sharp – latecomers fourteen days CB.'

'That still means confined to barracks,' I mumbled to Knowall, who kicked me in the ankle without taking his eyes off the officer.

'Now,' Lambert snarled, 'attention, and fall out!'

As we passed through the portals of the 'ship', I felt like I had been given the keys to the kingdom. The air out there was cleaner somehow and, once we were clear of the flag, we gathered at a safe corner and discussed our plans. Ignoring Knowall's suggestion that we pick up a couple of 'sorts', we counted our collective coins and opted for the pictures. Knowall, Ben Gunn, Show-off and the placid Hayseed – four musketeers on the town – walked into the high street of Gravesend. I felt so adult in my uniform; I noticed, too, that my three mates walked as I did, with a sailor's roll – that sway of the hips from walking the decks in a hundred and one force-nine gales. Who could possibly know that the nearest we had ever been to braving the deep was listening to Ben Gunn telling and retelling the tales of his heroes? But our time ashore was to be savoured – as our return to the dreaded gates of the 'ship' came ominously closer.

Over the coming weeks we advanced gradually to first-class service: preparing running buffets, selecting wines, making crêpes Suzettes, steak Diane, and *flambés* at the table, naming cheeses and taking orders correctly. It was pretty mind-consuming and nothing like any of us musketeers had expected – 'cept Knowall. 'It's all part of catering – that's why we're here,' he preached.

One night, late, Knowall came to my bunk and woke me up. 'Tom,' he whispered.

'What's up?'

'It's Hayseed.'

I sat up with sleep stuck in my eyes. 'What's the matter with him?'

'He's in the lavs, crying.'

'Crying?!'

'Yeah, like a baby – sobbin'.'

I followed Knowall to the head and, sure enough, there was Hayseed sitting on the can. Ben Gunn was standing over him, rubbing his shoulders, trying to comfort him, because he really was crying something awful.

'What's it about?' I whispered.

'He wants to go home.'

'Why?'

'He's homesick.'

Homesick?

That came as a real surprise. Hayseed homesick? He'd never mentioned it before – not even a hint.

'But why is he cryin'?' I asked.

'It's on account of his mother and the twenty-five-quid school fee,' Knowall said. 'He wants to go home and chuck the navy – but his family gave up a lot to get the money and if he quits he loses it.'

'It's no wonder he's upset,' Ben Gunn whispered. 'He wants to go home, but can't unless he has the dough. He don't want to look like a failure.'

'I thought he was enjoying himself,' I said.

'Well, he wasn't, was he?' Knowall said – ever the expert.

'Oim roight sorry, lads, abewt orl thus 'ere fess.' Hayseed spoke for the first time, taking deep breaths. 'But moi tether is quoit ended, Oi feel – Oi'm afeared Oi can't go, won way tor tother.'

'Becalmed,' I said thoughtfully. 'Like the *Flying Dutchman*, he's stuck to roam the –'

'Fuck off, Tom!' Knowall interrupted. 'Ain't 'e got enough trouble wivout you mixing 'im up?'

Hayseed didn't react, but he was calmer now, and the sobs had subsided. We four sat in a line with our backs against the damp wall, facing the urinal on the other side of the wash-house.

'So he can't quit,' we agreed, 'and can't get expelled without forfeit.'

Short pause for four in thought.

'S'pose he runs away?'

'Same as quittin'.'

'How about he's caught with a girl on leave?'

'Same as expelled.'

'How about he shoots himself?'

'Fuck off!'

The more we talked, the more frustrated we became. It wasn't until the next afternoon that Knowall had a chat with the secretary over at Admin. Slyly he got the conversation on to fee refunds – but she, like us, only knew how you *couldn't* get the twenty-five pounds back.

' 'Cept for compassion,' she said, as an afterthought.

'What's compassion?' Ben Gunn asked later, on the deck.

'He shoots himself!' I suggested again.

There were three more days to go before our group was free to go on half-term leave. This meant getting ashore on the Friday night and not having to come back until the following Monday at eight a.m. Those ratings who lived too far away stayed aboard, but me and the musketeers were going home – except Hayseed. Too far away, too expensive and too tempting.

He refused to go with me to Bermondsey, even though I swore on a pack of Woodbines that my mum would love it, but by the Friday morning he warmed to the idea. In fact, by that afternoon he was almost happy about it. At eight that evening after dinner we of the home-leave group assembled before Chief Officer Lambert. He gave us the usual lecture – no fraternizing in uniform, honour the service. Then he ordered, 'Attention! Right turn!'

We obeyed as one. Then, just before he marched us out of the gates and *home*, he said, 'And do the navy a favour.' He snorted. 'Don't come back!'

There was only one of us who would have granted him such a boon and that was the fellow striding out next to me – but Hayseed wasn't so dumb: he knew that to 'jump ship' meant 'no dough'.

'Oh, you poor little sod,' Mum said, clearing up the greasy newspapers in the kitchen. We had just had a slap-up coming-home meal of cod and chips. Hayseed nodded in self-sympathy and drained his Tizer.

'Sounds more like the Scrubs than a school,' Darbo said. 'Only you get in there for free.'

We could see tears welling in Hayseed's eyes.

Darbo started to chat again, anxious not to have our guest embarrass himself. 'So you can't get out of this gaff wiv the money?'

'No, Mr Hicks, Oi caan't. There bain't no way.'

''Cept death,' I said.

Mum dropped the cups in the sink.

Darbo's eyes twinkled. He went on, 'You've got a family at home – Mum and Dad?'

Hayseed nodded forlornly.

'And you don't want them to know about all this?'

Hayseed nodded again.

All of a sudden Darbo announced he was popping out for a bit. He was gone for hours. Mum went to bed with her usual: 'Oh, I don't know, I just don't bleedin' know any more.' She left me and Hayseed in the kitchen, wondering what the old man was up to.

Just before midnight the street door opened and Darbo came in, eyes dancing, hands rubbing and that gentle sway betraying the fact that he'd had a few. 'Y' better go to bed.' He chuckled. 'We got an important meet in the mornin'.'

★

It was Saturday – my best day. I got dressed in my uniform and took Hayseed round to Ginger Thompson's to say hello. And show off a bit.

Darbo appeared at noon and we left Ginger for this mysterious meet at the Gregorian Arms, a pub down the Jamaica Road next to St James's Church. There was a white wedding going on – the street was a mass of confetti blowing in the winter wind – the pub was laid out for a reception and, as we jostled through the carnation crowd, Darbo indicated a man standing at the far bar. 'There 'e is,' he called, leading me and Hayseed up to him.

'This is my boy, Tommy, and the kid I was telling you about,' Darbo said to the man. Then, 'Boys, say 'allo to Uncle Gorgeous.'

Uncle Gorgeous shook our hands. He was a tall, good-looking man, with a shock of black hair greying at the sides and a pencil moustache. He wore a Prince of Wales check suit with a red rose in the lapel, and spoke with a strong Cockney accent, fiddling nervously with his bow-tie. 'So you wanna get out of this navy nick really bad, eh?' he whispered.

'Reel bad.' Hayseed nodded.

'And this gaff don't give refunds.'

'No.'

'And you can't go without the readies? It's bleedin' robbery, that's what it is – there oughta be a bleedin' law against it.'

We didn't dwell on the subject – a few more drinks, a few stories, and we were pushing our way out of the noisy wedding reception, saying goodbye to Uncle Gorgeous.

'Now, don't you worry, son,' he said to Hayseed. 'Everyfing will turn out all right.' Then he spoke to Darbo: 'I'll start this Wednesday.'

On the way home Darbo gave cryptic orders to Hayseed: 'Fings will occur this Wednesday,' he said. 'If you get any questions at the gaff, use your loaf, act dumb and go wiv the moody.'

I could see that my mate was not following this conversation.

'Remember!' Darbo pressed. 'Whatever 'appens this Wednesday, you bite yer tongue and you go with the moody.'

'I'll explain it to him tonight in bed,' I said.

Darbo nodded with mild content, and led us into the Lilliput Arms, another pub just along the road. We hit the Rising Sun, too, about an hour later. Mum was not best pleased when we helped Dad down our passage and up to the cold dinner on the table.

Sunday evening arrived. Ginger Thompson came round and listened to our tales of derring-do. At five o'clock, me and Hayseed brushed and polished ourselves and prepared for our return to the dreaded 'ship'. Mum took me to one side, straightened my tie and pushed my hair back from my forehead. 'This place you're in,' she said gently, 'it's all right, ain't it?'

'Course it is.'

'I mean, you are enjoying it – it is worthwhile, isn't it?'

'O' course.'

'Cos if it ain't, you come right 'ome – sod the money.'

'I know that, Mum.'

'And look after that poor little tyke, too,' she said, referring to Hayseed. Then she called the other kids from the kitchen and we all said goodbye at the street door.

That Wednesday, at ten o'clock in the morning, the telephone rang in Admin and the caller asked to speak urgently to the captain of the school. It was the father of Rating Clive 'Hayseed' Mower. His accent was strong Somerset, but in spite of a few unintelligible words the captain understood that Rating Mower's mother was dangerously ill. The boy was summoned to the office. The captain told him not to worry: any more news would be conveyed immediately. The next call came on the Thursday afternoon – things had taken a turn for the worst and the father was coming up from Somerset to collect the lad and take him home – would that be convenient? Early Friday morning Clive 'Hayseed' Mower was dressed in his civvies and waiting outside the captain's office. His father arrived in a taxi and went into the office to conclude the arrangements agreed on the phone the day before. The captain offered his condolences, along with twenty-five pounds in cash and the official waiver of any agreement. Mr Mower signed the form, took the money and waited by the taxi while his son made his final farewells to his ex-shipmates.

'Sorry to see you go,' Knowall said, hiding his smile.

' 'Ope she gets better,' Ben Gunn spluttered, trying not to give the game away.

I walked with Hayseed to the taxi with my arm round his shoulders keeping up the charade. As he got into the back seat he started to falter, holding tight to my hand. 'Oi don't really want to go naow,' he said. 'Where'll Oi meet folk loik you agin?'

His 'father' got in beside him and winked at me. ' 'E don't know 'ow bleedin' lucky 'e is.' He laughed.

The taxi pulled off into that morning mist, me and the musketeers waving until it had disappeared with Hayseed, the farmer's boy and Uncle 'Gorgeous' George Pekinbright, the best con-man in England, nicely tucked in the back, bound for freedom.

Eventually, having passed my course and earned a proficiency badge, March blew into April and I spent my time at home mostly in daydreams. What kind of ship would I be given? When would the call come? Where would I sail to?

The library got a fair share of my time and the radio kept up its constant entertainment. All this, plus the pictures, helped me keep my sanity. But still the all important signal from Cunard had not arrived. With all those sailors on all those ships, I thought, maybe they had forgotten me.

On 5 April, they remembered.

The telegram held pride of place on our mantelpiece as I came in from a kickabout with Ginger.

'It's bin sittin' there all mornin',' Mum sang, from the kitchen. '*And* I gave the messenger thruppence.'

I tore open the envelope and speed-read the message: 'HICKS THOMAS STOP REPORT RMS SCYTHIA SOUTHAMPTON DOCKS 10TH APRIL INST STOP MUSTER 8.00 A.M. STOP SIGNED CUNARD'

Later that day I went through my list of instructions of what a seaman does when he is given notice of a ship. The manual said report to the Pool of London, Whitechapel, for discharge book, etc. I knew Whitechapel fairly well from visits to Petticoat Lane on a Sunday and to Cohen of the Lane for my triennial best suit. 'No, it's all right, Mum, I'll go on my own,' I insisted.

Even Ginger was barred from going with me – I was determined that I could do all this grown-up stuff alone. Sink or swim, I wanted to take this road to the sea without help. All of its mysteries would be revealed in time – but, first, a few short steps to take me clear of where normal people roam.

The area of Whitechapel in which the office of the 'Pool' was to be found seemed somehow foreign. I had got there by walking over Tower Bridge, thence past the Tower and into Aldgate. After the odd instruction from passers-by, I went down small, dank streets away from the main thoroughfares and into what Sherlock Holmes would have called the Limehouse Area. It was quite a shock. In my wildest thoughts I could not have conjured up such a place with such a strange array of people. There were Turks with fezzes, Indians with turbans, Pakistanis with astrakhan hats, Africans, Malays, Chinese. It was not just the faces and headgear that were strange: some wore their national costumes too – colourful folk. Some flitted, some walked, some were almost hiding in the doorways of shops that sold sweet-smelling spices, silk and other mysterious items.

This was not London – not *my* London! In those days, a multi-cultural mix of people wasn't common as it is now. It was alien – but now, here I was part of it.

Street after street passed as I searched, hands deep in my pockets protecting my telegram. Still no sign of the 'Pool' and now I was too scared to stop someone and ask. Then I saw the uniform of a sailor. He had suddenly appeared from another avenue and walked with a brisk, rolling gait. I moved after him, in and out of the 'foreign folk', down one street and up another. He stopped at a small shop and went inside. I decided to wait until he'd made his purchase. Then, back on the street, I would continue to follow him to where he was obviously going. The Pool.

I waited for almost half an hour – no sign of him – so I went to the door of the shop and looked inside. Apart from an old Chinese lady sitting at a wok frying, there was no one. My sailor had sailed. I ambled back across the street and tried to make up my mind which way I hadn't yet tried in my quest. Then, as if on cue, the sailor appeared again from the shop. I stood there like a kid before a conjuror, a big 'how?' on my lips, with 'where' and 'why' had he been hiding? Then he crossed the road towards me. A window above the shop slid up noisily, and a girl leaned out and wolf-whistled at him. The sailor stopped, turned and whistled back. Then, with a wave, he continued on past me. He caught my eye, saw my expression, grabbed his crotch and winked, saying something to me in a tongue I couldn't understand.

'Er . . . Pool?' I asked, more in shock than inquiry.

He smiled and shook his head. He hadn't understood. I tried again. 'Pool of London – office?'

'Ah! *Oficina!* Pool!' he exclaimed.

Then he rolled past me, indicating that I should follow. As I did, the woman at the window wolf-whistled again. The sailor waved without looking back. Within minutes, I saw a short queue leaning against the wall of a squat building. My sailor pointed at it. '*Oficina* – Pool.' He smiled, then rolled on towards the docks tacked on to the other end of the road.

The queue had strange people in it too, but when I got closer I could see and hear English seamen chatting to each other. I felt a little more at ease. I took my place, and within an hour I was looking up at a bloke in some sort of uniform on the other side of a counter. He looked down at me for some time – the sight of this kid staring up from a full four feet nothing much must have touched his funny bone because he tried unsuccessfully to hide a smile. 'Well, what can we do for you, Lofty?'

'I've come to register for –'

'The Good Ship *Lollipop*?'

'No, sir. The RMS *Scythia*.'

'That's not a ship, it's a bum-boat.'

'I beg pardon?'

'Never mind. Do you have your confirmation, birth certificate, parental release, Sea School exit form?'

I held aloft the wad of information.

'What's your rating?'

'Pardon?'

'What are you sailing as?'

'A sailor.'

'What *kind* of sailor?'

'A new one.'

On the bus home I read and reread my vital statistics typed on the crisp new pages of my Merchant Navy discharge book. Much like a passport, it would take me all over the world. I was a real sailor now – it said so: 'Hicks, Thomas, Seaman'.

'Oh, I say!' Mum squealed, when she saw it. Then she put it on the mantelpiece like some kind of trophy.

My time left at home was now short, what with the Pool and fast farewells to my relatives. There only remained one last kickabout with Ginger before I left for Southampton in the morning.

'I s'pose you *can* swim?' he asked thoughtfully, as he scuffed his shoe with a lob of a brick.

I hadn't thought of that. 'A bit,' I replied, remembering the odd afternoon at the Oasis swimming-pool in Southwark Park.

''Ow much is a bit?' Another lob.

I moved towards the brick and attempted a volley. 'I dunno – from here to the pub.' I indicated the Rising Sun a few hundred yards away.

''Ow quick can you get there?'

'I s'pose about a couple of minutes.'

'You'll never make it,' Ginger said, intercepting my shot and catching the brick on his thigh. 'My dad sez that once a ship starts to sink it takes less than a minute to go down and anyone in the water wivin two 'undred yards gets sucked down wiv it, so if I was a ship and you was swimming, I'd 'ave ya before yer reached the pub.' He belted another brick towards me. 'So if I was you I wouldn't go.'

But even the threat of Davy Jones's locker did not deter me.

We had our tea, Ginger and me, and then we parted at his street door. It was an uncomfortable moment for us, two lads about to say an adult goodbye for the first time. We stood looking out towards the railway arches, hands deep in our pockets, searching for the right words. Then, 'Well, I'll be seein' ya,' he mumbled.

'Yeah. I s'pose so.'

'Ta ta, then, Tom.'

'Yeah. Ta ta, then, Ginge.'

And I was gone.

As with my visit to Whitechapel, it was grudgingly agreed with my folks that I would go to Southampton alone. This was another bitter pill for my mum to swallow. 'It's bleedin' miles away – you could get lost,' she said. But no sooner had the words left her lips than she knew she had said the wrong thing. I was a man now – her first lad to leave the nest. She really had to let go and telling me I might get lost was close to insulting.

I just gave a long-drawn-out plaintive '*Mu-uum!!!*'

She shrugged and carried on chucking clothes into my new second-hand suitcase. The telegram was consulted yet again. 'It says you muster at eight a.m.,' she read. 'We've checked the trains and there's one gets in to Southampton at seven forty-five. 'Ow far is the boat from the station?'

'Dunno.'

'Well, if it's more than fifteen minutes, you'll be late on your first day – that ain't clever.'

'Is there an earlier train?'

'The two forty a.m. from Waterloo arrives Southampton at five forty.'

'I'll get that one.'

'Then you'll be there too early *and* in the middle of the night. You'll be cold – on your own *and* maybe lost . . .' She started to cry.

I didn't know how to handle that. What does the eldest son do on his last night when his mum starts crying? Does he get huffy and insist he be left to his fate as a man? Or does he weaken and convince the silly woman that there ain't nothing out there to worry about? Or does he keep quiet and let her cry?

I went for the latter and kept putting clothes in the suitcase so that it looked like I had other things on my mind.

I went to bed that night without the urge to sleep. I had said goodbye to the kids, who didn't seem to care one way or the other, and asked Mum to wake me at one o'clock. I lay there with constant newsreels running through my mind, flipping from one subject to another, nothing making sense. Just a mass of faceless people doing a mass of faceless things.

In the end I had to get up. My clock said midnight. I had been tossing about for two hours. I decided to creep downstairs, have a wash and a cuppa. A fruitful thought for once. I took the tiny stairs two at a time so that the usual creaks would be halved, then went along the dark passage past the coal-hole and into the kitchen.

When I opened the door Mum was still there, with just the glow of the coke fire for light. She was sitting on the floor with her head on Dad's lap. He was in his rocker, asleep, and Mum's jerk made him jump awake.

'Hello, son.' She half smiled, trying to make up for the tears running down her cheeks. 'Ain't you asleep?'

'No, I'm too excited,' I said.

She moved to the kettle and started some tea. Dad caught my eye and winked with the look of a husband who knows what a husband knows. ''Ow are you gettin' to Waterloo?' he asked.

'Tram or bus – it don't matter which.'

'A bit too early for the early one,' he mused. 'Come to fink of it, it's a bit too late for the late one.'

'For Gawd's sake!' Mum snapped at him. 'Leave the boy alone.'

'I'm only making conversation,' he said – his eyes dipped like a little fawn's.

Then she started sniffing again.

I couldn't wait to leave. I didn't enjoy seeing my parents like this – Dad unable to have his chat and Mum so sad, and all down to me.

At long last the time came. Dressed, packed and prepared, I paused at the street door just long enough to bid them both goodbye. Then, with a long list of don'ts, I left home and Frean Street.

I made for the top of Sun Passage, then went left to the bus stop on Jamaica Road. The streets were bare, the morning chilly and the bus stop open to the elements. As I stood I kept my eye on the turning into Sun Passage – Any minute now, I thought, my mum's coming round that corner and I'll go through everything again. I decided to walk along Jamaica Road to the next stop at Dockhead. Then I would be 'in my private'. As I walked down the hill I heard the sound of an engine – it wasn't the heavy diesel of a bus so I didn't bother to turn round. The police car came level with me and the copper in the passenger seat looked at me through his open window. 'G' mornin', son,' he said, staring at my suitcase. 'Been on holiday?'

'No, I'm going to sea,' I said, pressing on through the wind rushing up the hill.

'You're a sailor, then?'

'Yeah, I'm a sailor.'

'Where's yer parrot?'

'In me suitcase.'

The car stopped suddenly. 'We'd best 'ave a look, then,' the copper said, getting out.

The ride in the police car to Waterloo station was easily the most exciting I'd ever had, apart from the ambulance when I had purpura. The two policemen, once they'd checked my suitcase to make sure I wasn't Burglar Bill, had kindly offered me a lift. Now, today, I can imagine what it must have been like to them – a kid of fifteen, no bigger than a pennyw'th of coppers, walking the cold streets at one o'clock in the morning on his way to the seven seas: 'Poor little blighter, what kind of parents did he have that could allow such a thing?'

The station came. As I alighted, small groups of late-night revellers ceased revelling and watched me drag my case out of the police car and into the entrance. They think I'm a copper, I mused, a plain-clothes detective making my way to a secret rendezvous.

I could imagine them telling the tale to their friends.

13

I stepped on to the platform at Southampton at five fifty-five. I had two hours to find my ship – plenty of time. I gave up my ticket at the barrier and asked the half-awake porter where the *Scythia* was.

'What's a *Scythia*?'

'It's a ship.'

'This is a station, not a dock.'

'All right. Where's the dock?'

'Which one? Old Dock, New Dock, Royal Dock, Dry Dock? They're mostly that way.' He yawned.

I made for the general direction of all of them.

I'd been walking for what seemed like hours when somewhere a clock struck seven. It was freezing. I stopped by the modern civic centre and noted that here, too, the Luftwaffe had had a go: all around naked bombsites awaited resurrection. Then I went on, through the still empty streets towards the docks – which *had* to be round the next corner. At about seven fifteen I started to panic – three-quarters of an hour to go and then, if I'm not aboard, I'll be on a charge. Absent without leave – jumping ship! Clapped in irons!

I hurried on, too worried to freeze. Then I saw the high cranes, the soft smoke. My nose caught a smell that will never leave my memory. Fresh paint melding with anchor grease and oil and its accompanying sound of busy generators, throbbing pistons and the constant knocking of steel against iron.

I half ran towards my destiny. Then I saw the smokestacks. The high, majestic funnels of a host of ships, tall ships, great hulks of tradition waiting for me to climb aboard.

My run became quicker to keep up with my heart.

I saw a man. 'The *Scythia*, please,' I yelled. 'Which one is the *Scythia*?'

He pointed to the east. I peered through the mist, the smoke and steam. Suddenly it all cleared in a rogue gust of wind.

Then I saw her. Her three funnels, hissing a welcome.

Was she big?

I had seen St Paul's – but she was bigger!

Was she heroic?

I remembered my Spitfire, but she was more so!

Was she beautiful?

I was in love with Olivia de Havilland – but this girl was a knockout.

I ran down a ramp and to a dock gate. A policeman stepped out of a shed. I showed him my dock pass and credentials. He glanced through everything as if he didn't care that my neck was breaking to run up that long, long gangplank sticking out of my ship's side, daring me to board her. At last he gave me back my stuff and I was cantering closer to her – then at the plank. But before I threw myself into her bosom, I gazed up at my beauty for one last glance at her façade, admiring her strong stanchions, her magnificent decks, her long, majestic hull stretching from stern to stem and onwards, ever onwards, towards that name – the lovely, lovely name emblazoned on her bow . . .

Queen Mary!

'The *Scythia* is *that* one,' a docker told me. 'The one with the single stack, bobbing at the back of the *Queen*.'

I glared at the boat indicated – and, compared to the great *Queen*, it was indeed 'bobbing'! A bloody bobbing single rotten smokestack of a blinkin' bum-boat! Bugger it!

'It's a boat, innit?' I mumbled to myself. 'And, after all, it *is* mine and it's quarter to eight and I muster in a minute and I'm gonna enjoy it cos it's my destiny!'

So, I walked up the plank of the *Scythia*, looking across at the *Queen*, and I was fuckin' fed up.

But as my foot touched the iron of her deck I sort of grudgingly forgave her. She had a way with her, even at this early meeting. She was a kind craft: she swayed at her anchor and creaked as you passed her wooden bits.

I was directed to the Writer's Office. Such a place hadn't existed at Sea School. It was the nerve centre of the ship: every bill, docket, request, order and complaint came here, into the hands of the 'writer', a sort of clerk with the power of a Tsar.

'*And* I've got a proficiency badge,' I added, a bonus for the writer to what he had read in my credentials.

'You're to sign articles at eight after muster in the main tourist dining room,' he mumbled, ticking things off on a long typed list.

'Do I take my proficiency badge?' I asked.

'Your cabin is R45 – that's deck R, cabin forty-five.'

'Yes, sir.'

'I'm not a "sir", I'm a writer. You've got five minutes to stow your gear and turn to.'

I couldn't understand some of that.

'That means?' I asked tentatively.

'*That* means go to your cabin, unpack, go to the Tourist Dining Room and, if you're clever, you can stick the proficiency badge up your arse as you go.'

The way to R deck was a luxurious journey. Every deck, every staircase, every wall was pure elegance, great carved murals, oil paintings, carpets. I counted two lifts and took one down to R deck. The ship was still empty of crew. I came to cabin forty-five, which was next door to the Tourist Purser's Room. I guessed that he was probably in charge of the cabin boys. I knocked at my door. No answer. I opened it and dragged my suitcase in behind me. The cabin was breathtaking, all in polished wood, with a single bed and a double bunk. As I was obviously the first aboard, I took the single bed, under the porthole with the telephone next to it. I had barely put my case down when I heard a rumpus outside on the dock. I looked out of the porthole and saw a flotilla of taxis skidding to a halt at the ship's side with loads of men spewing out of them and charging up the gangplank. The crew were here.

It was one minute to muster and, unlike me, who had braved the freeze of the milk train, these boys had taken the later one and were going to be on time. I rushed out of R45 and galloped the decks to arrive at the Tourist Dining Room in time to join the crazy crew. They were a bonny bunch, all laughing and recounting their time ashore.

When the officers arrived, there was silence. Everyone jumped to attention and formed three lines in front of three desks. We were to sign articles, in which we promised to do our duty to God, the Queen and Cunard, so help us.

Someone slapped the back of my head. Christ! What have I done? I thought. When I turned round I saw the great grin of Ben Gunn. I could have cried, yelled, screamed – even kissed him. 'Fuckin' 'ell – it's not possible!' I cussed.

'It *fuckin'* is,' he cussed back.

'What cabin are you in?'

'R45,' I said. 'Y'know – the one next to the Tourist Purser's Room, with three beds and a telephone.'

He stared at me for a moment, searching my face for something more.

'I took the single bed cos I was the first,' I added. 'And you can still get the bottom bunk cos it's free if you hurry.'

The queue moved forward. Then I was signing on the dotted line. My wages were to be two pounds five shillings per week (£2.25p). From this I signed away thirty bob (£1.50) per week to go home towards the family budget, which left me, I decided, plenty of money to keep my head above water. Then I was told to report to the stores at ten a.m. for my uniform.

I trotted back to R45.

I had nearly an hour to unpack and maybe telephone the Rising Sun in Bermondsey. It wasn't an emergency, but the publican might not mind bringing my mum in to talk to her sailor son. I sat by my telephone and prepared to go into action.

The door to the cabin crashed open and there stood Ben Gunn and two other boys of our age. They grinned, grabbed me and my suitcase, and dragged us out of the cabin and along the decks.

I couldn't speak for shock. What were they doing? *Why* were they doing it? And, more to the point, where were they dragging me?

Soon the carpet under my feet changed to iron. The teak walls turned into greasy bulkheads. The staircases changed to paint-chipped companionways and my eyes smarted with wet paint and oil. At last, in what seemed to be the bowels of the boat, we stopped. All of us were out of puff, them still grinning and me still with the same burning question. Why?

Then they opened a door to reveal a cabin with twelve double bunks and a solitary porthole battened down with four unturnable screws.

'Welcome home,' Ben Gunn cried. 'This is CR45 to Cunard, but gloryhole to the rest of us.'

So there it was.

I had not realized that the C before a deck reference denoted *crew* and this rusty old room was my real home. Twenty-four men, back to back and belly to belly. All fartin', snorin', spittin' and smokin'. All together in one *gloryhole*. Some *glory*, I thought. Some *hole*!

But Ben Gunn was there and he was a mate, and by the time we had got our uniform from Stores, all disappointment had returned to hope. Hope of the adventure we had both promised ourselves – but Gunn's knowledge of the wheres and hows of seafaring was far superior to mine. All my stories concerning sea journeys were merely about 'getting there', like Hornblower on the way to Cádiz or Huckleberry to New Orleans. For Ben Gunn the *journey* was the adventure, the winds, the sea swell, the tops'l, the mains'l, the jib and the tiller, so while my mind was on our destination, his was on navigation. Our destination aboard the RMS *Scythia* was Québec, Canada. But we still had another day in port before we set sail. Still, on that first day at ten a.m., we four cabin boys paraded in our uniforms on the main deck square before Second Steward Rampling, known unaffectionately as Wankin' Ramplin'.

He was a long, thin man with small beady eyes that pierced

through you from behind thin wire glasses. He reminded me of a very tall Heinrich Himmler. With a clipped Liverpool accent, he handed out our tasks. Ben Gunn got the job of 'stand by purser'. This meant he reported to the Tourist Purser's Office and ran messages to passengers throughout the liner. It was a great job.

Mine was to 'stand by' in the Writer's Office. At first I thought this was a demotion – mebbe it had got round that I had made the silly mistake with the cabin. But I was wrong: it was a super task. Pete Lore was the writer, and in spite of his contempt for my proficiency badge, I found him a fine teacher. In spite of my youth he, in his thirties, always took the trouble to hold a conversation with me. I can see him now, sitting at his typewriter, chatting away in explanation of some question I'd asked, which most other men would have dismissed as not worth their time.

As well as the duties of bills and chits, the office was also the heart of the on-board printing. There were not only new menus to print for every meal, but the writer compiled a daily newspaper, based on 'on-board' information and world news from the Radio Room. Every day was a joy. I was rushing to and fro with the 'copy' and the 'rough prints', to the Radio Room (news), the purser (passenger information) and the galley (chef's instructions).

But this was still only my first morning with another whole day before we sailed. I was still new and my uniform was new, too, with blue serge trousers and scarlet jacket, gold epaulettes and one row of buttons, plus – just like the Savoy Hotel – white gloves, but with this job there was to be no backroom with benches and bells or, thank the Lord, a pillbox hat. Pete Lore sent me on enough errands that day to enable me to get the hang of the ship's geography. By the time I came off watch at five o'clock that evening I knew her pretty well.

At five past five she was empty again. Her wily crew knew their ropes, all right. Once more the taxi flotilla had screeched to the edge of the gangplank to take the lads four or five at a time out of the dock gates and into Southampton. The pubs and clubs would be full tonight as the seafarers drank themselves into the morning.

Me and Ben Gunn went to the cinema. Just before the main

picture the screen erupted with 'Coming Attractions' – next week's blockbusting movie in 'a U trailer advertising an A film'. Next week, I thought, I won't be here. When all them picturegoers come to see the film, I'll be gone – like I was dead. The pit of my stomach made a 360-degree turn. From tomorrow onwards, I will be no more.

All that night, stuck in the bunk by the door of the gloryhole, I thought of the life I used to have. The doubts came in floods, but I fell asleep eventually – to be awakened by the steady throb of the ship's engines. It was early morning and the lady was getting herself ready to go out.

We cabin boys turned to at eight, and by nine o'clock the stores were flowing aboard. I ran the deck betwixt the chef's office and the gangways, carrying dockets and chits from the head chef to the storemen – wines, spirits, vegetables, great sides of beef and a thousand live lobsters: these I followed to the main galley. I was fascinated. They were in huge wire boxes, their claws clutching at everything and anything. The noise of shell cracking against shell was almost musical – like some percussion piece on the radio. But that noise was nothing like the noise to come when we got to the galley. Standing over a great stainless-steel vat of bubbling, boiling water were three chefs with their high, white hats, tight kerchiefs and check trousers. In their hands they held shovels, which they stabbed into the cracking mass of crustaceans, dragging out of the boxes five or six lobsters at a time and tossing them into the steaming vat. An ear-splitting scream came each time a shovelful went into the water. I shuddered, remembering the purpura and my exploding guts.

'It's not a scream, and it's not pain,' Pete Lore explained. 'It's the noise of the shell as it reacts to the heat. Ask any chef.'

I wondered if anyone had bothered asking a lobster . . .

At midday I was introduced to a new tribe – the 'bloods', as the passengers were known. The terminal building stood opposite our gangways. It was on two levels, called embarkation stations, and on to these floors, first with a trickle, then with a flood, came the bloods. There were to be about fifteen hundred on this trip, moving like ants towards the ship, their hands full of luggage and tickets. The ship's baggage masters and their armies of stewards moved among them, receiving the suitcases and marking them 'State Room' or 'Not Wanted On Voyage'. Over on the far right, a railway line jutted into the building and at one o'clock a locomotive puffed in, smoke and steam everywhere. From somewhere above me, on a higher deck, the ship's orchestra crashed into a rousing medley. Then, from heaven knows where, a trio of men in tails and high hats floated towards the bloods alighting from the train, saluting and bowing to them. These were the men from Cook's. The train bloods were mostly first-class passengers and the beautifully dressed greeters knew every name and face, every cabin number, every like and dislike of their patrons. With a veiled snap of his fingers or a nod, the man from Cook's would have the baggage transferred, the ticket, passport and visa checked before the blood had reached the gangway. When they were off the gangway, the other three cabin boys and I took over.

As my first contact with a passenger, I had to lead Mr and Mrs Guggenberg to the main suite on the boat deck. They were like matching bookends – small, round and close to seventy, and thank God they'd travelled on the *Scythia* before. I got lost twice, but kindly Mr Guggenberg merely chuckled and, in his middle-European-American accent, gently put me back on track: 'I tink perhaps you should take the left, sonny.'

Once we got to the suite he asked me to bring the head waiter. I dashed past the traffic along the corridors, and waited in the first-class dining room for a glimpse of Mr Tappin, the head waiter, a short, fat man with black greased-back hair – Hercule Poirot with a Hampshire accent. He suffered from 'Cunard feet'. Whenever the vessel listed to port or starboard his feet would spread – left foot at nine o'clock, right foot at three – acting as stabilizers. Now, after years of stalking the dining-tables in search of a generous gratuity, this posture was permanent.

After a while he came into the room. I trotted over to him and presented the Guggenbergs' compliments and would he come? He snatched a table plan off an easel and waddled after me, mumbling about having to make such a journey at such a time. 'And for what?' he complained to himself. 'Just so they can see the passenger list *before* I make the seating plan. *I* make the seating plan on this ship, not the bloody Guggenbergs.'

He got this last sentence out just before we reached the open door of the main suite. The room was now full of cabin trunks, great black ingot-studded boxes of clothes opened by a brace of ship's stewardesses, a personal maid and a butler. Mr Guggenberg waved at Tappin from a table of champagne and canapés. 'Teppin, mine olt fren'.'

Mid–waddle, the head waiter segued into servile mode. 'Mr and Mrs Guggenberg, once more you honour us with your kind patronage. Your stay in London was satisfactory, I trust?' he said, rubbing his hands together like Uriah Heep – 'ever so 'umble'.

The Guggenbergs had a lot to say to Tappin! 'And where is the passenger list?' . . . 'Oh, I see the Rothschilds didn't make it but Lord and Lady You Know are with us!' . . . 'And that nasty woman, the Duchess of Gawd-help-us, is on A deck.' . . . 'But we must have Professor "Clever Dick" . . .'

Within ten minutes the dining-table of the Guggenbergs was on the plan, and those passengers invited to join it would be grateful to be among the *grande clique*. Those considered *non grande* were banished to the far corners of the saloon.

At four p.m. the open decks were crammed with passengers and their friends or relations who were seeing them off. A message came over from the loudspeakers: 'All ashore that's going ashore. The vessel will sail in thirty minutes.' Multicoloured streamers were distributed to the throng and in no time at all the friends and relations had filed down the gangway. The ship's foghorn had started its goodbye blasts and the live orchestra was belting out a march.

'Last call for going ashore – all ashore now!'

The ship's hull gave a little shake – her engines had caused the shudder: her screws turned just once, a powerful reminder of their presence as the tough, tiny tugs pulled her away from her capstans.

The band played on. The streamers stabbed the air like a mass of coloured lizard tongues.

People cheered.

The ship shuddered again and, now under her own steam, moved majestically into the Solent and Southampton Water.

I stood at the rail and felt a thousand eyes on me, staring across from the packed docks. 'There he goes,' their owners were saying. 'Off to the New World – lucky bugger.'

I stayed there mesmerized, feeling the wind in my face, for longer than I should have, but as the Isle of Wight came up on our starboard side, the passengers at the rails began to filter back inside the ship. Only then did I remember that I was working and went below. No one had missed me. Pete Lore gave me a few messages to run, but nothing that took me out on to the open decks again – but the inside decks beneath my feet reminded me that we were in motion. The *Scythia* bent her corridors as she rode the waves, her polished wood giving out a travelling creak that started at the forward end and finished at her stern. That same creak came back in reverse as if it had just rebounded off the propellers. I expected to go off watch at five p.m., like the day before, but now we were at sea and 'under articles', on call at the will of the authorities – within reason: it wasn't the *Bounty*!

At about six o'clock that evening Pete Lore sent me to get my dinner. After that I was to report to Mr Tappin, in the first-class dining saloon. I made my way down below. The companionways were not as easy to use now as they had been when we were in port – a sudden swing or jerk could send a landlubber on to his back, but I wasn't such a person any more and was determined to stay on my feet until I found my legs. I had my dinner in the tourist-class galley with most of the other crew. The place was pandemonium and the meal for the passengers hadn't started yet. There were chefs, underchefs and commis chefs, kitchen porters, waiters and commis waiters all screaming at each other, marking their territory during the dawn of this first battle. I learned pretty quickly that to survive in the serving game you had not only to hold your ground but go on the attack too, otherwise you, the meal and your bloods would falter and fall at the first fence.

The receiving of the passengers at their designated table was easy enough: they were *sent* to it, they didn't choose – unless they were Guggenbergs! The taking of their order for the meal was simple, too, as was conversation with them, and offering iced water, hot rolls and butter. Once you had settled them and instilled in them confidence in your presence, you had to achieve the same when you passed out of the saloon and into the galley – the 'den of din'. That stainless-steel trap of steam and sweat, that line of pushing, panting waiters, all shoving forward for the well-done steak they had ordered, the two lamb chops and the *filet mignon* that they swore was *theirs* and not the fellow's next to them. Then once you had the meat, the next skirmish was for the gravy and the sauce chef.

He towered over his platoon of pots, ignoring the yells, stirring his potions like a deaf warlock. Eventually he succumbed, and after the sauces, you were back for the vegetables.

And as the meal went on, so did the strain.

By the time dessert came, tempers were rising: the kitchen staff had been in the heat for five hours, the waiters for three. There was now more than one pressure cooker in that kitchen – there wasn't a meal went by that I didn't see a volcano erupt during serving. In years to come I saw fights almost to the death, once over a solitary teaspoon, but in all those battles, not one fight left the field to continue in the saloon. As far as the bloods knew, while the orchestra played its waltz the waiters moved likewise. Like ducks on a pond, graceful and serene on the surface with their feet going ten to the dozen below.

On that first crossing I read George Orwell's *Down and Out in Paris and London* – there were passages in that book I could identify with, although I wasn't yet a waiter. I saw the things to come.

Mr Tappin looked down at me and rocked back on his Cunard feet. 'This is a first-class dining saloon,' he purred. 'We don't 'ave no cowboys 'ere – do we understand all this?' He was referring to me and Ben Gunn. We were standing to attention by an enormous cold buffet. It had enough food on it to feed a fleet. Not long out of Bermondsey and rationing, the sight of it took my breath away. Once he had given his opening speech, Tappin left us with the saloon steward, a surly man who never smiled. His accent was soft and Scottish, but his tone was that of a hanging judge.

'Your job is those,' he told us, indicating the doors set to either side of the lift and leading from the saloon into the galley. 'You'll each hold a door and open and shut it as a waiter passes. You'll wear uniform at all times. You'll not leave your post for anything, and if I catch you skylarking, you'll be before Second Steward Rampling.'

Wankin' Ramplin': the name burned into me, along with the memory of Chief Officer Lambert. I knew that even if we were sinking and the sea was up to my ankles, I would not let go of that door, and even if I thought of the best joke in the world, I would never relay it to my shipmate across the way for fear of bringing a smile to the serious proceedings. I vowed that I would attend to my task with concentration and dedication. The meal began at seven p.m.

The bloods appeared at their own pace and in their own time. The majority of the men were in their dinner suits and the ladies looked wonderful. I noticed that Tappin had three different ways of greeting them.

Version one was accorded to those he knew were either important, big tippers or both. They got the full limp handshake for the male, the deepest bow for the lady, and the parade through the saloon to the designated table. Then came the overacted pulling out of Madame's chair, and the slow push back under her behind, bringing her safely down without a bump. The menu was produced and offered like a sacrifice – a sharp click of the fingers for the wine waiter – then another deep bow, which took him three paces backwards, followed by a waddled pirouette and a Cunard-footed walk back to the foyer. Version two was the same greeting in the foyer, but only half a parade to the centre of the saloon, followed by a flamboyant signal to the waiter of the designated table, who would take over the group mid-stream – like in those westerns when the Pony Express rider changes horses mid-gallop. Version three was an indifferent nod to the passengers as they entered the foyer. Then he would turn his back to move imaginary impediments on the cold-buffet table until they took the hint and, alone, braved the journey through the dining saloon. It was a real education, not only on the ways to get gratuities but on human nature. Here was a room filled with middle- and upper-class patrons, most of them travelling as VIPs and all of them posh, yet still being manipulated by those they considered servile. Under the auspices of the Cunard line, 'Getting there is half the fun', but on the way, you did as you were told without realizing it.

Mr Tappin was a professor of this particular college. As well as his art in greeting he also had a *coup de grâce*, his famous performance with his 'war-machine', so magnificent that it would have put anything Archimedes invented in the shade. During the five dinners on each voyage, he would approach his targets in order of importance and suggest something special: for the main course lobster *flambé* perhaps, or steak Diane or, for dessert, crêpes Suzette Grand Marnier.

It never failed. Of course they would love it! How kind! How absolutely wonderful!

Once he had secured the table's attention, he would wheel up his contraption of burners and pans, fruit or meat. Then he would fill his pan with goodies, chuck half a pint of alcohol into the concoction with a flourish and tip it towards the flame – whoosh! A column of napalm shot into the air. The bloods squealed with delight and looked round to see who else was admiring their 'special attention'. Once the heat had subsided, Tappin would serve from the pan and 'umbly accept the approbation of his victims. Up above their heads on the ceiling there was a black blob of scorched paint – those wounds were everywhere in the saloon, a constant reminder of past attacks.

Me and Ben Gunn worked the doors until ten p.m., our arms hanging off. Then the saloon steward waved us into the galley and told us to report back the following evening at seven after our daily chores. We made our way through the working alleyway of the ship and entered the *after* Pig and Whistle. This was the crew bar. In fact, there were two – the *forward* 'Pig' was used by the deck hands, but in the one at the rear of the vessel the catering department held sway. There was a bar with small tables and a few big ones with benches. I found a solitary armchair made of bamboo. Nobody seemed to use it, so over the course of the voyage it became mine. Me and Ben had a drink, him a light ale, me a lemonade, which was almost double the price of the alcoholic drink – nobody ever told me why. I only know that in my career at sea, whenever I ordered a soft drink I always got a dark look.

At midnight we made for the gloryhole. Then I saw the clock. It had stopped at twelve. 'What's happened?' I asked. 'The clock's stopped.'

'It's the time change,' Ben explained. 'The difference between North America and England is five hours, so to put things to rights the skipper stops the clock for an hour each midnight for the five nights we're at sea.'

'Great!' I cried. I had an extra hour to kill every night before I had to turn in.

''Cept going home,' Ben reminded me. 'Then you *lose* an hour.'

'But I'll be goin' home then,' I reasoned. 'It'll make it all the quicker.'

That night we sailed into the Atlantic and our first swell.

A swell is when the sea transforms itself from calm to not so calm. The ocean literally swells, thereby causing a ship to rise and fall sharply. It's nothing to an old sailor, but to a new one, like me, it was terrible. I lay in my bunk and felt my stomach roll around and suddenly spurt out of my mouth. My head swam in a muddy puddle, and any reason that I could muster told me I wasn't sea*sick* I was sea-*dying*. I dragged myself out of the gloryhole and into the washroom. Ben Gunn was already there, lying on the floor surrounded by his dinner. We didn't speak, not even to tell each other how we felt. We already *knew* that. By morning the swell had turned into a storm. At seven thirty a.m. as the crew were turning to – they were in and out of the washroom constantly – not one of them referred to the two cabin boys sitting under the showers. We had been dragged there by the night steward. 'Keep the showers on ya, then you don't 'ave to keep clearin' up the sick,' he advised.

We got quite a lot of advice that day, real useful stuff, like 'Try walkin' on your hands,' and 'Eat a big fry-up,' but the best one was that we should 'tie a slice of raw pork to a piece of string, swallow it and just as it reaches the stomach, drag it back up again'. We used none of those remedies, and were left to sort ourselves out alone.

Until nine o'clock that morning.

We had been throwing up for hours. Wankin' Ramplin' came below in search of the two missing boys. He found us in our bunks, wishing we were dead. We weren't in them long. He stood there glaring while we dressed in our uniforms like automatons. Then he led us up on to the open deck and dragged us to the ship's rail.

We held on for dear life.

'Look at the horizon,' he said.

I looked out over the falling waves. The sea was a dark grey mass, the sky was black, the clouds hung ominously above but, try as I might, I couldn't see the horizon. Just a host of ghostly images roaring at me through a curtain of cold icy mist, thrown up from the storm-tormented waves that surrounded the ship like some great monster.

'Can you see it – the horizon?' Rampling yelled, over the wind.

I couldn't even see him! Everything was a blur and my eyes were smarting with salt. I had lived by the Thames all my life, and had no fear of it, but if my benign river was the Beauty, this ocean was the Beast. The *Scythia* was taking the full force of its anger. It grabbed hold of her keel, lifted her like a cork and smashed her down into the void with a great wet slap.

Poseidon was venting his wrath and I was terrified.

'The horizon, for Christ's sake!' Rampling railed. 'Can you fuckin' see it?'

'Yes, sir,' I lied.

'Keep watching, see the horizon move, and as it moves, so will your legs. Accept the motion in your body, then your head will go with your eyes.'

'Yes, sir,' Ben Gunn said, not understanding a word of all this.

'You've got half an hour, then report for work,' Rampling rapped, and left us to work out the conundrum.

Gradually I became accustomed to the awful motion. I sought out that elusive horizon and gave it all the concentration my sick mind could call upon – and then, almost as quickly as it had come, the sickness went. My head cleared, and although I still felt rough, I didn't feel suicidal any more. But there was still no horizon for poor old Ben. However, in spite of the sheer hell he was feeling, he went below to report for work, and for most of that day he did his job. Pete Lore kept me moving about – printer's office, Radio Room, ship's stores. In idle moments he talked and talked, keeping my mind off the motion. I still felt sick but, by concentrating on the movement, I survived well enough to report to the dining saloon for door duty. Ben Gunn lasted only a few minutes before he was replaced.

The storm lasted three days, culminating in a force eight, which for seafarers is acceptable. For me it was purgatory, but for Ben it was hell. He was so bad that Rampling excused him duties. On the fourth day when we were approaching the coast of Newfoundland the weather cleared. Then, with my sea legs at last, I could stand on deck and look at the sheer wonder of it all. Four days before the mast with water, water everywhere, and now this far-from-Ancient Mariner was about to make landfall, proud to tell all that he had braved the storm and survived with honour – just!

The following morning RMS *Scythia* made her way down the St Lawrence river. On each side of the great waterway there was land, with buildings of unfamiliar architecture. I couldn't see live Canadians yet, but the further downstream we went the more defined the land became. I saw motor cars now, but not the vehicles of my mother country: these were the gasoline guzzlers of the movies. And that was how I felt – like I was in an American movie.

Then came the tugs, the ropes and the slow turn towards the docks of Québec. A nudge, a careful coax, and the liner slid alongside the terminal building. The gangways were out and a flock of blue-uniformed Customs and Immigration men came aboard, all officious, all foreign. I saw the red tunic of a Mountie and rushed below to tell Ben Gunn. He came to look. He was a bit better now, the blue-grey face flushed. We stood on the fo'c'sle head, taking it all in. 'I feel like I just discovered it,' Ben said.

Then the Tannoy crackled. 'Disembarkation will commence in fifteen minutes.'

Ben dashed below to his Purser's Office chores. I had a few more minutes. I watched the baggage build up on the quay, the white coats of the stewards buzzing in and out of the gathering crowds – just like in Southampton.

Then I remembered where I was – Québec! I was in French Canada, berthed in Wolfe's Cove. Up and to the right on the sheer cliffs of the Heights of Abraham was the Château Frontenac. There before me was history – *my* history. Here, in this very cove in 1759, the British General Wolfe led his men up those great heights at dead of night to surprise the French forces and capture the fortress.

By four p.m. the terminal was silent and empty. The ship was breathing a sigh of relief. I was getting ready to set foot on my first bit of foreign soil. Ben Gunn still wasn't very well. He went to the quack, who told him he had a stomach bug and to rest. 'We'll rest ashore,' he muttered. 'I ain't missin' nuffin'.'

So, we dressed in our civvies and waited at the gangplank for other crew members to go ashore. 'We'll follow them like we know where we're going,' I said. 'Then they won't know we're new.'

We slipped in behind half a dozen deckhands, who led us through Immigration, past Customs and out of the docks. They crossed the road and went into what looked like a bar. It had big picture windows with running lights round the frames. Above the door a sign flashed: 'DINER'. I was back in one of those American movies.

We waited for a few minutes till the other blokes had gone in. Then we followed them. As the door opened, the heavy rhythm of a jukebox jumped at us. It was in the corner to my left. Just as I'd expected it to be: a real live jukebox with lights running round its hand-painted pictures of palm trees. Its loudspeaker was covered with carved hula girls and throbbing bass notes accompanied Doris Day singing 'Sugarbush'. It drew me like a magnet. The closer I got, the louder the bass, and the louder the bass, the deeper the trance.

> *Oh, Sugarbush I love you so*
> *I will never let you go . . .*

The record ended. But I wanted more music, more throbbing bass. The instructions on the front of the machine told me what to do. I obeyed without question, feeling in my pocket for the coins. *Five cents one play, six plays a quarter.* The coins dropped. The red light flashed impatiently: *Make your selection. Make your selection.* I tried to focus on the long list of titles running along the machine's front, like rows of gnashing teeth. But all I could see was ' "Sugarbush" – Doris Day, A22.' So I selected A22 six times and the record played continuously for twenty minutes. By then I was well into my 'film'.

I was sitting at the counter with a steaming cup of Java and ham 'n' eggs smothered with ketchup, mesmerized by the actions of the short-order cook. That chap ran the diner before your eyes: he took the orders, cooked the meals, washed the dishes, made out the bills, gave the change, cleaned the counter and kept up a lively conversation with the customers. All on his own.

'Stick a broom up his arse and he sweeps the floor,' one tar joked.

I couldn't take my eyes off him.

I think that out of all the jobs I have seen performed in the service industry across the world, the short-order cook's is the champion.

He mixed my first chocolate malted and grilled my first hot

dog. I ate five that day. Crisp red frankfurters lying on a warmed roll, swimming in mustard and ketchup, topped off with a quarter-inch-thick layer of relish, and devoured in seconds.

Ben Gunn didn't join me: although he, too, was bathing in this brave new world, he didn't warm to the culinary pleasures because of his aching guts. He just sat by the jukebox telling me about some bloke called Vancouver, who came this way in search of new lands. 'He's buried in a little church in Richmond, Surrey,' he lectured. 'Funny place for a man who could have picked the Pacific.'

I nodded in mute agreement, then yelled, in my perfect American, 'One dog, one malted to go!'

The short-order cook echoed the call, and as he went into his act, I fed my last nickel into the jukebox, inviting Doris to sing us home:

> *Sugarbush what can I do*
> *Mother's not so pleased with you . . .*

The next day was our last full day in port, but as we were not at sea I was back on the nine-to-five watch. The ship was in the full flow of cleaning and repair. My job at the Writer's Office followed the same pattern as it had in Southampton. Dockets and invoices rushed from one department to another. On those trips I saw Ben Gunn occasionally. He still wasn't eating much and cried off going ashore that evening because he had to wait for the quack to come back from an appointment in the city. When the time came to leave I prepared to hit the diner alone.

I was on my third hot dog and malted when a group came in. They were 'donkeymen', tough blokes who worked in the ship's engine room, mostly Jocks and Scousers. For some reason I spurned Doris Day, and joined them for a trip into Québec. We walked away from the docks and caught a bus, then took another walk up a series of quaint hills with lovely smart houses on either side of the cobbled sidewalks. It was a most beautiful city.

The bar was dim with photographs of ice-hockey players on the walls. 'I'll have a lemonade,' I said.

A fat donkeyman cursed. 'You'll 'ave a *drink*, lad, no' a mouthwash.'

He bought me something called a Tom Collins. It was served in a tall frosted glass with a slice of lemon and a straw sticking out of it. It looked innocent enough, so I took a deep suck. It tasted a bit like Galloway's Cough Syrup, but I finished it and mebbe even had another one – I don't really remember.

All I do remember is waking up.

I was still in the bar but the donkeymen had left. There were just two men sitting by the door – strangers.

I asked them where my mates had gone. They just looked at me. '*Je ne sais pas,*' they said.

I didn't understand. 'Me mates, they've gone – d'ya know where?' I asked again.

'*Allez-vous-en,*' they mumbled, and dismissed me with a Gallic shrug of annoyance.

I had absolutely no idea what they were talking about. I went over to the bartender and asked the same question, but he, too, talked foreign. I left the bar – it was pitch dark outside. How long I'd been asleep I didn't know. All I knew was that my head was heavy and my legs were slow. I found the small hills and the houses after about half an hour, but I hadn't an inkling of where the bus stop or the docks were. All I had, now that dawn was breaking, was the gnawing feeling that I was lost and would be late for muster. It was now perhaps six a.m. A few people came on to the streets on their way to work, but every single one spoke French. I knew that Canadians also spoke perfect English but somehow, on hearing my accent, they took on an overkill of pride. There was no way that these Froggies were going to talk the Queen's English, especially to an Englishman.

I walked and walked. Daylight came and with it more anxiety – now I wasn't just going to miss the muster, I was going to miss the bloody boat. God help me, I could see it all: 'Young seaman jumps ship in foreign port, never to be seen again!'

On I went. Then it came. I heard her foghorn in the distance, throwing out that mournful cry over the high spires and copper roofs. That long call told me it was well past muster . . . well past nine – probably *eleven a.m.*!

She sailed at midday!

Christ!

That horn! *Run, bugger, run.*

Down past the last of the city, the warehouses and the diner. Finally I neared the dock gates, the lines of empty taxis coming towards me, away from the ship. God, they were all on board!

The Immigration official took for ever to check my identity card and discharge book. The ship gave two long blows: she was now very impatient.

I made to pass the Immigration desk, but the officer pulled me back. 'Vaccination certificate,' he said. 'I need your vaccination certificate.'

'It's on board,' I said, pointing at the ship, watching her two main gangways tilting back into the bulkheads.

'That's England.' He smirked. 'This is Canada. And in Canada you have to have a certificate.'

They took me into a small room at the back of the terminal. A man in a white coat was resting on a bunk. He and the officer spoke in French.

'Please, Mister, me boat's going!' I cried. Now I knew the meaning of sheer panic.

Outside, the calls of the ship's bridge came from her Tannoys: 'Stand by after spring. For'ard lines easy now.'

Another long blow on her horn.

'Please, Mister, please.'

The man in the white coat slowly selected a needle, pushed up my sleeve and rammed it into my arm. I didn't feel a thing. I was too numb with the knowledge that I was going to miss my ship. Then he scribbled on a piece of official paper and stuck it into my discharge book nonchalantly, stapling it as though he had all the time in the world. Then, at last, he waved me away. '*Bon voyage.*' He smiled. '*Tout de suite – allez, allez.*'

I passed over the remaining *terra firma* betwixt dock and deck without touching it, making helter-skelter for my last chance of salvation – the crew gangplank still hanging from the after end. Two deckies were coupling it to the rotating capstan preparing to hoist it up. The plank rose two feet off the ground. I banged my heels into the concrete floor and soared towards it – up, up. It was as if I was in slow motion. I could feel the soft wind of the open space between the ship and the dock. I could smell the salt of the river and I could hear voices, faraway words, chastising words. Then with a wooden thump, I hit the plank. The aroma of paint, oil and grease told me I was home – back on my lovely *Scythia*. I felt her shudder as the screws under my feet gave a gentle turn. She blew once more, which came now as a welcome rather than a reprimand.

There, shaking with a combination of fear and relief, I swore I would never allow alcohol to put me in that predicament again, and those I had considered shipmates, who had left me, a fifteen-year-old kid, in the middle of nowhere, I would neither forgive nor forget.

14

On our third night at sea the weather was building up into its usual threatening pattern. We had passed the light swell and were now well into a heavy one bordering on a storm. I had finished the dining-saloon doors and had had my evening meal. Most of the crew quarters were turned in. I went to the lavatory.

There I was, sitting tight to the seat, toes biting into the deck swaying under my feet. All was quiet except the creak of the ship as she rode the waves. Then I heard something new. A rustle – just to my left. At first I thought it was a rat.

It came again. Rustle, rustle.

It was definitely coming from my left and I decided it *was* a rat. I took a deep breath and looked at my feet, hidden under my trousers. Christ! If it *is* a rat, it's under me *strides*!

The rustle came again, but now that I was facing left, I was *looking* left and I saw the true cause. A small hole, about half an inch in diameter, had been drilled into the partition opposite my left shoulder. In the hole, as a 'filler', there was a wad of toilet paper, which was now, as I watched, being pulled away slowly by someone in the next cubicle. I sat dumbfounded, transfixed. I didn't consider calling out, or running away or even mounting the wall and looking over it. I just wanted to watch the next chapter unfold.

With one last tug the wad vanished. Then came a huge eye, so close to the aperture that I could make out the lashes, and a pupil, bright and searching. Staring into my privacy.

My next move came without much deliberation. I took careful aim and smashed my fist into the Cyclops. A scream came from the other side, then the crash of a door.

Now I was up, the strides were up and so was my blood. I crashed out of my cubicle and confronted the phantom voyeur.

He stood at the mirror poking a handkerchief into his eye. His nickname was 'Greta' and he was a tourist waiter. He was more than six feet tall, about thirty-five and had been a paratrooper during the war. He also wore makeup. 'That fuckin' hurt!' he cried, rubbing his eye.

'You shouldn't have been looking. It's dirty,' I snapped – not in the least bit alarmed. 'And don't do it again,' I added, walking out of the place *à la* John Wayne.

'Not with you I won't, you filthy little sod,' he screeched.

Although I was satisfied with the way I had handled the episode, it preyed on my mind. I had known irons before – but Frankie and Barry in Bermondsey were like the 'uncles'. They had sung and played at parties in our house and had taken me to other people's parties to do my record act. I'd never thought twice about *what* they were, only *who*. But now, at sea, with this phantom voyeur, I was starting to worry.

Pete Lore sorted me out. I told him about Greta the following day, so he took me below deck to the cabin of QB. 'He's called QB because he's the Queen Bee,' Pete said. 'I think you and he ought to have a chat.'

I walked tentatively into the cabin. The Queen was well into his fifties with a shock of dyed blue-white hair backcombed to perfection. He was a first-class bedroom steward, a sought-after job. He arose from a deep sofa with chintz cushions, a small man with smiling eyes, and shook hands warmly. He moved in a feminine way, which told me I was in the presence of a lady.

'Welcome to my home,' he said, in a high-pitched Bristol accent. Then he pointed to a big bloke lying on one of the two single bunks. 'This is my friend Flicka, son of Thunderhead.' Flicka waved and went back to his book. I thought, How lucky can you get? A cabin for *two*.

'Would you like a drink?' QB inquired.

I shook my head. He offered me the room's other chair.

I sat and watched him pour a drink first for Flicka, then for himself. He sat opposite me and drank deeply. 'Hmm,' he purred, 'a nice drop of mother's ruin.' There was a pause as he studied me studying him. Then he said, 'I hear you've had a to-do with our Greta – silly cow. It's not the first time, dear, and it won't be the last. She'll have to go, dear, she really will *have* to go. I was saying to my Flicka that Greta is going to send me to my grave. And she will – she will.'

'She – I mean *he*,' I explained, 'took a diabolical liberty – and it was out of order.'

'It was, it was. And what you did was quite right. You showed our Greta that she wasn't welcome. And now she knows, dear, and so do all the girls.'

'Knows what?'

'That you're not available, love. That's all.' He pulled his chair closer and patted my arm. 'Believe me, Master Tommy Hicks,' he smiled, 'there isn't any danger here, no terrible people, just a lot of men living together, hoping to get along and enjoy life. Most of them are straight, some are queer. The queer will see someone he likes and make an advance. A simple *no* tells him to stay away and that's that. You gave Greta a shock and now it's all over the ship. All the girls are saying, "Stay away from the new kid. He isn't interested," and that's it.' He patted me again. 'I really do promise you, love, so no bad dreams, no dark thoughts, OK?'

I nodded and left.

What QB told me that day proved to be true. Throughout my years at sea I never once saw or even heard about youth moles-tation: the gay community mixes with the straight without inter-ference on either side. We see in films and read in novels how huge men in hard prisons make for young men and force themselves on them – we see sadism and violence. I saw none of it. A ship is not a prison, and those on it are there by choice.

The Atlantic had become angry. We were again riding out another force-eight storm. I staggered to work and at six o'clock in the evening of our last full day at sea I went to the Pig to meet Ben Gunn. He wasn't there. 'He hasn't turned to all afternoon,' a purser told me. 'I only know he was going to see the quack again.'

I went to the ship's hospital. The chief sister, Miss Chalmers, let me into the surgery. The doctor was in his cabin dressing for dinner. I asked if she had seen Ben.

'I'm afraid he's here,' she said, 'in the sick bay – very, very sick.'

'I know,' I said. 'He's 'aving trouble with the motion. Every time we get a swell he's Pat and Mick, but he'll get used to it, won't he?'

She studied a file on her desk. 'Are you good mates?'

'Oh, yes, Miss – ever since we was kids.'

'Then you know how he loves the sea.'

'Yes, Miss, he loves it.'

'And that nothing in the world is more important to him.'

'Nuffin', Miss, not in the whole world.'

'And that if he were taken away from it, it would break his heart.'

'Break it, Miss, in two.'

'And if his heart were broken, he would need a mate, a good mate.'

'Yes, Miss.'

Sister Chalmers took me into the small ship's ward. It held four neat single beds with gleaming white sheets. Ben Gunn was the only patient, lying with his back to the door. 'I'll leave you two together,' she whispered, then left me standing in the semi-darkness.

The decks rose and fell with the storm. The only source of light was the one over Ben's bed. He looked bloody rough – the blue tone had returned to his skin. He stared up at me, his eyes like a trapped rat's. The pillow and sheet by his head were wet and greenish like a soft watercolour.

''Ow are ya, Ben?'

'I've been thinking about Horatio Nelson,' he said, as if he was living in another world. 'Did you know that he was always seasick?'

'No, I didn't.'

'Well, he was. They said that was why he always got his battles over quick – so's he could get back to port. It never stopped him going to sea, Tom, ever.'

'Well, it wouldn't, would it, 'im bein' Nelson?'

'So, once I get this trip over, once I get meself straight, I'll be all right, won't I?'

'Course you will.'

The ship gave another lurch, which caused him to retch again. His throat gurgled and he choked green bile.

I stayed for a little while, until the quack came in with a hypodermic needle. He was a tall, elegant man, all the more so because he was in his dress uniform – wing collar and bow-tie. He sat by Ben's side and pushed his hair off his sweating forehead. I thought of my mum then – and I thought of Ben, the bile and the needle.

'How's our Horatio?' The quack beamed at him.

'Much better, sir.' He flinched as the needle went into his arm. 'Will it go away now, like last time?'

'Yes, just like last time, son, and tomorrow we'll all be home.'

The sister tidied the bed and I followed the quack into the waiting room. I asked him, 'Will he be all right, sir?'

'Yes, he'll be fine tonight. Tomorrow depends.'

'Thank you, sir. He has to be a sailor, you know.'

'So he tells me.' I made to leave, but then, as an afterthought, he said, 'He won't go back to sea, son. He's brought up the lining of his stomach and he can't be doing that again. I'm afraid your friend is beached indefinitely.'

'It'll break his heart, sir, when he knows.'

'He already does,' the quack said.

The ship listed to starboard.

I waited for the quack and the sister to go to dinner, then slipped back into Ben's room. 'They said the Vikings were the first to cross the Atlantic,' he said. 'In them longboats they used sail and oars – can you imagine how . . .' He fell asleep before he could finish.

The next morning came. And with it 'the Channels'.

It isn't easy to explain the feeling that comes over a sailor when he and his vessel are in the last knots of their homeward voyage. Is it euphoria? Is it bliss, bordering on a sort of happy madness? I suppose it's both those things. It first hit me when the BBC news was relayed over the ship's Tannoy at eight a.m. and the refined voice of the perfect Englishman assured us that we were entering British waters and all was well. The crew went around with a constant grin, everybody was bouncing, goodwill in the air. The passengers were over the top with their greetings. The noticeboards spelled out the orders with references to 'port' and that wonderful word 'Leave'! Apart from those selected for 'working by' the ship, the rest of us were to 'job and finish', then free to go. This meant that after five o'clock that evening I could have the next day off.

What would I do?

I met Ben in the gloryhole. He was out of the hospital and, although pretty weak, was packing his stuff. We made small-talk, neither of us wanting to discuss his signing off. As I was on duty at the Writer's Office I couldn't stay long. 'See you later,' I said.

But I didn't. What with the extra work attached to our arrival, I didn't get back until we had berthed and by that time he had gone. The note on my pillow read 'Land Ho! Ben.'

We never met again.

15

The train to London left at six twenty p.m. and there was no way I was going to miss it – I was on my way home. I had decided that, even if it was one solitary day, it was going to happen – and, besides, it was more than a day, wasn't it? One night, one *whole* day, then another night and an early morning before the train back. But should I let the family know I was coming? Should I telephone or just turn up at the front door?

I decided on surprise.

It wasn't until I stepped out of the station at Waterloo that it dawned on me that I was home. The accents of the passers-by were of London, there was a grey fog, red buses and a black taxi. I hailed it. It rattled along the roads past the Old Vic to the Royal Eye Hospital, then on through Elephant and Castle, across the Old Kent Road, past Bacon's School for Boys and the Trocette cinema, along Abbey Street and under Druid Street arches. Turn right into Spa Road and there it was, Frean Street, the best port of all. Strangely, everything seemed much smaller than I remembered, the street, the church, the houses. It was as if, during my weeks away, some magic spell had been cast and the neighbourhood had shrunk. The taxi pulled up outside number fifty-two.

My pulse was in overdrive.

I fiddled in my pocket for the half-crown to pay the driver. Then, as I looked up again, my dad was standing at the door in his Sunday best, smart tie, starched collar. He beamed and yelled into the house, 'Bet! Bet! 'E's 'ere!'

Mum came out, dolled up to the nines too. Her eyes were tired but her beauty glowed. She gave an excited cry and then she was surrounded by the kids, all peering from the house like Sickert's paintings of an audience at the old Bedford music-hall.

Colin gave a traditional Cockney 'Oi!' Roy, too. Sandra held

Back at the family home in Frean Street.

on to Mum's skirt coyly and peeped at me from under her blonde fringe.

The taxi drew away, and I stood there with my sea-bag, just looking at my folks. Dad referred to his attire: 'I've bin in this since four o'clock.' He laughed. 'Yer mum finds out you docked at twelve, which, according to 'er, gets you on the one forty to Waterloo, then the bus and, bingo, you're 'ome. Then she says, "Gotta look smart, got to go out, make a night of it." Five hours I've bin like this.'

I don't know why, but it seems we never left the pavement. My mum ran into my arms, the kids skipped around pulling my coat, Dad kept ruffling my hair and I handed out the presents: a bottle of perfume for Mum, export Woodbines for Dad, an Indian doll for Sandra, a baseball mitt, bat and ball for Colin and Roy. The neighbours came to their windows and doors, waving. The church bell rang – by chance! Then Mum scolded everyone into the house and things were back to normal.

That evening and the next day was a combination of pub crawls,

Home on leave. Here I am with my little sister Sandra.

my sea stories (selected!), and constant cups of tea. When my last night came, I was exhausted. I went round to Ginger Thompson's for a rest.

'So wot was they like, then, the Red Indians?' he asked, trying not to sound as jealous as I knew he was.

'Mostly big on account of their fevvers,' I lied.

'Makin' a lot of noise, I s'pose.'

'Yeah, you know, wiv their drums and their shouts and whoops.'

'And their bows and arrows and Winchester rifles and warpaint?'

'Peacepaint,' I corrected him. 'They ain't allowed the war stuff any more.'

'Who said so?' he asked.

Pause.

'The United Nations,' I said.

Come the next dawn, I set off for the five forty – this time! – back to Southampton Central. There were quite a few of the lads on the train. At seven fifty we all jumped into the waiting cabs, yelling the name of our ship and demanding 'full steam ahead'.

At eight sharp I was in the tourist-class saloon answering my name along with everyone else.

The next day the *Scythia* shook her timbers and aimed once more for Québec. The first night at sea brought my first fight. It was all over the bamboo armchair in the Pig and Whistle. There I was, sipping my lemonade, when a large wide steward came up to me. 'Get up,' he snapped.

I'd never seen him before so he was obviously new crew or just back from long leave. My first inclination was to ignore him, which I did.

'I'm talking to you, kid,' he snarled. 'Get up. I want that chair.'

Now I had to reply. 'Bollocks!' I said, toasting him defiantly with my lemonade.

Whack!

He slapped me hard across the face. If he had punched me I'm sure I would have reacted differently: he was a big bloke and I would probably have had to take it like a kid. But a slap? That was an insult.

I jumped up and punched his chin. With absolutely no effect. He didn't even blink. Christ! I thought.

He slapped me again. Another insult. But what could I do? I was angry – and psychologically hurt. I looked around for some kind of advantage. On my right there was a table with a chef sitting at it, his kerchief wrapped round his kitchen knives at his side. I drew one and waved it in front of the steward's fat face.

'Piss off!' I threatened. 'Piss off or I'll do ya.'

He smiled, took me by the wrist, turned the knife towards me and stuck it a full inch into my right thigh. I was astonished, watching the blood pumping through my trousers. Then he pushed me aside and sat down in the chair as if nothing had happened. Nobody else bothered to interfere. Everyone carried on with their evening.

I eased the knife out of the wound and literally dropped my trousers for a closer look. It was an ugly hole going blue round the edges, still pumping blood and now beginning to smart.

The chef indicated his knife lying on the deck. 'You'd better

clean that, son,' he murmured. 'I've got to cut meat in the morning.'
As I was going to be sick, I picked up the weapon gingerly and
hopped to the washroom outside the bar with my strides still round
my ankles. There, I took half a ton of toilet paper and rammed it
into my wound. I washed the knife, threw up and looked at myself
in the mirror. I was a sickly white with dark rings under my eyes.

The chef came in to retrieve his property. 'You silly bastard,' he
murmured. 'Let's have a look.'

He eased away the wad from the wound. Half of it was stuck,
so he filled a glass with water, threw it at the paper, then dragged
it off. 'Fuckin' 'ell!' I cried.

'It's a bit deep,' he said. He began to pull the cut open, which
hurt more than the stabbing had.

'Fuckin' bloody 'ell!' I exclaimed.

'Right,' he said. 'You've got a deep cut there and you've got a
big problem.'

Shit! I thought. He's going to amputate!

He went on: 'If you go to the quack, he'll want to know *how*
you got it. When Wankin' Ramplin' comes down, he'll want to
know *who*. When the skipper turns up, he'll want to know *why*.'

'I don't want none of that,' I said. 'It's my cut and I'll handle it
me own way.'

'How?' He smiled. 'You've got to do something with it cos it
won't just go away.'

'I'll put a plaster on it,' I said firmly.

'You do that.' He laughed – and left.

I pushed another pile of paper on to it, pulled up my trousers
and went in search of Pete Lore. He listened to my tale and shook
his head. 'You should report it,' he warned, 'and you shouldn't
involve me.'

I realized that he had his career to think about and now, given
the opportunity to think clearer, I knew I'd placed him in a bad
position. But he got dressed and helped me along the decks to the
cabin of the Queen Bee and Flicka.

QB was worse than my mum. He scolded and screamed at me.
Flicka gave me a cuff on the head and Pete left us to it.

'He'll have to have stitches,' QB wailed at Flicka.

'Not if he wants to stay in the navy.' He snorted.

'Who cares about the soddin' navy? He could bleed to death.'

'No, he won't,' Flicka said, calm as a millpond. 'Just get me some antiseptic powder, lint, cotton wool and a few six-inch strips of Elastoplast.'

'And where do I get them, may I ask?' QB said sarcastically. 'Boots closes at six.'

'You can get anything, doll.' Flicka smiled. 'Just run along and do your Lauren Bacall bit.'

Later that night they carried me back to the gloryhole, and at seven the next morning Flicka came and uncovered the wound. 'Very nice,' he whispered. Everyone else was still asleep. Then he dusted it and put on a fresh dressing. 'Can you walk?'

I got off the bunk and gave it a try. My leg had stiffened, but Flicka took me outside the cabin and it eased as we walked up and down the deck. Then he asked, 'Do you think you can turn to?' He was very serious. He knew that if I couldn't work questions would be asked, and answers would have to be given.

'I think so,' I replied.

'Don't *think*, son. Can you work?'

'Yes, I can work.'

'OK. That means moving about, running up and down companionways, standing around opening doors. You can do that?'

'I can do that.'

'And what do you do if the cut opens?'

Pause.

'I dunno.'

'You tell 'em you've got diarrhoea and you find me.'

'Yes,' I said. 'I find you.'

'Right,' he said. 'Now fuck off back to sleep.'

I went to my bunk and lay there worrying.

What I hadn't mentioned to Flicka was the thumping in my ears. It was as if I had a bilge pump in my leg, throbbing loudly each time my heart beat, but the beat was very fast, faster than it usually was. Anyway, I turned to and managed to get through the day. The cut didn't open, but the throb stayed.

The evening came and I was on the doors. It wasn't so bad, but every now and then when the ship went into a roll, I had to grip the deck with my leg muscles. *That* hurt. I prayed we wouldn't hit a storm.

I finished at ten and went straight to the gloryhole and my bunk. I lay there depressed and anxious. There were more than twenty men in the cabin, but I felt terribly lonely. My leg was throbbing and so was my head. And I had to deal with the fact that I had got into a fight over a soddin' chair and drawn blood – my own! At about eleven the cabin door opened and the Queen Bee came in. He was dressed in full drag and full makeup. I think I swallowed every fly in the room. He called to me in his Bristol accent, touched with not a little high camp. 'Who's been on his own, then?'

Now he had the full attention of every man in the room. I could have died. Christ!

He walked the floor like an aristocratic old bird in an Oscar Wilde play and sat with a thud on the end of my bunk, ducking under the one above it so that his picture hat didn't bend. Then he produced a bunch of grapes from his handbag. 'I thought you might like these.' He smiled. 'And it's no good you lyin' around mopin' – that's no way to get better, is it?'

'No, it's not,' I mumbled, embarrassed to know that everyone in the gloryhole was listening.

'So, I've brought some company, dear,' he went on. Then he gave a loud feminine 'Cooee!'

The cabin door opened again and in waltzed half a dozen more queens, all in drag with wigs and full makeup. They fussed about me, pinching my cheeks, placing lemonade, chocolates and comics at my feet. Then they pulled up chairs and gathered round my bunk like a spell of witches. All was silent for a while. Then QB spoke. 'Now, tell your aunties all about it,' he cooed.

I could have died again!

Eventually the voyage ran its course and Flicka strongly advised me to get the cut stitched in Southampton. However, with visions of opening up another can of beans, I decided to leave things as they were. It was a daft mistake. I still have the wound – it healed, but never really 'joined up'. It has a thin layer of skin over it and is still liable to open up if it has a knock.

Two more voyages passed without incident. The next one, however, impressed on me that there are 'more things in heaven and earth' . . .

The *Scythia* had just entered the English Channel outward-bound. It was early evening when the order came from the bridge that the four cabin boys were to report to the bosun's mate. Me and the lads had a quick wash and brush-up, then padded forward to the fo'c'sle head. From there, we were directed to the chain locker, an area well below decks that houses the anchor chain. There, in a cold, unfriendly corner, a small group of men had gathered round a soft light. We four crept forward.

The bosun and his mate were laying out a large square of white canvas on a trestle paint table. Then, with a silent nod, the group reached down to the other side of the table and lifted up a dead body. It was a man, white and stiff as a statue. Now they wrapped him in the canvas. The bosun took a long, thick needle, threaded with twine, and began to sew the body into it. The others watched every stitch without a murmur.

My thoughts went back to the *Victory* and Trafalgar. My mind's ear heard the ship's surgeon advising Captain Hardy that his lordship was mortally wounded. I saw Nelson lying across the gun-wales, his white shirt torn down below his waist, and heard his last memorable words, 'Kiss me, Hardy.' I held back a cry because I was among men – just like I was now in the *Scythia*'s chain locker.

The bosun spoke softly: 'Right, that's it, lads. Break out the grog.'

A bottle of rum was produced. The bosun addressed us cabin boys: 'I'm about to effect the last stitch.' He moved to the uncovered head of the corpse and talked as he worked. 'This last stitch I place through the nose.' The needle went in. 'You will all affirm that there are no tears from the corpse.' It's an age-old custom of the sea: should the stitch bring tears, the person isn't dead – yet!

Men and boys uttered a solemn 'Aye.'

With the body now covered, the rum was handed round for each of us to toast it. A Union Jack was produced and laid over the silent package. Then, the men lifted it, still on the trestle table and, with us four cabin boys in attendance, we took it along the decks and the working alleyway, and then up on to the after end of the ship.

There, the orchestra played a lament as a small collection of people assembled round the skipper, and a lady in black. Later that day we were told that special permission had been granted for the body of an old sailor to be buried at sea. The ship's horn sounded a long note. Beneath us the engines idled and the *Scythia* shuddered to a slow, slow stop. Now there was just the sound of the sea and the wind.

We took the body to the ship's side and held it fast.

Eventually Captain Maclean's beautiful voice spoke: 'And now we commit his body to the deep.'

The canvas was tipped forward. The body slipped from under the flag and majestically entered its watery grave. The band played as we sang, 'Oh, hear us when we cry to thee, For those in peril on the sea.'

16

Autumn came, and waned into a freezing winter. The Atlantic became cold and unfriendly – only the porpoises that occasionally swam alongside us had any frolic left. Storms hit with varying degrees of threat and, once we neared Newfoundland, the feeling of dread was upon us: we were now entering the silent world of the iceberg. During the daytime these white mountains were breathtakingly beautiful. On one occasion I saw a pair of polar bears hunting from one. But during the night, when the ship was on 'ice routine', with the watertight doors closing on those of us below the waterline, my thoughts were of uglier things. Like the sinking of the *Titanic* – she had struck a berg in these same waters.

At six thirty one night in November, I was typing in the Writer's Office when the ship shook with such force that it sent me and the giant Underwood typewriter flying across the deck. I had barely time to collect my worst thoughts before the intermittent ringing of bells told me and the ship's company to make for their lifeboat stations – lively!

My lifeboat was up on the main deck. I grabbed a lifejacket and pulled it over my head as I ran, tying the reef knot without looking and wondering if it would hold when I hit the sea. As I ran, the Tannoy gave instructions, the calm voice of the announcer fighting the panic of the ringing bells.

'Would all passengers please go to their stations. Please wear warm clothing under your lifejackets. Do *not* go to your cabins. Do *not* congregate in the public rooms.'

Because of the emergency drills ordered by the Board of Trade we, the crew, knew where we were expected to go, and what our duties were without running around like a bunch of headless chickens. The passengers, too, knew roughly what was expected of them. Cunard was rigorous when it came to safety: within hours of sailing the bloods were paraded on the open decks regardless of weather and drilled in what to do during an emergency.

But this was not a drill.

And the engines had stopped. Just like the *Titanic*.

When I reached the main deck there were only two cooks, a greaser and a stewardess at my station. Up above our heads was our lifeboat with two deck hands checking the ropes and pulling away the tarpaulins. 'Where's the coxwain?' I yelled to the deckies.

'Up for'ard,' one answered. 'That's where we hit.'

''E's s'posed to be wiv us,' I yelled back.

'Not if he's needed up for'ard,' came the calm reply.

Our cox was an engineer – and he was up front. Just like the *Titanic*.

I stood there for a few minutes more – the cold night was about us and the decks were filling with people in lifejackets, which gave the impression that everyone had turned into a hunchback. The combined condensation of their cold breath seemed to compete with the mist wafting in from the sea. Above us the ship's horn blew ominously at regular intervals. Again and again the *Titanic* came back to me.

More and more people were arriving now, children skipping along, enjoying the game, mothers scolding, men carrying the very young, and crew members giving directions, plus a thousand explanations as to what had happened.

Suddenly an officer appeared. 'Are you warm under that?' he said, pointing at my red tunic.

'A bit, sir, yes.'

'Come with me,' the officer ordered, striding off towards the fo'c'sle. 'I need you.'

We went through the chattering crowd.

'Don't run,' he snapped, as I tried to keep up with him. 'Stride purposefully.'

We passed the public areas and moved down towards the working part of the ship – no covered ways or teak doors here, just cold open decks with small pockets of crewmen swinging out lifeboats.

Judging by their clothes – sou'westers and sea boots – they were going over the side. They reminded me of a crew in a Melville novel, preparing to hunt whale.

I followed my officer to the fo'c'sle head. A group of men was there, peering out over the bow into the mist. I knew then that the real action was here at the bow. Back among the passengers there was just rumour. I joined the group and concentrated on staring into the night. I had no idea what I was looking for, but as everyone else seemed to know I decided that a still tongue would make me wiser. Sooner or later things would become apparent. Like how big the iceberg was that we had hit and how deep the hole in our side was, which even now would be filling with grey ocean, and how long we had before . . . That damn *Titanic* again!

Just then a crackle came from the giant Tannoy speakers housed in the bridge wings. Every head at the bow snapped towards the sound.

Captain Maclean's voice came, his words calm and measured. 'What ship are you?'

Once more our heads snapped – this time back towards the mist.

Blimey, I thought. There's another vessel out there.

The captain's voice came again: 'We are *Scythia* out of Québec. I repeat, what ship are you?'

A faint cry came from within the mist on the starboard quarter. A seaman pointed, yelling up towards the bridge. 'There, sir, I see it – to starboard!'

Then we all saw it, a ship moving out of the fog like the *Mary Celeste*. The captain's voice again – more agitated: 'What ship? What ship?'

'I have men in the water,' a voice shouted, from the distance.

Our two crewed lifeboats swung out and down into the ocean.

'Engage the bow lookout,' came the order from the bridge. My officer took off my lifejacket, directed me to the bosun standing at the point and ordered, 'Take him up, Bosun.'

The top sailor lifted me up on his shoulders. 'Now, you keep a good look out, son,' he said. 'You watch careful at the waters and if you see a man, or what you *think* is a man, you shout, point and *hold* your point till the boats get to what you've seen – all right?'

'Yes, Bosun.'

Once I'd settled on his shoulders, a shaft of light hit me from the bridge, lighting up my red tunic like a beacon. Then the huge arc lights to either side of the bow began to sweep the sea as if it were the perimeters of a prison.

God, I was cold – but my shivers were nothing compared to my one big fear: supposing I missed someone? I peered into the port quarter. Then, almost at once, I saw another ship, moving in fast towards us. I yelled, to the bosun below me, 'Ship, port quarter! A ship – comin' in to the port!'

I felt him jump. Then he pinched my arse so bloody hard that my eyes watered. 'It's a berg, you bleedin' charlie, just a berg.'

To me it was the *Ark Royal* and I would still swear that it was moving towards me. It was, in fact, *us* moving towards *it*. Although we were under power we were not using our screws, because people were in the water so we were drifting. But the bridge had taken note of my sighting and the ship shook itself to safety.

I saw the first man in the water during that manoeuvre, just to starboard, lying on a mattress resting his head on his arm as if he was reading a book. 'Man to starboard,' I yelled. 'Reading a book,' I added.

I pointed straight and held until the nearest lifeboat got to him, then I watched them pull him aboard. The other ship was coming closer. Before I returned to the search, our Tannoy crackled again. 'What ship are you?'

A pause, then a voice came from a distant loud-hailer: 'We are the Canadian collier *Wabana*, bound . . .' Crackle! Crackle!

'We are *Scythia*.'

'We have men in the water.'

'We have boats out. Do you need assistance?'

Long pause.

'We have no power, no steering. You have sliced through our after end. We have injuries and are rigging sea anchor and bow chains.'

Pause.

'Do you understand?'

Our captain's voice answered — there was a waver in it: 'We understand. I am sending a rigging crew and hospital staff. Will you accept a line? Will you accept a line?'

'Send your crew. Send a line — we have men in the water.'

I heard more of our boats hit the waves and then I saw them move strongly into the mist towards the stricken collier. Now I was back to my search.

Two men were taken out of the sea that night — the man on the mattress was one. Both were dead. Sister Chalmers told me that the shock of either the collision or the cold had killed him instantly, leaving him petrified on his bunk.

It was an eerie thought.

After the search was concluded, the questions came about *our* state.

Were we stricken too?

Were we holed?

Were we, in fact, sinking?

We were damaged at the bow, but not so that we couldn't make headway. The stricken collier had no such advantage because her rudder had gone down with the rest of her after end, plus her screws. All power and steering had gone — but the icebergs hadn't.

Now that the search for survivors had ended, the main task was to keep what was left of the collier away from the certain destruction of a collision with the mountains of ice around it, waiting to pounce like a pack of hyenas. Due to the extensive damage, the vessel was pretty close to sinking. Captain Maclean sent one lifeboat after another to try to get a line to her but, with the combination of continual drift and worsening weather, they had no success. In the end he tried a desperate measure. He would risk his ship and take the *Scythia* nearer the *Wabana*. Then, from a better height, and with more power, he might negotiate an exchange of life lines. The danger lay in that power, which could work against the operation: if the skipper turned just a few revolutions more than

his careful calculations, the crippled collier would take the force
of our mistake and drift quickly away from us in *any* direction.

I watched the skipper pace the freezing bridge, arms behind his
back, snapping orders to officers all round the ship. He looked to
me like Hornblower, full of doubt, racked with the fear of doom
yet determined to win the day. He coaxed us closer, ordering
'Astern', 'Ahead' and 'Midships' and 'Stop', until we were so close
that the bridge officer and the quartermaster on the wheel could
barely draw breath.

In the second hour of the operation, a line was exchanged and,
to the cheers of the passengers, we towed the *Wabana* away from
the iceberg area. But the next morning we lost the line and she
started to drift again. Thankfully, by that time ocean-going tugs
had reached the area and they took charge.

We decided to return to Québec for a close inspection of the
Scythia. But just before we left the scene, a message came from the
Wabana's skipper. He wanted his dead back. They were lying in
our hospital. Our captain sent them with his condolences. The
message was ignored.

A day later we arrived back in Québec. The dock was full of
people, gathering to see the ship hobble into her berth with a
bent bow.

We were not welcomed as heroes.

By all accounts, we had spread ourselves over the Atlantic,
clinging to the myth that Britannia still ruled the waves and God
help any lesser craft that got in the way. Hence the collision. That
was the French version.

Once the passengers were disembarked the crew were informed
that we would be in port indefinitely to assess repairs. We were
also assured that our families would be advised of our present
safety, but should anyone wish to send a message home they could
do so on the company.

I joined the queue outside the Radio Room. When I eventually
gave my message to the officer he pushed it back at me testily.
'You can't put "shipwreck",' he snapped. 'And you can't put
"many dead" – and who's this Alfred Thompson anyway?'

'It's my mate – in Bermondsey.'

'Immediate family only,' the officer growled, and chucked another blank form at me.

I settled for 'Dear Mum, Still alive – tell Ginger.'

That first night ashore I was the centre of attraction in the diner. Even my beloved Doris Day had to stay silent while I told of the 'great search'. By midnight I was bloated with malted milk shakes and hot dogs, but by morning my celebrity had dimmed. The docks were now quadrupled with crowds.

'More people than the Ascot Gold Cup!' I told Pete Lore, who had followed me up on deck to see for himself.

We watched the multitude pushing and shoving each other, jostling for some sort of advantage.

'Have you noticed something strange?' Pete laughed. 'They're not looking at us – they're looking in the other direction.'

And they were. I couldn't understand it. If *we* were the attraction, what was going on over there where the lights blazed? And there was the answer. The lights!

'It's Alfred Hitchcock,' Fred, the master-at-arms, said mournfully. 'He's making a film called *I Confess*. He's got Montgomery Clift, Anne Baxter and a thousand extras down there all acting their arses off, all making a fortune, and here we are up here used as background for nuffin'. It's a bleedin' disgrace.'

Hitchcock, Clift and Baxter – lights, camera, action! Wow!

I reached the dock in record time and gradually, with a lot of push and shove, I got to the bright lights. The film camera was on a swing crane like a magician's black box, skimming the heads of the crowd, seeking out Montgomery Clift in army uniform returning from the troop ship (ours!). The fat bloke with the fag in his mouth shouted, 'Cut,' and talked to the mob.

'There ain't nuffin' worse than people lookin' at the camera,' he rasped. 'So do me a blinkin' favour and ignore the lens.'

'That's Alfred Hitchcock,' someone says.

'Nah,' I muttered. 'He's a bloody Cockney!'

'So what? He's still the best director in the world.'

I spent the rest of the day watching him and listening to his voice. Mr Clift got the odd glance from me and Miss Baxter a few more. But it was the fat bloke with the fag who mesmerized me.

That evening back on board I gave a lot of thought to this Hitchcock. I could not equate his accent and manner to the silver screen. Going back to my earlier decision that you didn't get into showbusiness without a pedigree, I could not accept that he was who he was: words like 'nuffin'' and 'lookin'' and especially 'blinkin'' did not come from the mouths of gods – yet there he was, barking like a butcher's dog, dropping his Gs and Hs yet directing classics like *The 39 Steps*, *The Man Who Knew Too Much*, *Rebecca* and just about every other film that had kept me on the edge of my seat till the end titles. I had yet to learn the philosophy of Feste – 'Some are born great . . .' Anyway, the next day he was gone.

A week later so were we. With the ship passed fit for sea, we set off for England with no band, no streamers and no waving well-wishers. Two days into the voyage we were out of the land of the icebergs, so everybody breathed again.

On the third day I awoke with an itch that could have raised the dead. When I looked at myself in the mirror I got a shock. I was covered with a rash – but not a usual one from prickly heat or allergy: this was thick in places, as if it had been stuck on my skin. I tried the usual remedies, hot and cold showers, calamine lotion, without success so I went to the quack.

'It's not contagious, but you do have acute dermatitis,' he said.

'You mean like the clap?' I ventured, having heard the word mentioned once or twice by men talking about contagion.

He looked at me over his *pince-nez* and smiled. 'No, it's nothing like that, but we must treat it. I'm going to put you through a course of phenobarbitone so strip down and I'll get Sister Chalmers.'

I stood in the ward, thinking about Ben Gunn and dermatitis, paying off and going home beached. Sister Chalmers came in with a paint-pot and a brush. Then, ignoring my nakedness, she daubed me with a thin white paste until I was completely covered and looked like a ghost. 'It'll sting for a while,' she said, 'but don't worry – and don't get dressed for fifteen minutes till it's dry.'

She hadn't left the ward for a second before I was feeling as if a host of piranhas was biting into my skin. This pain was so bad that I jumped up into the small bay holding the open porthole and jammed myself into it to get the full thrust of the cold wind blowing outside. And I cried. I didn't care whether Sister Chalmers saw me or even the quack. I was really hurting. Later that night I was still itching, the next day too – and the next. Even QB and Flicka had a go.

But on the last day, in spite of the Channels, I went back to the quack. Things were getting worse: the rash was spreading. He wrote a note to my local doctor at home and advised me to see him. 'Does this mean "paying off"?' I asked, praying it didn't.

'Just take your leave as usual,' he told me. 'Then, if he agrees, come back. Everything will be fine.'

We arrived in port late at night, but I made for the station – I had two days' leave and I wasn't missing a minute. Anyway, I wanted my mum to see my rash and to look after me.

Besides, I'd been in a shipwreck and I had stories to tell.

I stood on the freezing, deserted platform at Southampton Central for hours – I had missed my intended train and didn't get to Waterloo until just before midnight. In London it was raining and taxis were thin on the ground. My journey to Frean Street was not a happy trip. As well as being terribly cold I had a splitting headache and the itch still hurt. Even the surprise of my arrival at home didn't exactly raise the spirits. Mum took one look at me and her excitement turned to worry – a cup of tea, yes, but we dispensed with the stories and the presents. She put me to bed and sat by me, speaking in the soft lullaby that only mothers know and soothing my forehead.

When I woke the next morning, she had gone.

So had the feeling in my legs. I lay there with my aching head, trying to work out what was going on. I tried to sit up, but I had no control over my lower body. I did my best not to panic – my first thought was to yell out – but I had to come to terms with what had happened. I forced myself to relax and try once more to move. I couldn't. I was paralysed.

So I yelled.

Roy came into the room and told me not to shout cos Dad was asleep.

'Where's Mum?' I asked.

'Gettin' Sandra ready.'

'Ask her to come up.'

'Why?'

'Just ask her to come up.'

'She's gettin' Sandra ready,' he said again, then went away.

Panic took over.

'Mum!' I roared. 'I can't move my legs,' I told her, as she came to the door.

She froze for a minute, then went into Dad's room. I could hear his voice, first annoyance, then concern. He came to me with just his vest on and felt my head. Then he pulled back the sheets and saw the rash.

'Can you move even a little bit?' he murmured, feeling my calves. I tried again – but it was useless. 'Call an ambulance,' he told Mum.

She ran out of the house and made for the telephone box in Jamaica Road. She came back in a state of frustrated confusion. 'It's broke,' she cried. 'I tried dialling nine-nine-nine, but it's dead.'

Dad didn't say anything. He went to his room and seconds later he was back in mine with his clothes on. 'Don't you worry, son, don't you worry.' He smiled reassuringly and rushed out of the house up Sun Passage and rang the private bell of the Rising Sun pub.

Within minutes the publican had kindly reversed his car out of the loading bay and brought it to our door. He and Dad lifted me out of bed and, Mum following with a blanket, they eased me into the back of the vehicle. Then, with a screech of gears, we sped off towards London Bridge and Guy's Hospital. I don't remember much more, but Mum never forgot.

'We carried you into Casualty – there was a lot of people sitting in rows of seats – and two nurses. One was seeing to a little girl with a bad cut, the other was helping a young doctor with an old lady. Your dad went to the doctor and told him about you. He sent the nurse over – she spent ages with a form listening to what we had to say about symptoms, then writing it down along with your name and address. Then she goes back to the doctor. All this time me and your dad was holding you up on one of the seats with the blanket over you – you had your eyes closed. We thought you was asleep. Then a porter comes with a trolley and we helped him lay you on it. We thought that maybe things would happen now, but he just pushes it against a wall and goes away again. We waited an awful long time, then your dad gets angry. He goes off to find this nurse again – she comes to the trolley and just looks at you, straightens your blanket and goes back to the other people, filling in forms again. We didn't know what to do next – we was in their hands and we didn't want to make too much fuss.

'Then an Indian gentleman walks by. He stops by your trolley and looks at you – I didn't want to ask, but I wondered why he was doing it. Then he calls over to the nurse who brings him a stethoscope and a little torch. Then he listens and looks in your eyes, rips the stethoscope out of his ears and starts to push the trolley down the passage really fast, shouting at the nurse as he went. Me and your dad jumps up to follow – but we're overtaken by the young doctor, who chases after the Indian. I honestly thought for a moment that you were being kidnapped. All of a sudden the trolley and the Indian and the others chasing turn sharply into a side room with big lights – and the door shuts. "Well, I never," I said to Dad. But he just leaned against the wall and shook his head. In the room the Indian doctor explained to the junior that in his opinion you had meningitis – and he wasn't to be ignored. Although he was just a visitor to the hospital that day, he was a consultant with no time for argument. There was poison in you and it was climbing up your spine towards your brain. He decided to perform a lumbar puncture, which he hoped would drain the poison from your spine. They gave you some anaesthetic, then they went in with the big needle and started.'

'Now we can only hope,' the visiting doctor told my folks in the waiting room. 'He has meningococcus septicaemia. If we were in time, we may have stopped it reaching his brain.'

'And what if you ain't in time?' Mum asked, gripping Dad's hand.

The doctor answered honestly but with compassion: 'He'll be dead, Mrs Hicks – or at best brain-damaged.'

'Is there nothing else you can do, then?' Dad asked.

The doctor thrust his hands into his pockets and walked a few paces to the window, which overlooked the aged Georgian façade of the great hospital. It was raining hard – young nurses going off duty ran through the puddles arm in arm, laughing, seemingly unaware that a thousand stories were being enacted in the wards above their heads.

'Streptomycin,' the doctor said finally, as if he had just thought of it. 'I'm going to give him streptomycin.'

This was a revolutionary new drug called an antibiotic. I don't know whether he had used it before – but he went back into that room and injected it into me.

I woke up in the middle of the night. I had screens round my bed and just above my head a small light was on. As I began to focus, a small rubber ball came over the screens and landed on the bed. I could just reach it with my right arm. I held it for a moment, then threw it back. I heard it bounce. Then came the excited sound of a child's laughter – and the patter of feet chasing it.

Back came the ball.

I threw it again.

More bounce, more laughter, more patter.

By the third throw I was on my knees.

For the fourth I was on my feet, balancing on the end of the bed.

That was the last throw. The patter of feet and the laughter faded away.

I fell asleep again.

The next morning I was out of danger. The doctor admitted to my parents that, in his experience, my sudden improvement was a miracle of modern medicine. When they took away the screens I saw, to my surprise, that I was in a ward full of old men.

'It *was* a little kid,' I insisted.

But the sister didn't believe me. 'There are no children on this ward – you're the youngest.' She smiled, then left me and Mum alone. Mum held my hands in hers. They were shaking and I could see that she was trying to say something, but couldn't.

'What is it, Mum? Tell me,' I begged.

She took a deep breath. 'It's the ball, son – and the laughter. Don't you see?'

But I couldn't.

Then, with a sigh in her voice, she said his name: 'Rodney.'

Suddenly the fog cleared and in my memory I saw my little brother, lying in the cot next to my bed at home with that crafty look in his eye, waiting for me to go to sleep before he chucked that bloody ball at me.

'Aunt Bec [my mother's cousin] saw him that night – the night he died,' Mum explained. 'She was watching over little Roy at Frean Street while Dad and me went to the hospital. At half past midnight she saw something move in the yard and went outside. Just then a train went by, and as the smoke came down from the arches, she saw a little boy by the rabbit hutch throwing a ball in the air. When she called to him, he vanished into the smoke. Rodney died at twelve thirty that night – and when Aunt Bec told me what she saw we buried him with his ball.'

Mum and me sat there quietly for a while, each of us in our own thoughts, seeing in the story what we wanted to or what we *needed* to. I came to the conclusion then, and I have never changed my mind, that my brother came to me that night either to take me away or to make sure I stayed.

My mum always believed the latter. 'He came to wake you out of it,' she insisted. 'You've got a whole life ahead of you – more than he ever had – and, you mark my words, he'll be lookin' after you all the way through it.'

My stay at Guy's was lengthy, but Sir Walter Scott and his Waverleys kept me company. I also delved into a collection of Agatha Christies and, having decided who 'done it' by the second murder in every tale, I would rush to the last page to beat Old Mother Marple and Co. to the culprit. I was always wrong, and decided eventually that in every case Mrs Christie had cheated by changing the killer towards the end of the plot. So I returned to the more serious side of my hunger. Churchill's *The Second World War* enlightened me. The man wrote with such passion – his love of his language cried out from every line, and in some passages I allowed the performer in me to speak the words out loud, using his long vowels and endearing wet syllables. I also read a good helping of Pepys – 'I met my Lord Mayor in Fish Street who bade me go to Pudding Lane . . .' Here was no jobbing historian: here was a man on the spot, telling me about the Great Fire of London and other happenings in Stuart England. I left hospital full up.

The meningitis was conquered without any side effects; only the dermatitis remained. It had taken such a hold of me that, no matter how many treatments, I still had the rash and the itch. But, apart from a mask and the gloves I had to endure, I lived a pretty normal life. The mask was a sort of paste with coal tar in it, painted on my face and left to harden. It worked very well in beating the rash, but it was embarrassing when I went out in public, which was rarely. I must have looked like the Phantom of the Opera sitting on the bus with that ghost face on.

The nights were tough. I had to wear the gloves to bed or I would pick at the mask in my sleep, which made my face bleed, sending long red lines of blood down the scratches. It wasn't funny! Well, not as funny as tying my wrists to the headboard before I went to sleep, which was how we'd started out until Mum thought of the gloves. Gradually as the weeks went by I reached my sixteenth birthday. As a present, Providence caused the rash to disappear – she also gave me a gnawing desire to go back to sea.

★

During my illness Cunard had arranged for me to be 'paid off sick'. This meant that my name was on the list at the Pool of London as an available seaman. I made a few trips to the office to inquire about possible vessels but none wanted a cabin boy. Besides, I still saw myself as a Cunard rating and the thought of sailing with a lesser company did not appeal. Then I saw something that excited me. The Furness Withy Line was touting for cabin boys to join a ship called the *Queen of Bermuda* in New York. New York! The city of Broadway! I asked for details, but when I read them I realized I would have to consider going away for two years. Mum wasn't too happy about that – she and Dad had got used to my getting home regularly from the *Scythia*. But I was dying to taste salt again and the prospect of going to the States was too good to miss.

The *Queen of Bermuda* sailed between New York and Bermuda like a glorified ferry service. The voyage took thirty-six hours each way, with a day 'turn around' at each port – that was in summer. In winter she cruised the islands of the West Indies – wow!

And there was an even bigger carrot.

I would be on American wages, a good three times more than the British equivalent. And in order to join the ship as soon as possible, I was to leave for America as a blood on a French liner, the *Flandre*.

I left home in July.

Two other lads went with me – first trippers – so on the way across the Atlantic I spent most of my first-class voyage taking them up on deck, and teaching them to watch the horizon and not to be sick into the wind.

Eventually Nantucket passed us on the port beam and I, with every other romantic, rushed to the rails to wait for the great lady to appear in the distance.

And there she was, the Statue of Liberty, standing proud, her robes, her torch, her great crown and that face! The wonderful classical expression that promised fulfilment of the American dream. 'Give me your tired, your poor/Your huddled masses . . .'

★

The Hudson river, with the New York skyline beyond, blossomed in the sharp sunshine. I felt myself drifting into that American movie again. As the *Flandre* fussed herself into her berth on Pier 101, I saw the *Queen of Bermuda* on Pier 102, beside it. She sported three funnels – an important plus in a sixteen-year-old's mind and, running my experienced eyes over the docks around her, I could tell that she was preparing to take on passengers. She was also flying the Blue Peter, which told me she would sail within the day. I gathered the other lads together and, as a team, we walked down the passenger gangway of the *Flandre* and headed to the crew plank of the *Queen* – from riches to rags in about fifty yards.

I looked beyond the terminal buildings as I went, and saw my first New York cop smoking a cigarette with his nightstick under his arm and a gun in his belt – a real gun! Then a yellow cab bounced by with a bad-tempered hoot of its horn, followed by a police car with the familiar siren and lights – but this was just a mere glimpse of the city. A tempting sample, but before I could wake up from what was obviously just a dream, I was running a new deck.

As the *Queen* poked her head out of the Hudson and headed for Bermuda, New York and her lovely lady were on the starboard beam. Only three hours ago we had said hello and now it was goodbye. I could hardly catch my breath. The great city disappeared in our wake, like a gift taken away just as the package was opened.

The consolation was that the *Queen of Bermuda* was a happy ship – I could tell as soon as I boarded her. Her crew were about three hundred, made up of British, Bermudan and American sailors. The second steward was not of the Wankin' Ramplin' ilk: he was the image of Arthur Askey, with humour to match, a lovely man called Atkins – an Englishman, like all the officers.

He beamed at me in his office as he gave me my orders. Elevator operator from nine to six, break from six to nine thirty, then to main lounge to assist with horse-racing and bingo until one a.m. A long day – but what a day!

To begin with I found life in a lift a lot more rewarding than

I'd expected. People use lifts, and when they're in an alien environment, they talk. Add to that my natural tendency to be nosy, and I was soon having the time of my life going up and down, asking and answering multitudes of questions.

It was mostly Americans who took the ship, and once they'd heard my Cockney accent they opened up like the Red Sea. I loved it. After dinner I had the fun and thrill of mixing with these self-same passengers again, as I took their wagers and delivered their winnings during gambling games.

I also got tips, which came at first as a surprise. I had never yet been in a position to accept gratuities, but now after one day at sea, with something approaching five bucks in my pocket and not yet in Bermuda, my mind boggled at the prospect of retiring at twenty-one.

It was indeed an affluent vessel. You could feel it below deck in the gloryhole. To begin with all the portholes were open – the Atlantic was at its most friendly in this part of the world. Then, every other member of the crew had a radio or a gramophone, so there was constant music about the place. Once we got to port the array of fashion the lads demonstrated showed there was plenty of money about.

After thirty-six hours we docked in Hamilton, the island's capital. The tranquillity of the place was quite a surprise. The people, a mixture of black and European, were laid back and full of the islander confidence that I was to experience for the next year and a half. Hamilton was also Oxford Street: everything on sale was English, clothes, food and attitude, and that, apart from the weather, was the great draw for the Yanks. To them England was a day and a half away of pure pleasure, and they were willing to pay for the privilege. We had a quick turnaround – this meant an exchange of passengers – a fast clean-up, and off we went back to New York.

By now I had settled aboard. Less than a week had passed, but I had happily made my bunk and I was in the company of good friends. New York was on the horizon again and, with a pocketful of dollar tips, I was really going to see her this time. As with most things new, I had decided to make my first reconnoitre alone. I knew there were plenty of blokes on board who could show me the ropes – but I prefer to do my discovering alone, so that I can enjoy the moment without sharing it, I suppose, or suffer disappointments without admitting publicly that I was wrong.

Anyway, I hit the corner of West 57th Street and the docks at nine p.m. I wore a charcoal grey suit with an American pink shirt and striped tie. Despite the shirt, I felt more English than our new Queen! But I had to look my best if the evening was going to be as exciting as I hoped. Neglecting to take a yellow cab, I walked east up 57th, taking in the fire hydrants that sprayed the summer-hot children, and the high steps to the brownstone houses, with their hosts of apartments front and back housing families like the Dead End kids. The burly city cops all looked and talked like William Bendix, swinging their nightsticks as they walked, like baton twirlers leading a parade. One by one I crossed the wide avenues that ran across the streets from north to south until I came to the widest avenue of all. When I got to the corner, the pedestrian light warned 'Don't Walk' – but the street sign above dared me to ignore it.

Broadway!

I waited an eternity for 'Walk'. Then, at last, it flashed. I went across the road with an impatient line of huge cars throbbing at the lights, pulling like horses at the start of the Grand National. Now I was half-way across the road – and I was going to do what I'd promised myself a hundred times I'd do.

I stopped right in the middle of the road and looked to my right. There she was. The 'Great White Way'!

A vast thoroughfare of dazzling lights, white lights from a hundred marquees, blue and green lights from shops and arcades, and warm lights from grand restaurants and bars and, melded into this vista, a million red rear-lights from herds of automobiles, still in flight, going away from me towards the blinding flashes. I ran the last few yards to the pavement and watched the avenue for a little longer, then moved further into the dream. Barkers called from penny arcades and 'Can you believe it?' sideshows. Schleppers invited me into shops 'just to look' – the windows filled with all sorts of all sorts, clothes, toys, jewellery. After four blocks, Broadway seemed to get a little tired: I thought that maybe the thrill was over as the shouts died away, but the lady was merely having a breather before she went into her finale.

They call it Times Square.

It isn't exactly a square – perhaps it was once, but any sign of four equal sides has gone. It's still unforgettable, though.

On my left, just like the Palladium at home – set between shops and a delicatessen – was the Palace Theater, and on a small island in the middle of the road a statue of the great man of the musicals, George M. Cohan. He stands with hat and cane and a smile that must have set the stage alight. A small man but a giant in musical history. The epitaph at his feet reads, 'Give My Regards to Broadway.'

Just ahead, no more than an eight-bar travelling time step, protruding from the buildings on the same block, I saw the giant head of the Camel Man, the cigarette advert that paved the way for all kinds of moving posters. I stood hypnotized by the 'show'. The head of the man was as high and wide as a four-storey house. He had a huge open mouth, as if he was about to blow a smoke ring, and he did! Every fifteen seconds a cloud of smoke pumped out, in a perfect ring every time. On still days with little wind, that rolling circle could make it straight across the square to the Paramount Theater opposite. The Paramount Theater! More history! I had seen some pretty impressive cinemas at home – we had then the finest example of art-deco picture-houses in the world – but this place, this Paramount, was as wonderful as it was enormous. It had entrances on two streets – uniformed flunkeys attending the doors – and inside a dozen elevators took you to your designated balcony along wide, handsome, carpeted corridors with deco mirrors and decorated windows. The place was so big that when I went to see *A Star is Born* I queued (inside) for over two hours, with more than three thousand people spread over all the floors.

That first night as I passed the Paramount I glanced up at the street numbers for yet another look, satisfying myself that it would come soon. Soon!

I was now at 43rd Street. Next it would be there. That tune came tapping into my head, the anthem of the showplace of the shows.

> *Come and meet those dancin' feet*
> *On the avenue, I'm takin' you to*
> *Forty-second Street*

And then it appeared, right on cue: 42nd Street!

Compared to Broadway, it was very small, a busy street, though – more people crowded its pavements – and the number of theatres was far in excess of those on the 'Great White Way'. But all of them, alas, had been demoted to picture-houses. Even so, the smell of the greasepaint still hovered over the names of those past palaces – the Ziegfeld and the New Amsterdam were the dominant marquees, with their chasing lights advertising a double feature, 'Alan Ladd in *Shane*' and 'Humphrey Bogart in *The Maltese Falcon*'. That night I saw six films in three theatres until my eyes gave up. Now, in the early hours of the morning, only 42nd Street was still awake – even Broadway was dark. I walked the avenues back to the docks. I was very tired, and very full of hot dogs and popcorn.

But I'd had my first date with a girl I'd thought I'd never meet. And she was as vital and exciting as she'd promised.

Until the time I joined the *Queen of Bermuda* I enjoyed listening to recordings by popular artists and stage musicals, but walking the gloryholes of my new home introduced me to tunes and rhythms that opened my ears. The Bermudans had the calypso: a simple beat with a guitar lead, and the lyrics were in the local dialect, love songs with a comic rendering:

> *Matilda, Matilda, Matilda,*
> *She take me money,*
> *Go run Venezuela . . .*

The American contingent, however, leaned towards country music, love songs with sad undertones and messages of hope or unrequited love. The first country singer who held my attention was Tennessee Ernie Ford. He had a deep-throated voice that twanged with a drawl and made Roy Rogers sound like a college boy. The words of these country-folk songs with their hyper-sentiment are pure hokum, but for me they never fail.

> *There are three things a man must do*
> *Before his days are done,*
> *He must plant a tree and take a wife*
> *And give the world a son . . .*

Those songs, too, had the guitar lead. That instrument had taken the place of the usual shipboard entertainments, like the piano or the concertina. At least five of the lads could play it and every night, on deck beneath the summer stars, I would sway with the calypso or tap my feet to the infectious country song. It wasn't long before I was singing along, watching the fingers of the guitarists forming the chords. I was happy to stand around, sipping my lemonade, enjoying the renditions. Then I heard Hank Williams.

His was a voice that could draw tears with just one of his mournful words. He wrote all his songs from his soul, the first country writer to make the transition across to the popular charts with great hits like 'Cheatin' Heart', 'Jambalaya', 'Settin' The Woods On Fire'. The list goes on, and would have been longer, had he not died tragically in his twenties. To me, of all the country songs, his were, and are, the best of the bunch.

There was one of his that I *had* to learn, 'Kaw-Liga', a simple story about a wooden Indian standing outside a shop, who fell in love with the Indian maid over the road at the antiques store. They never met, they never touched, and they couldn't cry because their hearts were made of knotty pine. Once I had learned the words and practised the 'Williams drawl', I had to find someone to accompany me so I could sing it. I would sit in the Pig and Whistle – crew bars had the same name on every ship – every night and wait for the resident guitarist to run out of numbers, then sidle over, offer him a drink or a cigarette and ask him if he knew 'Kaw-Liga'. Then, I would sing it, feeling my way with the lyric, picking out the places where Hank would want a desperate cry to underline his plot. The trouble was, I didn't stop. I would sing the song over and over, begging the bloke to play it just once more – it must have driven the boys stark raving mad. Eventually my ploy was so well worn that I couldn't even bribe them with a drink or a fag to play for me. Except one. A black plate-cleaner called Cookie.

He never said no. He was a calypso man – but he enjoyed playing so much that he wouldn't even turn down a sob song, sung far too often by the corny Limey. So 'Kaw-Liga' became my party piece and now I found it a bit more satisfying to sing a song live than mime while Danny Kaye did it.

17

As the summer boiled on so did my love of sea life. It seemed that I had found a world that would suit me for ever. I had money, a job, a home, friends and two ports of call that came so quickly it fair took my breath away. Mainly because they were complete opposites. Hamilton had grace, tempo and a people who lived by *mañana* – it'll wait till tomorrow! New York had rush and bustle and now! Now!

During my third month aboard, Second Steward Atkins offered me an opportunity that came like a bolt out of the blue. 'I want you to watch the tiger,' he said.

I knew very well what 'watching the tiger' meant. It meant that I was to grow up. I was to leave the land of the cabin boy and be a man. I was close to seventeen – only three months to go – and Atkins had decided I was ready. 'Tonight would be a good time,' he went on. 'Stand at the buffet – you won't get in the way there – and when you watch the tiger you wear white tie and wing collar, white gloves and polished shoes. No gum!' He sent me to the stores with a chit.

At five o'clock my mates gathered round me in the gloryhole. I had two hours to get ready, and each of them was giving me yet another tip on how to tie a bow-tie or tease a collar or keep chewing-gum in my mouth without detection. Then at last it was time to go, with my hair slicked back, my neck stiff from keeping my bow-tie straight against my Adam's apple, my tongue tingling after keeping a Juicy Fruit tight against my lower teeth, allowing the sweet nectar to flow on to my taste buds, without moving my lower jaw. I went in search of the tiger.

As I walked into the dining room, the wingers smiled and, in their nonchalant way, wished me well. I was placed ceremoniously behind the cold buffet and, after a once-over by the head waiter,

I stood transfixed, watching the swing doors leading into the galley. Soon the tiger would come.

At seven twenty-eight precisely he appeared. He moved across the pastel room with such balance and poise that you didn't notice the speed. He carried a huge silver salver with two silver jugs of iced water and placed them on his dumb waiter, straightened his tie and consulted his watch. At seven thirty the entrance to the dining room swung open and in strode Captain Banyard, the skipper, with his fifteen dinner guests. The tiger moved to the big round dining-table and prepared to seat the ladies.

His name was Pat Futcher, the captain's waiter or, in ship's parlance, the tiger. He was in his early forties, an Englishman, no more than five feet six but strong and good-looking. His brown hair was curly, with tufts of grey at the temples, and his smile was, like the rest of his temperament, kind and engaging – but as a professional servant he was a tyrant to those he considered 'below the call'. He had a commis working with him but they were not getting on too well.

The first sign of that came soon after the skipper's party had settled themselves for the meal. The tiger was circling the table with the menus when the galley doors crashed open. The commis came through into the saloon at a rush, carrying a tray with a great basket of hot rolls, which he slammed on to the dumb waiter. The tiger carried on with his menu distribution, showing no sign of his anger at such a crass performance.

I knew then why I was there.

Second Steward Atkins had told the tiger, or the tiger told him, that he wanted a fresh cub. Lo and behold, guess who got to stand at the cold buffet. Lucky me! I swallowed the Juicy Fruit and watched that meal like a hawk.

I saw the great tiger stalk his prey. I saw a table laid to geometrical perfection and a meal presented with such panache that if you could have framed it it would have hung at the Tate as a work of art.

By the time dessert was served I was exhausted. I had stood at the buffet for three hours, not taking my mind off the 'performance'. Then he came over to me, the tiger, the best winger in the world.

'Petits fours,' he said, fixing me with those smiling, yet testing eyes, studying my clothes and appearance as he spoke. 'Take a salver up to the skipper's cabin and lay out enough side-plates for twenty, then for coffee. Cups, saucers, spoons, two pots coffee, plus cream, hot milk, sugar and napkins – *now*!'

I moved out of the buffet and made for the galley. I didn't rush, though God knows I wanted to. I got to the swing doors with at least a suggestion of dignity. Then, once they had closed behind me, I dashed around like a dervish, getting the order together and into the cabin before the captain and his guests got there. I knew that was what the tiger had meant by '*now*'! I knew, too, that this was my test. I couldn't do much harm, taking up petits fours and coffee, but the way they got there, the pace and presentation once the bloods arrived, was the true examination. I also knew that the tiger's commis usually did this chore, yet Pat Futcher had told *me* to do it, so mebbe – just mebbe – I was next in line.

Captain Banyard's drawing room was enormous. It reminded me of a country scene at the pictures – very English. I laid out the coffee and petits fours, then stood by the door admiring my work. In came the tiger. He gave the scene a quick glance and nodded. 'That's fine, kid, fine. Report to me tomorrow at seven thirty sharp,' he said, and ushered me out to make way for the approaching guests. 'Study the dinner menu,' he whispered after me. 'Study it well.'

The next night I was back at the buffet, as ordered.

The tiger entered with the iced water as usual at seven twenty-eight, only this time he beckoned me to his dumb waiter. 'Did you study the menu?' he asked.

'Yes, I did,' I replied.

'Did you understand it?'

'Yes, I did.'

'What's the main ingredient of mulligatawny soup?'

Pause.

'Er, owl?' I suggested.

'Owl?'

'Yes.'

'Is it fuck! It's curry.'

'I thought it was owl.'

'Never *think*, kid, *know*,' the tiger rapped. He wasn't finished with me yet. 'What is *tournedos moutarde*?' he muttered.

'I think I don't know,' I said.

'Is that what you'll tell a passenger, then? "I think I don't know, madam, but perhaps I could recommend the flippin' fish and chips"?'

I shrugged, embarrassed. I hadn't followed his instruction properly. When he had said, 'Study the menu,' I'd thought he meant *read* it, not learn the content of the dishes.

'It's fillet of beef with mustard sauce,' the tiger explained. 'What is *cantaloupe melon à la mode*?'

I was on better territory with this next question: it was my favourite dessert. 'Melon and vanilla ice-cream.' I smirked confidently.

'Not necessarily,' Futcher snapped back. 'The passenger *chooses* the ice-cream – it could be chocolate pecan.'

'Oh, Christ!' I cringed. 'Chocolate pecan with cantaloupe melon is disgusting!'

'No, it's not.' The tiger smiled. 'It's an *order* and the passenger is always right. Get it?'

'Got it.'

'Good!'

It was a lesson well learned. Pat Futcher taught me that a few minutes spent in the galley asking the chefs the ingredients of a dish is not only enlightening but good manners. I was never caught out again – and on the next trip I was summoned to the bridge where the skipper told me that I was to be the next cub and that he had every confidence in me.

The first dinner out of New York put a little doubt into that statement. As usual, the skipper had fifteen guests at his table, and made up the number to an even sixteen (odd numbers are unlucky!) and, as always, he had a lady at each side. I had just arrived with the hot rolls and was about to pick up a giant silver jug of iced water to pour each guest a glassful. But, as the tiger had taught, I had to wait for the start of the skipper's opening joke. It was always the same. It began: 'This reminds me of the time we had the Hobsons travel with us. I sent my compliments and asked if they would like to dine at the captain's table. "Not on your life," they replied. "We didn't pay all this money just to eat with the crew."' As he started to speak, I would begin to circumnavigate the table anticlockwise, quietly pouring water without drawing attention to myself. I had to time it so that by the time he got to the tag-line – '*eat with the crew*' – I was at his left shoulder. As he gave the line, he and all the others laughed. Then, and only then, I would go in to fill the lady's glass at his left hand and retreat to return with the rolls.

But he didn't keep to the routine. For some unknown reason, he changed things. Instead of delivering the tag as usual he added a playful tap to the hand of the lady on his left. The melodrama played thus: '. . . We didn't pay all this money just to eat with the crew.'

The table laughed.

Tommy moved in with his silver jug to serve the left lady.

The captain slapped the left lady's hand, hitting Tommy's jug into the air. Tommy's right elbow snapped up taking the captain's left epaulette off his dress jacket. The silver jug landed in the middle of the table smashing four crystal candelabra and a water-filled flower-bowl, which, with the half-full jug of iced water, produced the splash of a lifetime.

Not one guest escaped.

The skipper sat wet, red-faced and 'out of uniform'.

Me, with my feet welded to the deck? I couldn't even summon up an apology. Instead I kept repeating, 'It wasn't s'posed to go like that.'

Anyway, somebody said something funny and the table erupted into laughter. The tiger pulled me away from the hot spot and shoved the basket of rolls into my hands. 'Hurry up – they're gettin' cold,' he said, as if nothing had happened.

'I can't!' I muttered.

Tommy the waiter.

'Why not?'

'Somethin' else might happen.'

'It couldn't be worse than the fuckin' water, could it?' he retorted. 'That *would* be a miracle. Do you believe in miracles?'

I nodded.

'Well, then, serve the bloody bread before it turns into fish.'

For a month I served the iced water and hot rolls to the bloods, and that was as close as I got to being a real waiter. The rest of the time I was in the background carrying my huge tray in and out of the galley, under the guidance of the tiger and with continual quizzes on the menus. I learned the true meaning of first-class service.

Then one evening, just after dinner the tiger said, 'What's the hardest meal to serve?'

'Dinner,' I answered, confidently.

'Breakfast,' he corrected me. 'Because it has no shape – no control. From seven thirty a.m. to eleven you have fifteen passengers all arriving to break their fast at their own time and pace. They have different tastes. Some like cold cereal and hot eggs, others hot porridge and cold meat. If you can think of one daft, impossible permutation, you can bet they'll think of a dafter one. Their moods, too, are not those we may see at night when they're

With some of the boys from the diner.

wide awake and anxious for company. Their temper in the mornings is sometimes short, their conversation often non-existent. You have to recognize their moods and make that meal like all the others – effortless and a pleasure. So, you speak soft and short, accept all their shortcomings.

'And by the way,' he added, 'you're serving breakfast in the morning – alone.' Then he walked away.

Tomorrow I would serve!

Alone!

That evening went so fast that I don't remember it. I *do* remember not sleeping and going down to the dining room to lay and re-lay the table from five o'clock onwards. When seven thirty came, there I was, standing stiff at *my* dumb waiter, awaiting the arrival of *my* first bloods and *my* first order. They were a couple from California, quite young for the captain's table. They ordered pancakes and prunes. Only three more couples showed themselves that morning and at five past eleven the doors closed. I breathed a sigh of relief. I had served my first meal alone without incident. It was a red-letter day.

What I didn't know was that, like the instructor of a young pilot flying solo for the first time, Pat Futcher, the captain's tiger, had watched my every move from the window in the galley doors, noting everything.

I was on my way!

By the time my birthday came I was serving *with* him, luncheons and dinners. He gave me a twenty-dollar tip each trip, but now that I was like a (very junior!) partner, I was allowed to keep any extra gratuity a grateful blood might give me.

There was one such person on an outward-bound voyage. He handed the tiger and me an envelope each after the last meal, with a cartoon drawing on the front of us in full cry, serving an ancient lady. First chance I got I rushed into the galley, ripped the envelope apart and found the crisp ten dollars inside it. I threw away the envelope and stuffed the money into my pocket, then I walked nonchalantly into the saloon like the cat that got the cream. The captain's table was empty. Pat Futcher was standing at the dumb waiter studying his envelope. 'Never in all my years at sea has something as wonderful as this happened,' he said. He went across to the saloon steward and the head waiter, who looked at his envelope as if it were a treasure map.

Later I discovered that our grateful blood was a bloke named Giles and that he did a bit of sketching for a newspaper back home. 'He gave me ten dollars!' I exclaimed – but most of the lads wanted to see the cartoon I didn't have any more.

18

The tips meant that during stays in New York I could afford to go to my beloved Broadway and enjoy its many entertainments. Diamond Jim's became a favourite, with its live country music. It was a bar with a long thin stage running behind the barman at head height, and I had to lie about my age to get in but sat in a corner with my lemonade. I thrilled to the bands, which were unusual even in New York – here, country music was still a poor relation.

Then the Paramount Theater began a series of cine-variety shows, a new innovation: a feature film was followed by a live show and, this being America, what a live show! At my first, I saw Dean Martin and Jerry Lewis, two performers who were perfect for that kind of venue. Martin, the handsome Italian-American, sang beautifully and 'fed' Lewis, the tall, lanky comic genius, with such charm that you would have sworn they were from the same embryo.

The highlight was their singing of 'Every Street's A Boulevard (In Old New York)'. It had been a big number for me in my record act back in the days of my Danny Kaye impressions so it conjured up memories of home and my family. I had been away for months now and I had a strange feeling, sitting there: I thrilled to what was going on in front of me on the stage, yet longed to be with the people I loved and missed.

At another show I saw the Mitch Miller Orchestra, with their French horns, a full chorus and their effervescent guest vocalist Guy Mitchell, with his catchy hits 'She Wears Red Feathers' and 'Truly Fair'. It was during that show that I realized he had been a country singer: he devoted a great part of his act to the kind of songs that my idol Hank Williams had written. It made me an

I loved being at home with the family, (from left to right)
Mum, Dad, Sandra and Roy.

Some young adoring fans.

even bigger fan of the little bloke with his straw boater and lively personality.

God, how I loved that life! Could there be another job better than mine? Another world better than this? I had music, movies and shows, hot dogs, milk shakes and youth – and if the pangs of homesickness ever went away, I also had my future. I could do this for ever, I thought.

One day I found the perfect remedy for homesickness. It came in the shape of 'Speak a Letter Home!'. The 'personal recording machine' had arrived and it brought me closer to my folks on the other side of the world. I went into a sound booth in an arcade on the corner of 58th and Broadway and for fifty cents I could make a voice recording on to a black lacquer disc that ran for a minute. From then on every time I got ashore I went into that booth and told the family all about my week, then posted it home like a letter. 'It was better than a letter because it was like having you in the room, all to ourselves,' Mum said.

At Christmas the *Queen of Bermuda* began a series of winter cruises, visiting islands in and around the Caribbean Sea. I thought I'd had enough adventures for one life! How much more could a person learn? Our first port of call was Nassau in the Bahamas. It was very much like Bermuda so, *blasé*, I told myself that the rest of the islands on our itinerary would be just like it so it wouldn't be worth going ashore.

Until Haiti.

We had been at sea for a week and the weather was so hot that many of the lads slept on the open deck under the stars. It was so tempting that I decided to join them – but I needed a camp bed. As we eased ourselves into the berth at Port au Prince, I got a few dollars together and walked ashore into a culture shock. I had seen poverty – or I'd *thought* I'd seen poverty – but it had been nothing like I encountered in Haiti. I had never seen beggars or cripples *en masse*, dragging themselves along the hot dirt road that made up the main thoroughfare. And such afflictions.

Within a hundred yards of the ship's gangway a line of shacks stood on either side of the road. They were ramshackle, made from unrelated sun-parched wooden slats, with roofs of corrugated tin and dry, balding thatch. When I was level with the first building, people surged out shouting, '*Secours!*' Many were either limbless or blind, and all were starving. They spoke French with a West Indian accent, and their plight woke my conscience. I dragged myself away from their gnarled hands and tried to avoid their eyes. I felt ashamed: I had money in my pocket, but I knew that if any of those desperate souls saw one penny piece they would become a pack of jackals.

Soon the majority of the crowd fell back, exhausted, and eventually there was just me and a small boy of about twelve. His right foot was badly malformed and caused him to dig a trench behind him as he followed me into the main street, which was like a dozen Covent Garden markets stuck end to end. Such colour, too – bananas, watermelons, pineapples and songbirds in huge cages with feathers that, even in the bright Caribbean sun, hit the light like a rainbow.

But there was something else about Haiti. Somewhere behind the façade of a busy, sweating population I could feel dread – and it was catching. I had felt something like it before when the Nazi bombers chased me round London during the blitz – but to stand among a crowd of paupers and watch the street corners clear as the Tontons Macoutes came into view was even more terrifying. It was as if they had stepped out of another world.

The Tonton Macoute were the secret police of the Haitian government, which was then headed by President-for-life 'Papa Doc' Duvalier. Their reign of terror has been well documented. Their laws were their own and, with the threat of voodoo, their control of the people was as much spiritual as political. They wore black silk three-piece suits, immaculate shirts, ties and pork-pie hats – but it was their black sunglasses that chilled the onlooker.

They stood in pairs on street corners and were never jostled or spoken to: they just stared ahead, taking in the crowds, who all slowed to a walk as they passed, in case they caused a speck of dust to fall accidentally on a highly polished shoe.

The possibility that mine was the only white face around made me feel that the searching eyes behind the sunglasses were all on me. I pressed on, still trailed by the boy. I thought of doing a runner back to the ship – but a combination of false bravado and the desire to sleep on deck that night drove me on towards a place that might sell camp-beds. I found it deep in the belly of the market: a hardware store that sold everything rusty.

The owner nodded as I pointed to the very thing I needed, hanging on a palm tree. 'Dem gonna be free dollair, *mon ami,*' he said, through the pipe in his mouth that stank of some opiate, as he took the bed down.

The boy pushed him away and hauled the contraption on to his skinny shoulders. The owner shrugged and took my money. 'Dat kid wanna help – maybe give few cents only, OK?' he murmured.

I looked at the boy as he stood there, thin legs shaking under the weight of the bed. How could I say no and how could I say yes?

I was able-bodied enough to carry the thing myself: how would I look letting him do it? I decided to make a compromise. I took a twenty-five cent coin out of my pocket and offered it to him. His arms were full, so he took it between his teeth and held it in his mouth. Then I tried to take the bed off him, but he pulled away, staggering against the wall of the shop. He muttered something in French.

'He just want carry dat bed – like you pay for,' the shop-owner said.

'But I don't need him to carry it.'

'He *want* carry it – no matter.' The man smiled. 'Eet ees what you call *obligation*.' Then he disappeared into the rear of his shop.

I tried to talk to the kid again, but he had steadied himself and, ignoring my protests, was heading towards the crowd and the dock with my bed on his back. I gave up – his will was stronger than his body – and followed him into the flow of sweating human traffic.

As we pushed into the middle of the crowd, I felt an ominous presence behind me. I turned to face two Tontons Macoutes. One grabbed my ear and pulled me off the road round a corner. The people cleared a path and went cautiously about their business – in another direction.

'You visit here?' Tonton One said, patting my pockets. His black glasses were fixed on me.

'Yes, I'm English,' I said, feigning the power of the British Empire. 'I'm a sailor.'

The two men conversed in French. Then, 'We don' beliff you – we think you slave-trader,' Tonton Two said, with a crooked grin, as he in turn patted my pockets.

My eyes closed against the sweat that had formed a swamp on my forehead. *Slave-trader?* Fucking hell! The trouble was that I agreed with him: hadn't I let a crippled kid carry my bed while I walked without effort? I could imagine a Haitian court sitting in judgement: 'Guilty and the sentence is . . .'

'*Cinque* dollair *américain*,' Tonton Two murmured. 'Five dollars fine for misuse of native population. You pay now – *tout de suite*, you savvy?'

I savvied all right! They wanted five dollars and I was willing to pay anything to get off that corner and away from those black glasses. Except that the last of my money had bought the bloody bed.

'I ain't got five dollars,' I said, as firmly as I could.

Tonton Two patted my pockets again. Then his rough fingers pulled out the material, proving I was skint. 'You got no dollairs, you got beeg trouble,' he murmured.

'I can get it off the ship,' I stammered. 'It's over there.' I pointed to the huge liner as if they hadn't noticed it before. Tonton One grabbed me by the neck and together they took me behind the row of shacks. A cluck of chickens scattered before us in the dust. Oh, my God, I'm gonna get me throat cut! They had dragged me somewhere quiet, and now that we were out of the sight of witnesses they were going to kill me, I thought.

Instead, while Tonton One held my head still, Tonton Two took out a small bottle with an eye-dropper in it. He took out the dropper and squirted my forehead with a yellowish liquid. 'Now you got voodoo on you,' he said. His deep bass voice throbbed – I think I nearly fainted. 'You come *tout de suite avec les* dollairs – or tonight we send the zombies for you. Now you have the mark, no matter where you hide they find you.' They stepped back and indicated that I could leave.

'You come back queeck,' Tonton Two called after me. 'We wait here short time only.'

The liquid on my forehead felt like it was burning into my brain. What was it? And what was voodoo? And who was this zombie bloke?

I walked away fast and when I got to the ship's gangway the kid was waiting at the bottom with my bed, which he transferred to me with obvious pride. Then he dragged himself back towards the dust.

Once I'd got myself and my bed on to the ship I paused for breath. I could see the returning passengers alighting from their tour taxis, puffing their way through crowds of Haitians whose arms were full of local produce and souvenirs. On board the luncheon gongs were sounding and the crews were preparing to serve. The orchestra was playing around the swimming-pool on the rear deck and beggars were massing at the dock entrance, engulfed by that ever-present cloud of dust. It didn't seem fair that life could be so cruel to one, yet so kind to another. The ship was like a predator, floating in a sea of luxury, taking the sun and the beauty of this island, enjoying the sight of its people until, with a fond farewell, we sailed off in search of another day in Paradise without another thought.

Just then the two Tontons Macoutes came into view, staring up at the decks through those dreaded black glasses, trying to find me. Thankfully I had to go below to serve the meal, so for a couple of hours I didn't have time to worry about the voodoo curse.

As soon as I had cleared away I went in search of someone on board who could advise me on what I should do.

'Two things you do,' Cookie, the black guitarist, told me. 'One, you forget giving them bastards the five bucks, and two, you find somewhere to hide tonight. Then, when we sail in the morning, you'll be safe.'

'Safe from what?' I gasped.

'The coming of the zombie.'

'Who *is* this bloody zombie?' I blurted.

'The living dead up there in the hills, they wait, stiff and wide-eyed, coming to life only when the drums play. Then when Papa Doc tells them your name, they come for you and give *you* the voodoo.'

I paused to catch my breath. Then I asked, 'What's voodoo?'

'The rules of the living dead,' he explained, eyes wide. 'The one that has the mark is the one who becomes the ghoul who becomes the zombie who becomes the slave of Papa Doc and the drums.'

'Why don't I just give 'em the five fucking dollars?'

'It won't change nothin', man. You got the mark, ain't you?'

I felt my forehead. 'Yeah,' I murmured, 'but I gotta do something. I don't wanna be a bloody zombie all my life.'

Cookie gave the matter much thought as he washed the mountains of plates in front of him. Finally he said, 'Give me a dollar.'

'What for?'

'We gonna fight the voodoo with the only thing we can.'

'What's that?' I asked, with faint hope.

'A little voodoo of our own.' He smiled. 'You meet me on the after deck tonight just before midnight. I'll have it ready by then.'

For me dinner at the captain's table that night passed in silence. Even the tiger noticed. 'That's a bloody first that is,' he remarked, as I cleared the table. 'You haven't said a word all evening.'

I forced a smile. I didn't want too many people in on my dilemma. It was now close to eleven thirty and my meet with Cookie was only half an hour away. All I could think of now was what he had in mind that would only cost me a dollar yet save me from a living death.

At eleven fifty-five I ventured into the black night.

The after deck was deserted. All was quiet. Then, from the distant hills, thickly forested, it came: the throb-throb-throbbing of the drums. Now I could see the faint glow of fires and the movement of tiny lights, dodging in and out of the trees like glow-worms. 'Blimey! They're coming,' I muttered, holding tight to the ship's rail. I wanted to run but somehow I needed to stay there, anxious to be safe yet curious as to what might happen next.

The ship's bell announced midnight.

Then Cookie's voice came from the shadows: 'Hey, are you there?'

'Over here,' I called, in a half-whisper, half-shout.

He approached me with a small bundle in his hands. 'Diss is good voodoo.' He thrust it into my hands. 'You keep this with you all night till we sail. Then, come morning, it's all over. No more voodoo, no more zombie, but don't let it go till then, man. If you let it go, you're a goner.' He padded back into the shadows, leaving me holding on to the bundle for dear life.

But what was it really, this voodoo in my hot hands?

It was an old table napkin covering something warm and – alive!

What was small enough to be concealed in a table napkin and alive?

A head popped out from the folds – and I almost dropped it with fright. Then the 'thing' struggled and a sharp point dug into me.

I fought not to scream. What was it?

The thing must have read my mind because it answered immediately: 'Cluck! Cluck! Squawk! Cluck! Cluck!'

It was a chicken. A warm-blooded, napkin-covered, voodoo-breaking, dollar-costing, cluck-clucking, fuck-fucking *chicken*!

My next thought was to chase after Cookie, get my dollar back and ram the bird down his throat. But those drums came again, and as they throbbed the chicken strained to listen: its body became stiff, its talons, like my hands, began to shake, but somehow I felt safe. Perhaps Cookie was right – this was voodoo, wasn't it? Who knew what he knew? And who says a chicken can't ward off the evil eye?

'Keep it with you all night,' he had said. 'If you let it go, you're a goner!'

It wasn't a night to remember! Naturally, I didn't sleep much with the thumping of the distant drums — but I held fast to that there chicken for dear life. I nodded off on occasion, but if it wasn't the drums that woke me, it was that bird! When it was free of my desperate grip, it fluttered and pecked its way up and down inside the sheets looking for a way out. But I didn't let it go until first light, when the drums had stopped. Then I watched it tear down the gangway, off the ship and on to the dock road. As it passed the shacks, a cloud of beggars' dust rose and my voodoo passed into other hands.

I was left with a sense of relief and suspicion, but Cookie swore on a stack of Bibles that his actions had been based on true knowledge. 'Anyway,' he pointed out, 'wasn't them Tontons real, and didn't you get the mark of the living dead, and didn't the voodoo drums play and the zombies stay away?'

'Yes, they did,' I exclaimed.

'Then thank me and thank dat cotton-pickin' chicken.' Cookie grinned, took up his guitar and strummed out a tune:

> *'Chick chick*
> *Chick chick chicken*
> *Play a little song for me*
> *Chick chick*
> *Chick chick chicken*
> *I'm as blue as I can be . . .'*

19

Once Haiti was out of sight, it was, thankfully, out of mind. Now the times I spent on the after deck were truly fantastic. As I slept, I felt the warm air of the sultry evening mix with the cool breeze caused by the vessel cutting her way effortlessly through the Caribbean. And every night, just before I fell asleep, I would gaze up at the stars above me, sharp as diamonds on a black velvet cushion, and feel free as a bird among the camaraderie of our motley crew.

The after deck was now packed with the lads' beds and we had parties almost every night – and crew concerts. They were organized by Eric Firth. He was as lithe and strong as a jockey, with a great sense of humour and a talent for putting shows together. 'I need a feed,' he said to me, one night.

'Don't tell me, tell a cook,' I replied mischievously.

'I want someone to feed me jokes.' He laughed. 'You know, "Who was that woman I saw you with last night?" sort of thing. If you fit the bill you can sing that blinkin' Indian song of yours, all right?'

All right? I'd have gone into a double somersault if I could have done one. Eric was inviting me to join a show! I couldn't say yes quick enough.

I fed him for two concerts and then I sang 'Kaw-Liga'. After that I did a Norman Wisdom impression *and* sang my first calypso, 'Hold Him Joe'.

The lads loved those shows. Our skipper came to one and afterwards told Eric that he could put one together for the passengers in the main lounge. Well, that did it! As each curtain fell on each performance, the adrenaline in my heart kept me alive till the next overture. Pretty soon I was doing songs *and* sketches. Eric pushed and pulled me through those extra bits and I was always surprised by an audience's laughter. Everything went just as Eric

Me on the left – as the resident comedian.

said it would. 'Just keep to the plan,' he would say. 'Remember the words and don't bump into the furniture.'

I couldn't believe my good fortune. If there was an angel on my shoulder he was working overtime. It was like I was living in a garden of constant summer – even my dreams were over-shadowed by reality.

Nothing, absolutely nothing, could have tempted me away from my job. I was working at the captain's table. I was with good mates, sailing round beautiful islands in the sun and, above all, I was performing on a stage. Strangers laughed with me, applauded my songs, and as I walked the deck during the day, passengers would stop to ask if I was the kid who had entertained them – and would I be doing it again soon?

Bloody 'ell! It was great!

Our arrival in the Dutch Antilles on the February cruise brought about a change in the mood of the crew. After an early breakfast we had discharged our bloods ashore and as the last tour taxi pulled away the majority of the lads got into their swimming-trunks and hung around the after deck sipping cold beer and soaking up the sun. Suddenly a shout came from the rail: 'Shark! *Shark!*'

Everyone rushed off, including me – I'd never seen a shark

before. I stood among the sweating bunch searching the sea below
as it sloshed against our hull. The locals on the dock didn't seem
to share our excitement: they glanced casually at the ripples in the
water, then went about their business. It was just us sailors who
cared, stretching our eyes for a sign. For a while there was nothing.
Then, in a flash, it broke the surface just off the starboard side –
the fatal fin, black and shiny, like a rubber triangle, cutting a line
so thin and straight that it looked mechanical, and silent, not a
splash even when it turned sharply, just that quiet cut into the blue
water. The crowd around me overreacted at the sight of that fish:
they seethed and swore and gnashed their teeth, running in all
directions, shaking their fists and spitting, 'Bastard! Devil! Killer!'

I watched them in amazement. I knew these men: many were
friends and some were idols – Pat Futcher, Eric Firth and Cookie.
But that was before the shark. Now they were rushing around like
the other mortals, eyes wide, mouths wet, voices raised to a scream.
Then, after a matter of moments, as if someone had pressed a
button, everything was calm again. They had formed a circle in
the middle of the after deck, out of sight of any passenger deck.
There, as if a Haitian ritual was about to take place, they assembled
three buckets of blood from the butcher's galley, a side of beef, a
huge metal meat hook, sixty yards of ship's rope, three inches thick
and spliced at one end to a length of iron chain, which was soldered
on to the hook. Then the biggest, strongest fishing tackle I could
have imagined was taken ceremoniously to the ship's side. A chef
poured a bucket of blood into the water, where it floated, a red
puddle, on the surface. Now all eyes were on the fin as it cut its
way right and left, searching.

Then, as if someone had called it, it turned towards us and the
blood. Faster and faster it cut. Closer and closer it came.

Closer, closer.

'Now! *Now!*' someone yelled.

The side of beef flew through the hot air attached to the thick
rope with the chained hook and a score of crazed sailors. The 'bait'
hit the blood puddle, causing an almighty splash. A fountain of
bloodied water shot into the air. The black fin sliced into the spray

and, without touching the beef, dived out of sight into the depths.

Now, silence.

The red spray had settled back into a puddle. The water around it had calmed. The side of beef floated in the centre.

The crowd at the rail took time to breathe.

It struck! From nowhere – no fin, no splash! Just a flash of teeth hit the light, like a line of knives. Then, with the beef, it went! I was thinking – like everyone else – I could have been lying in that water, getting a tan, bothering nobody . . .

Another shout came from the rail as the rope men prepared for the gigantic tug that must come soon if the shark had swallowed the 'bait' and was on the hook.

'Steady, lad, steady.'

The rope creaked and straightened and then, with a dry *twang!* it went taut, stiff as a poker. It shook – like my knees. The shark was sounding – going deep – taking the beef away. Then it ran out of rope and came to a sudden stop. With its jaws full of hook it was now being tugged back towards the remains of the blood puddle by the sweating sailors.

A big deckhand, his back soaked with perspiration, was hanging over the ship's side peering into the deep. He was the Fisherman – the leader: in the crew hierarchy there were a dozen Captain Ahabs above him but *he* was the guide for landing the beast. *He* was the one who had done it before. ' 'E's goin' to zound agin,' he yelled. 'When you feels the pull, let 'im go till oi zay.' They relaxed their collective grip.

As the monster raced away, the rope ran across the rail biting into the teak, ripping a scar into the polish as a puff of friction exploded out of it. A hose pipe played on the hot spot preventing fire and keeping the tackle moist.

The rope was running out again – pretty soon the lads would have to take the strain.

'Stand by to pull,' the Fisherman yelled.

The men flexed their muscles. They blinked in anticipation, hands smarting from sweat-soaked friction burns. The Fisherman shouted: 'Pull, you bastards – pull!'

The rope men dug in their heels and rocked back, hauling as one.

'Heave!'

'More!' the Fisherman cried.

'Heave!'

'More! More!'

'Heave – *h-e-e-e-a-v-e*!'

Once again the dark shadow beneath the water edged towards us, once again it was allowed to sound away. On the fourth pull we saw the whole shark, big, white and angry. Then it lost the will to go on, its strength spent, and floated to the surface, still and dead. The Fisherman lowered himself over the side with a loop of chains in one hand, gripping the outside rail with the other. Tentatively, he leaned close to the shark. Then with a fast lasso-type swing, he looped the chain over its head and used the other end to secure the tail.

'Down with the rope, lads,' he half whispered, as if he was scared of waking it up.

Hands lowered another few yards of rope. The Fisherman threaded it through the chain, then pushed it back up to be tied to the starboard capstan. Now the catch was lying stiff with the hook and line in its mouth and a chain between its head and tail.

Secure . . . ?

The signal was given to raise the shark to the rail.

'Now, watch the devil,' an old salt cried, lips quivering. 'Watch what he does when he has no water.'

The rope men heaved.

The body of the beast cleared the water –

Suddenly it struck out with such power that every man on that deck gasped. Some dropped the rope and made to run. Others froze.

Those who were brave enough to hold on were dragged to the rail and came face to face with their opponent. Its great jaws snapped. Its huge tail slapped the ship's side. They let go of the rope and it crashed back into the sea sending a gusher thirty feet into the air. But it couldn't escape. The rope and chain at its head and tail were still secured to the capstan. It had lost and it knew it. It lashed out just once more when the lads found the courage to retrieve the rope with the hook attached to it, and heave again. After that it went into a sort of coma.

At last it hit the deck. Beached and vulnerable. It was only then that I realized how big it was. More than fifteen feet long with a head three feet across. Its eyes stared at me, without fear. It was as if the shark was lying in wait, preparing to take another bite.

But if this was an animal, what were its captors? I confess I could not have called them human. Not then. Not when they knew for sure that they had won. It was as if a spell had been cast on them, forcing them to fall upon the shark like mindless predators. They strung it up tail first to swing helplessly. Then they produced an array of knives and fell upon it. I watched but I couldn't believe what I was seeing. Surely these were not my shipmates – my idols. My respect for them was cut away with every slash of those blades. Someone ripped open the shark's belly – the contents fell on to the deck as if someone had emptied a dustbin: there was the side of beef, still intact, old tin cans, bits of iron and coral, fish and lots of bones – at least one was identified as human. Then they went for its head, shouting expletives, cutting and slashing. To the victors the spoils but there was no honour here. I felt it was an act of vengeance – an act that I could not comprehend.

Until four days later, when we anchored off the island of Martinique.

In the early afternoon Jack 'Taffy' Phillips, Al Frederiks, Cookie and I went ashore in search of a clean, quiet beach. We found more than we'd bargained for. It was a small bay, shaded by a host of royal palm trees bending with the breeze over a talcum-powder beach. The sea was turquoise, with white foam tumbling over a coral reef two hundred yards away. It was as if we had discovered a secret Paradise. We rushed out of our clothes and ran towards the water. But Cookie ran faster. Ahead, he turned and held out his arms to stop us in our tracks. 'Wait!' he called. 'Don't haul ass till we know.'

'Know what?' Taffy laughed.

'You jus' wait there, man,' Cookie grunted, and went back up the beach to a ramshackle hut. We watched him gesticulate to someone inside, then an elderly beachcomber came out. Together, they joined us at the water's edge.

'Diss is ol' Mo,' Cookie said, introducing the man. 'How long have you bin living here, Mo?'

'All my life,' ol' Mo said, in surprisingly good English.

'Ever seen shark or barracuda?' Cookie asked.

'Nope. Never here, not shark. It's dat reef – dey can't get over it. Mebbe barracuda sometime, but never shark.'

Cookie gave him fifty cents and he ambled back to his shack. Then the four of us raced into the warm sea. Cookie stopped short of going out of his depth – Al, too.

'C'mon, let's dive the reef,' I yelled, splashing further. But they shook their heads. They were old-school sailors, who never ventured further than their waists. Only Taffy took up the challenge, striking out strongly for the white foam. He got there well before me and had dived at least twice before I reached him. He was waving to me with a beautiful piece of coral in his hand when he vanished.

I stopped swimming and stared, wondering how he had achieved such a feat. I knew he hadn't dived . . .

Just then he came back into sight. He crashed up from the water and into the air as if he had been shot from a gun. 'Tom! Tom!' he screamed. Then he hit the water again, arms flailing. 'Tom! Tom – Christ, *Tom!*'

I saw red around him and, to my eternal shame, I swam away. I tried yelling at the distant figures of Al and Cookie playing catch, but every time I opened my mouth it filled with water – that warm foreign water was all around me, stopping my escape and hiding whatever was swimming under me, choosing its moment to take me down to where it had taken Taffy. Any moment now I would feel its bite – I could feel it chasing me. I imagined I could see it too. Fifteen feet long, its stomach full of cans and coral and whatever it had taken off Taffy. After every few strokes I turned on my back and kicked out with my legs, then turned and swam on strongly.

At last my feet touched the bottom. Now I was making headway towards my mates and I could shout: 'Quick! Quick! It's Taffy!'

Al and Cookie stopped throwing the ball, looked beyond me – and froze. I turned, dreading to see that fin coming in my wake – but all I saw was somebody floating.

Al and Cookie ran out of the water and on to the beach. Ol' Mo came out of his shack, looked out towards the reef, then rushed past us and dived into the sea. His stroke towards Taffy was unbelievably strong for someone of his age, but it was his bravery that impressed me. He knew full well what was hunting out there, but he powered himself to Taffy, took hold of his hair and dragged him back to us three, quaking on the beach.

We ran down to help him, but stopped in our tracks as one when we saw the horrific injury to our mate. His left leg was gone from the thigh. Jagged strips of skin hung like red ribbons from the exposed white bone. The rest of his body was like ivory – and he was still alive.

He was muttering deliriously, 'It hurts, Mum – take it away, Mum.'

They were the last words he said. The last words he *heard* were those of ol' Mo: 'Dass the first time I ever saw a shark in this bay.'

After an inquiry, the authorities decided that it had been a young shark, small enough to clear the reef yet big enough to take the life of an eighteen-year-old boy. It was a long, long time before I dreamed of anything else. My shame is constant, as is my fear of the sea and what it hides. Nowadays I never swim out of my depth. And if I see a shark in an aquarium I ache to get at it with a rope and hook.

20

The normal winter cruises of the *Queen of Bermuda* ended in February. Now the ship changed character again: we embarked on what were called 'liquor cruises'. These were different. The ship carried extra crew, which meant fewer passengers – but those few were very special and only the best cabins were used. An extra outside pool was opened and *everything* (especially the booze!) was free. Those passengers seemed to know each other, too, because in most instances the ship was taken by a company like General Motors or other industry giants, anxious to please its salesmen or directors by giving them a break in the sun. The captain's table was not wanted on voyage – to the skipper's delight, but the tiger's and my disappointment.

It was only for a month but there were four separate trips. Pat Futcher continued to take care of the captain in his quarters, but I was offered a new job. I was to be in charge of the outside swimming-pool *and* I was to take a series of lessons from the gymnasium attendant in the gentle art of massage. Massage was an extra on those cruises and as demand was generally high (because it was free) so an extra pair of hands had to be ready to take the overflow. Mine!

By the fourth and last liquor cruise I was so proficient that I was in demand as a masseur, and my time on board was full. The pool and other entertainments took care of my days and the early evenings found me in the massage room, pummelling and squeezing the various bodies that presented themselves to me. The room, with its subdued lighting and the gentle roll of the ship, was a most relaxing place – away from the fun and frolics on the other decks – and the atmosphere prompted the clients to talk freely about themselves.

On that last cruise I had a client called Mr Cicci – a very

important man. In fact, that voyage seemed more important to me than all the others . . . And different – *very* different!

Only half of the passengers joined us in New York, and it wasn't until we anchored off Miami, Florida, that the rest came aboard. It was a strange group: the men were apparently of Italian extraction and most were accompanied by much younger wives, all of whom were unbelievably beautiful. I thought at first that it was coincidence, but a rumour soon got around that the women were unmarried, and their escorts belonged to a secret society, founded in Sicily, with family businesses in every major US city . . . They were a frenzied mob of loud-laughing wise-guys. But they were friendly too, joking with each other, mixing English with Italian. They partied till late, and the men hovered at the bars forming card schools or heavy drinking teams. At midnight huge vats of spaghetti arrived, with a selection of sauces, meat and seafood. More groups, more drinks, more jokes. In the early hours the bars emptied as the men, red-eyed, made for the cabins, which had been occupied since eleven p.m. by their 'wives'.

On the first morning at sea, a passenger called Manny paid me a visit at the pool. He was large and swarthy with a cigar jammed into his folding jowls, and wore a gaudy Hawaiian shirt over badly creased dress trousers. 'Are you da guy who gives da rub?' he asked.

I told him I was and that I massaged every day after five.

'I need to book for dat exact time – five o'clock,' he mumbled. 'For Mr Cicci.'

I checked my appointments book. I already had a client at that hour.

'Who is it?' Manny asked, a little ruffled.

'Mr Graziani,' I explained, showing him the name in the book.

Manny roared with a dry laugh that drew the eye of every swimmer in the pool. 'Dat bum! Shit, move da guy to anudder time already.'

'I can't do that, sir.'

'Why can't ya?'

'Because Mr Graziani has preference – he booked first.'

'Preference, my ass,' Manny growled, drawing out of the top pocket of his shirt a stack of crisp twenty-dollar bills. He peeled one off, and dangled it in front of my nose. 'Change da times, an' if diss Graziani hollers you tell him it's on account of Mr Cicci – *capisce?*'

I nodded and took the tip.

Manny lurched away with the roll of the ship. 'Don' forget, kid – Mr Cicci,' he called back, through his smouldering cigar. And then again. 'Mr Cicci – after five. Bring strong fingers. *Capisce?*'

I made the change in my book, but I still had to find Mr Graziani to explain. I didn't want two clients fighting over a double booking because that would end up with me doing two quick, ineffective massages with no tip at the end – not good business.

I found him playing deck quoits with a couple of his friends. Their 'wives' were sitting in deck-chairs at the rail, wearing full makeup under the blazing sun. Mr Graziani was very tall, bronzed from what must have been an earlier holiday, and wore the fashionable Jantzen swimming-trunks. A range of gold medallions, half hidden by the mass of hair that curled from his huge chest, hung round his neck. He was in his mid-forties, gentle in his speech. I waited for the players to change ends, then said, ''Scuse me, sir, may I have a word concerning your massage time?'

He smiled genially and swung a heavy arm round my shoulders. 'Sure, kid – shoot!'

'Would it be all right if I changed your "after five" to an "after six"?'

'No, it wouldn't.'

'Only I've made a mistake and double-booked another gent.'

'No problem, kid. Tell the other guy he ain't gettin' his rub and you're off the hook.'

I couldn't answer that piece of logic. I just stood there dumbfounded, watching another 'end' of the game, wondering what to do, or say, next. The men changed ends once more. I went back to Mr Graziani and took the plunge. 'Do you happen to know a Mr Cicci?' I asked.

He nodded, lit a cigarette and took a cold drink. 'Only I've never met him,' I continued, 'and I have to find him and explain about this mix-up. Do you know where I might find the gentleman?'

Mr Graziani took the longest drag of a cigarette that I have ever witnessed. He held the smoke deep in his lungs, allowing the nicotine to bite. Then, slowly, it drifted out through his nostrils as if a fire was building deep inside his brain. 'What was that other time you had free?' he asked noncommittally.

'After six, sir.'

'Yeah, OK, after six,' he repeated to himself. Then he snapped his fingers at one of his friends – a roly-poly man. 'Give the kid a ten spot,' he murmured.

The roly-poly man slipped me the note with a wink.

'Thank you, sir,' I said, relieved, to Mr Graziani. 'I'll explain things to Mr Cicci. I'm sure he'll appreciate your kind gesture.'

'You don't explain nuthin', kid.' Graziani grinned coldly. 'You take the ten and shut the fuck up. *Capisce?*'

I *capisced*.

That evening just before five in the massage room, I checked the towels and my own mixture of alcohol and oil. Then, having prepared the table, I put two electric fans in strategic spots on the side shelves. They were the only source of air as we were below the waterline. Then I sat and waited for Mr Cicci. At five fifteen I heard someone move in the anteroom. 'In here, Mr Cicci,' I called.

The door opened and Manny popped his huge head round it. 'Hiya, kid, how goes it?'

'Fine, thank you, sir.'

He rolled into the room and walked around looking in the wardrobes, as if he had lost someone – mebbe Mr Cicci, I wondered. 'Is Mr Cicci coming, sir?'

Manny nodded, sending a two-inch stub of hot ash off his cigar on to my massage table. 'You got everything you need here?' he murmured.

'For massage, yes, sir.'

'So ya won't need to go out again after you start the rub. Is that a fact?'

'That's a fact, sir . . . Is Mr Cicci coming because I have Mr Graziani after six and the massage takes –'

Manny interrupted my flow by placing one of his club-like fingers on my lips. 'Da massage for Mr Cicci takes as long as it takes, kid, OK?'

My eyes hooked on to his eyes, and his meaning became ominously clear. Then his stern look softened – he knew he had made his point and that this kid's understanding him was no great conquest. 'OK?' he asked again, attempting a rare smile.

'*Capisce*,' I said.

My sudden command of Italian caused him to splutter something through his cigar – but he was laughing too much for it to make sense.

Then the door opened. Another big man looked in. He nodded at Manny and glared at me.

'Mr Cicci?' I ventured.

The big fella ignored the question and moved away from the door, making way for a small man in a dressing-gown far too big for him. His hair was snow white, but his eyebrows were black – like his eyes. He walked to the massage table and pressed down on it with his thin arms. Then, satisfied, he concentrated on me. He spoke in a low growl: 'You got a name, kid?'

'Yes, sir, Tommy, sir.'

He shook my hand and took off the dressing-gown. Then he positioned his naked body on the table. 'Give it to me hard as ya got, Tommy.'

I turned the interior light to a soft glow, covered his upper torso with a towel, filled my hands with oil and began.

The massage took its usual course. Mr Cicci's body relaxed and conversation started.

Manny spoke first: 'Are you goin' into Caracas, Mr C?'

Mr Cicci grunted, then answered as if he had just come out of a deep sleep. 'No. I've seen that dump more times than you've had pussy.' The other man laughed and repeated the gag: 'Had pussy . . . had pussy. Ha-ha!'

Then Manny said, sounding a little hurt, 'I like da place – it's got class.'

Mr Cicci grunted again. 'Yeah, it's got class – all steerage.'

'All steerage . . . all steerage. Ha-ha!'

Mr Cicci continued: 'The only class thing Caracas has in its favour is one Vinnie Capizzio!'

Manny nodded. 'Wasn't he the guy who had that heist in his desert business?'

Mr Cicci half turned to me and signalled that he wanted me to continue elsewhere on his body. I went to his shoulders and neck. He exhaled, eyes closed, and told the tale of 'Big' Vinnie Capizzio. 'His casino was doin' great – the skim was high and so were the rollers – then in 'forty-nine he gets robbed for a whole week's dough. The caper was run by two Mick brothers from Detroit. They took the joint for two million – cash. Vinnie's in Florida when he hears about the job. He makes a few calls – Chicago, New York, Tahoe, LA – who done it? He wants to know – "I want names!" Two days go by. Then he gets the whisper about these two brothers.'

'The Floyds,' Manny interjects.

'The flyin' fuckin' Floyds,' Mr Cicci agrees.

'Two punk Micks – clever kids but unwise. Once Vinnie had the names he put out the word. The Micks broke ground in some shithouse east of Encino. A "person" caught up with them in their Buick convertible at a set of traffic-lights right in the middle of the town. And that's where they stayed, dead as dodos. One kid slumped over the wheel, the other in the back, and here comes the touch of class . . . He still had the two million in his lap, which was Vinnie's way of saying, "It ain't the money – it's the fuckin' insult."'

'Some guy, dat Vinnie,' Manny says.

'Yeah!' Mr Cicci sighed, and turned over.

The massage ended just before six. Mr Cicci left to get ready for dinner and the other man followed, then Manny.

'Ya did great, kid.' Manny smiled at the door. 'Did ya like the stories?'

I paused for a moment, the answer poised on my lips. Then, I must have been struck by a touch of nous. 'What stories?' I replied, fingers crossed.

Manny peeled a twenty spot off his wad and winked. 'We got a word, kid, *omertà*.' He smiled. 'Silence earns you money and long life – *capisce*?'

I had Mr Cicci for two more appointments before we arrived in Venezuela. The conversations followed the same lines as the first – anecdotes and references to Big Vinnie Capizzio. I could see him in my mind's eye, tall and handsome, dressed always in the tropical whites of Hollywood stars in the forties, cigarette hanging from his lips and a gun in his shoulder holster. During the last massage before we docked Mr Cicci mentioned that Vinnie would be joining the cruise in Caracas and staying with it until Havana.

The ship had been berthed alongside the Caracas dock for most of the morning when the three limousines arrived at the gangway. I knew that Big Vinnie had arrived when Mr Cicci and his entourage gathered at the main-deck entrance. All the doors of all the cars opened in unison, a host of white-suited European males got out into the hot day and made their way up the 'plank'. But which one was Vinnie? Mebbe the tall bloke in the lead – the one who looked like Clark Gable. Mebbe the one with the Humphrey Bogart look. Or was he the one like Alan Ladd or Wallace Beery?

The two groups met on the main deck, shaking hands, holding each other and kissing cheeks. Mr Cicci and Manny were talking earnestly with one of the new arrivals. I couldn't see the man because Manny's bulk was blocking my view, but it was even money that once Manny moved Big Vinnie Capizzio would be there.

And even as I thought it, so it happened. Manny lurched to the left and there he was. Groucho Marx!

Big Vinnie Capizzio was *not* big: he was small – *very* small. He walked with a stoop. And with his big cigar, horn-rimmed glasses and thick black moustache under a long nose, he was the image of Dr Hackenbush in *A Day at the Races*. I was disappointed – Big Vinnie and my imagination had let me down.

That evening in the massage room my disappointment doubled. He came with Mr Cicci and Manny and he even *spoke* like Groucho Marx. Mr Cicci gave up his rub and 'Groucho' took his place on the table. 'Just polish the skin, kid,' he wisecracked. 'Leave the bones for the vultures.'

He came the next evening, too, when we were about to reach Cuba. By now legends about the man were circulating. How he had been at the forefront in selling illegal liquor during Prohibition. His dealings with Albert Anastasia (Murder Incorporated) and Lucky Luciano. His part in the St Valentine's Day Massacre with Al Capone, then his arrest, incarceration and deportation from the United States as an undesirable alien in 1941. He had been sent back to Sicily, his birthplace and what many people called the Gutter of Gangsterdom. Now, homesick for America, Vinnie Capizzio lived as close as he could. With homes in South America, he could almost touch Texas and, with cruises like this, he could join his old friends and party in Havana with the lights of Miami blinking at him from the Florida coast just a few miles away. Once we docked, he would leave the ship: he had business in the city.

The massage room was silent, full of smoke, garlic and sweating men all gathered to wish Big Vinnie a fond farewell.

Mr Cicci sat in the only chair and Groucho lay on the table, talking to the assembly in comic Brooklynese. 'I'm gonna have to take this Limey with me,' he cracked, referring to me as I pushed into his body. 'These days, it's the nearest I get to a wank.'

The room rocked with laughter.

I wished a hole would open up for me to hide in.

More jokes followed until, at last, the massage ended. Vinnie sat on the edge of the table and lit a cigar. 'Well, kid, I guess that's it, eh?' he drawled. 'Let's discuss what you get by way of gratuity. How about fifty bucks?'

I nodded gratefully.

'Or a piece of ass?'

I froze mid-nod. I could feel my face filling with red like a wine glass.

'Did ya ever have a piece of Cuban ass?' he pressed. I shrugged in a way that I hoped would convey yes – but the 'boys'' reaction told me they didn't accept it.

'One gets a hundred da kid ain't yet lost his cherry,' Manny growled.

Groucho studied me, surrounded by a pack of joking hyenas. At that moment he had my father's eyes. It was as if we were standing in our passage at home, me with a problem and him with the solution. Somehow I knew that *he* knew I was a virgin. 'D'ya ever get off dis floating crap game?' he asked.

'At night when we're in port,' I replied.

'What time d' we leave for the joint?' he asked Mr Cicci.

'Whenever you say so, Vinnie,' Mr Cicci said.

'You got a suit and tie, kid?' Big Vinnie asked, and before I could answer, 'You come to the Copacabana at eight, you ask for Mr Capizzio, you join us for dinner. You eat, you drink, then you fuck till your teeth bleed.'

The whole crowd gathered around me, laughing good-naturedly and ruffling my hair like my childhood 'uncles'.

After they'd left, I sat in the massage room and thought about the Copacabana, the food and drink and 'da boys'. I felt excitement, mixed with fear, curiosity and anticipation. I couldn't wait for the engines to stop and my adventure to begin. I was determined to take everything as it came. Whatever was waiting for me out there, I had a 'cherry to lose' and a 'piece of Cuban ass' to lose it with – and mebbe my teeth might bleed a bit too.

As we were not allowed to fraternize with passengers, I couldn't spread my exciting news and, to my knowledge, there wasn't one member of the crew who had ever been inside the Copacabana. It was the most famous, most exotic nightclub in the Americas, and the nearest I had ever been was outside, looking up at the shafts of coloured lights that stabbed the Caribbean night sky through the open roof, the music of the mambo wafting up – with those wonderful orchestral brass sections hitting fantastically high notes, the cacophony of rhythms from battalions of percussionists – and those guitars, with their hypnotizing chords throbbing from stacks of amplifiers. And I was about to see it. I had to tell someone.

Eric Firth stood in the shower, spluttering beneath the downpour. 'Don't go,' he warned me. 'You stay away from that lot. They're bloody nutcases.'

'But it's the Copa, Eric – I'll be inside, watching and eating, and listening. I've *gotta* go,' I pleaded.

'Not in my best tropical white Brook Brothers, you ain't!'

'But I haven't got a suit like yours,' I begged. 'You've got to lend me it, Eric. I gotta look smart – it's the blinkin' Copa.'

He stepped out of the shower and started drying himself. 'And s'posin' they 'ave a gunfight,' he growled, 'cos they 'ave a lot of them, y'know.'

'It won't involve me,' I argued. 'I ain't a gangster.'

'You don't 'ave to be a gangster,' he said. 'You'd be an innocent bystander, dead as a doornail with bullet holes all through my fuckin' suit – *and* my fuckin' shirt. So, the answer is no – go in something of your own.'

'I can't lose me cherry in a pair of jeans,' I cried.

Eric stopped mid-rub. 'Who said anythin' about cherries?' he asked, surprised. 'You said you was goin' to the Copacabana.'

'At first yes,' I explained. 'I'm losin' me cherry after dinner – with a bit of Cuban ass.'

He tried to hide it, but I saw the bastard laugh behind his towel. I followed him from the shower to the gloryhole, watching his shoulders shake.

'Are you takin' the piss?' I murmured, once we got to his locker.

He shook his head, unable to speak – I could have punched him on the nose. Here I was, on the threshold of manhood, and one of my best mates was killing himself laughing. But he didn't answer. He just reached into the locker and took out the white linen suit I coveted – with the shirt and tie. 'I don't want no creases and no bloodstains,' he grunted, and handed it all to me, eyes watering.

I took it gratefully, feeling lucky that I had such a great mate and thankful that I hadn't mentioned the bit about the bleeding teeth.

At last my big night came. I finished my work on board at six p.m. and by seven I was standing at the front of the queue at the crew companionway, which led down to the waiting ship's tender. This was the only way to go ashore – the berths around Havana did not have the depth to take a liner like the *Queen*, so the tenders ferried between the ship and the docks five hundred yards away. It was a romantic way to travel, sitting in the open craft, feeling the sultry night breeze ruffling your hair, watching your beautiful ship at anchor behind and the amber lights of Havana ahead, thinking about those promises for a night ashore.

The tender eased up to the wooden dock. The mooring ropes flew through the air into the hands of a couple of Cubans. The smell of cigars and bubbling brown sugar wandered through pine trees that had seen better days. A small band played a samba beside a makeshift bar, giving free slugs of rum to the arriving passengers. I took a taxi to the centre of Havana City – it was an American Dodge and the driver spoke with that fascinating Cuban accent. 'You gat soomwhere to go, *amigo* – soomwhere *terrific*, eh?' he asked, admiring Eric's freshly pressed suit.

'The Copacabana,' I said proudly.

'You gotta have plenty *dinero* for dat place, I theenk.' He laughed.

I decided to let him believe I was a millionaire slumming it – it meant adding an extra quarter to the tip, but it was worth it.

At that time Havana was probably the most beautiful city in the Americas, with its noble Spanish architecture – original rococo, built with the care and quality of anything you might find in Cádiz or Madrid. Its roads were spacious and full of honking American cars, all in bright colours with chrome plating. The shopping streets had hosts of open arches running the length of the buildings, inviting the pedestrian to walk in the shade, out of the sun and the sudden showers that came and went without the warning of a cloud. They gave the island its permanently green foliage, which complemented the terracotta buildings with their magnificent pink and grey marbled touches of high Spanish tradition. And then there were the posters. Vast bright pictures of Batista – El Generalissimo! El Presidente! A big man with a Zapata moustache and military uniform. Cuba in the fifties was a dictatorship, where the president was all-powerful. The posters told me that, and so did the voice echoing from the loudspeakers on the political vans that drove constantly through the streets. I couldn't understand what the voice was saying in Spanish but, from the attitude of the people, I concluded that it was a vocal form of Haiti's Tonton Macoute. However, when I arrived at the Copacabana, all thoughts of doom and gloom disappeared.

I walked up the vast steps between banks of bougainvillaea and royal palms, past the carved fountains, with their cooling spray filling the hot night, into an open square with more fountains and more foliage. Then the terracotta tiles beneath my feet started to reverberate. The mambo was beckoning and the pedestrians were better dressed. I came to the polished mahogany of the head waiter's podium. Like the majority of Cuban men, he was unfairly handsome. 'You are expected, Señor.' He smiled and led me across the open-air dance-floor through the tables to the Cicci party, which was closer to the orchestra than the conductor. Big Vinnie and Mr Cicci stayed seated, but Manny rose to welcome me.

'Right on time, kid.' Groucho grinned. 'I hope you washed your balls!'

So there we sat, me in Eric Firth's best tropicals, Mr Cicci in a white dinner jacket, Big Vinnie in a tight-fitting black one that made him even more Hackenbush than handsome, and Manny, the ever-watchful Magog.

I don't remember what I ate, except that it was mostly fish. I drank a non-alcoholic fruit concoction in a glass the size of a birdbath to hold the garden that came with it. I watched and listened to the most exhilarating floor-show I can remember. Las Vegas has its moments with such extravaganzas, Paris too, but beside the music and the undeniable beauty of the Cuban girls, they faded into shadow. Here, tall, elegant females paraded with high feathered headdresses falling over vital faces, with dark eyes, tantalizingly full lips, and scintillating sexy smiles that promised not only this mambo but the next, and mebbe the samba . . . and after the show perhaps . . .

Later we assembled at the top of the pink marble steps beneath the royal palms at the entrance to Copacabana. The show was over and I was on my way to the next part of my growing-up. 'It's cherry time, son.' Groucho grinned as the huge Cadillac crept up to the waiting quartet of doormen.

Before any of us could get in, Manny checked the interior and glanced at the surrounding rooftops. Then Groucho and Mr Cicci got into the back and I got into the front with Manny. We were away, crawling through the busy streets. It was after midnight, yet if you were to put a searchlight on the dark pavements, the crowds there would have convinced you it was morning. The long Cadillac swung away from the throng and squeezed through narrow streets. After a few blocks we stopped outside a building whose façade was plastered with pictures of naked women.

'We call it an *exhibition*,' Vinnie explained as we entered the building. 'Just for you, kid.'

I followed the men without asking questions – I had no idea what was coming but I didn't want to look daft. I was being given an 'exhibition' of I knew not what.

We stopped in a foyer, surrounded by more pictures of more naked women.

'OK, kid. Pick two.' Vinnie smiled.

'And *only* two, you fuckin' pervert,' Mr Cicci growled.

I honestly thought they were offering me a choice of two sexy pictures to take back to the ship. I thought of Eric and his preference for blondes: for him, I chose one who looked like Jean Harlow. For myself I selected a dark girl with lips like lifebelts. A man sitting in the foyer with a fedora and a toothpick took the photos and slid out through a small door, leaving us with another man who led us into a theatre with a semi-circle of no more than ten seats facing a thrust stage, dominated by a giant bed, with a host of lights over it and loads of mirrors. We four sat in the red plush seats and the house lights dimmed. Recorded music came from somewhere and red lights came on over the bed. 'Jean Harlow' walked on to the stage, in a tight-fitting cocktail dress. She was *not* a photograph! Then the dark girl with the lifebelt lips came on – topless. *Definitely* not a photograph!

The music became a little hotter. The two girls began to fondle each other. I wanted to squirm in embarrassment, but stopped myself – the men around me were entirely calm.

Now the girls were undressing each other. Oh, Christ! Sod the clan! I knew that if I didn't change cheeks soon, my arse would fuse itself to my chair. I squirmed.

'Yeah, kid,' Big Vinnie encouraged me, patting my neck. 'Go for it!'

The girls were kissing on the bed when this bloke walked into the scene. He was big – bigger than Manny – he was naked, and he was half man half donkey. He threw himself on to the girls and gave us his impression of a cross-eyed cockerel. He 'hit' each girl in turn, and they went through the same procedure twice more, sheets flying, pillows tossed, legs pulled into extraordinary positions. Eventually Jean Harlow and Lifebelts gave satisfied screams and collapsed, hanging out of the bed, exhausted.

Donkey Dick walked to the edge of the stage to accept the applause of my mentors. Then he grinned down at me. 'Hey, *amigo*!' he said, offering his hand. 'You must be Tommy.'

Big Vinnie roared with laughter and said, 'Shake hands wid da guy, kid.' I took Donkey Dick's hand. He gripped it so tightly that I knew there was more to this genial greeting than met the eye. With a tug he pulled me up on to the stage and threw me on to the dishevelled bed. Harlow's breasts were in one eye, Lifebelts's privates in the other.

The boys yelled with glee. 'Go, Tommy, go. Lose that thing!'

I deduced that they were referring to my cherry. The two girls came to the same conclusion and began to tear off Eric Firth's tropicals. I felt a rip under the right sleeve and another just below my trouser leg. Fuckin' hell! Eric'll kill me!

Then my tie was snatched off, the buttons of the shirt twanged away and Lifebelts was *biting off* my fly buttons. Now I wasn't just squirming, I was fighting – for Eric Firth's tropicals and my honour. I decided that cherries were for giving, not taking. Those girls were not having mine, and the hyenas laughing in the stalls, cheering every embarrassing move, weren't going to watch. I tore myself away from the red fingernails and bouncing breasts and jumped back into the auditorium facing Big Vinnie, Mr Cicci and Manny. Now I was more angry than embarrassed. 'I don't like this,' I cried defiantly. 'And I wanna go 'ome.'

'It's a once-in-a-lifetime, kid.' Vinnie laughed. 'How many guys d'you know get to screw two broads on a first date?'

'I don't know none,' I fumed. 'And I don't wanna – and I don't want this, and if you don't mind me saying so, sir, I fink you've took a fuckin' liberty.'

By this time the girls had come to the edge of the stage. Manny and Donkey Dick grabbed me again. Up in the air I went towards those red fingernails clawing at me. I was preparing one last scream of defiance when Mr Cicci's voice cut through the laughter: 'Enough!'

The action stopped. His voice wasn't loud or insistent but it had such authority that it dominated. Manny froze, and I was lowered to the floor. The girls and Donkey Dick walked off the stage while Big Vinnie joined Mr Cicci at the exit.

We walked to the waiting Cadillac. The journey back to the ship took place in utter silence. They dropped me off at the jetty and a waiting tender. Big Vinnie took my arm as I left the car. 'There was no harm intended, kid,' he said gently. 'But that don't stop the hurt, does it?'

'No, sir, it don't,' I said.

'Anyway, I'm sorry – OK?'

'OK,' I said.

'Likewise from me, Tommy,' Mr Cicci called from behind.

Manny took a wad of money from the pocket of his tuxedo and offered it to me. I refused it – insulted.

'You fuckin' jerk,' Mr Cicci snarled at him.

'I know, boss,' he murmured. 'I got no class.'

The Cadillac pulled away and headed back towards Havana.

The next morning the *Queen* sailed for Miami. Mr Cicci, preceded by Manny, came once more for his 'after five'. Big Vinnie Capizzio (a.k.a. Groucho) stayed in Havana to continue his business and his exile. Mr Cicci and his entourage left us in Miami, and when we returned to New York there was no sign of 'da boys'. The ship returned to normal. But we had one last cruise to complete before we went back to our Bermuda run . . .

21

As with all the fruits of life, the moment came for that cherry of mine to fall off the bough. It was just before my seventeenth birthday. We were anchored off the French island of Martinique in the West Indies and, as with all ports, the area round the docks was packed with bars. They had no windows, no doors, just open gaps to let in the breeze and passing sailors. I went into one with Cookie to buy some 'fire'. I had no idea what it was, except that it was liquid and came in an unlabelled bottle.

'Um goin' in de udder room.' Cookie smiled in the direction of a table of working girls. 'I might be some time, man.'

I sat at the rickety bar, sipping ginger ale, when a refined English voice called, over the crackle of an ancient gramophone, 'We few, we happy few!' An old man resembling Walter Huston in *The Treasure of the Sierra Madre* was standing in the gap to the street. He held a book in one hand and a tequila bottle in the other. A piece of rope was tied around his waist, attached to a small dog, which trotted behind him as he stumbled towards a table. 'Innkeeper, a stoop,' he called, as he collapsed into a chair.

The bored barman shuffled over and landed a great jug of beer on the old man's table. As he turned to go back, the little dog's rope got tangled round his ankles, earning the mutt a swift kick in the tail. First it yelped, then it drew itself up defiantly and spat. No bark, no bite, just a long wet lump of saliva winged its way towards the barman, hitting him right between the legs.

'Let loose the dogs of war!' the old man exclaimed, and poured a puddle of beer on to the floor. The dog dived in and started lapping.

The gramophone went into another collection of crackles, and I ordered more ginger ale. Minutes later a vision of loveliness tapped my shoulder. She was tall, unbelievably beautiful, and almost wearing a sarong that clung to her carved hips. Her skin shone like polished mahogany, and all this was topped by a mass of black hair falling over her dark eyes down to her breasts. She said something in French.

'I don't want none,' I replied, lying my head off.

She spoke again.

'I'm waiting for someone,' I said, pointing towards Cookie's retreat.

With a fiery toss of her head she went back to the working table.

Then I caught the old man's eye. 'Methinks you protest too much.' He grinned, showing a row of black teeth through a thatch of stubble. 'You sound English, which may account for your total lack of tact. The girl was paying you a compliment.'

'Well, I'm sorry.'

'Don't tell me, tell her. She asked, "Will you fuckee for love?" This is a minor falsehood in that the love is free, but the room will cost you two dollars.'

I smiled in her direction, half in apology and half in hope. Still looking miffed at my earlier rejection, the girl came and sat next to me at the bar. She touched my thigh with her naked foot as the old man fell asleep, joining the dog in a drunken snore. Then her toes reached their final destination. God, what should I do? It didn't take a lot of thinking about!

The small room on the ocean side of the bar was just big enough to keep the bed from the salt spray, but I didn't care about the damp. I was in that place called heaven, and somewhere in the dark an angel was teaching me to fly. I don't remember how long I was there, but when I returned to earth, Cookie had left for the ship.

The old matchmaker was still at his table. 'Ah, the infant mariner.' He grinned. 'It's the hair, you know. Blond boys are so rare in this neck of the forest that an albino could be king. And there's the rub,' he mused. 'We are, all of us, characters in search of an author.'

'Me?' I said.

'Not just you, you selfish swine – all of us! And what author would write of you?' He studied me for two more shots of tequila. 'Conrad! You are a Conrad, the wide-eyed innocent abroad, in search of love and, above all, adventure!'

I liked that thought, me in the middle of a Conrad novel. I sat there, wondering what kind of plot would suit me. Then the old man scratched his stubble impatiently and steadied himself for another pounce on his tequila. 'Well, c'mon, boy,' he muttered, 'who would my author be?'

The name came instantly. 'Somerset Maugham!'

'*Somerset Maugham?*' he snarled. 'You have the audacity to align my life with that poof? Do I *look* like a damn cocktail-drinker to you?' He pulled himself up from the table and staggered towards the swing doors of the bar, dragging the dog in his wake. Then, brandishing the half-empty bottle of tequila above his head like a mace, he announced, 'I'm a *Hemingway*, you uneducated prick – and don't you forget it.' Then, with the flourish of a latterday Lear, he vanished.

The whole bar fell quiet; all you could hear was the buzz of a thousand flies. Then my angel gave me a kiss and floated back to the other girls.

As I left the place the gramophone crackled back into life and the working table giggled to a whispered secret.

After that cruise, the *Queen* left the Caribbean and we returned to the Bermuda run. It was almost eighteen months to the day since I had joined the ship and what had been a rumour suddenly became stark reality: 'All UK crew will return to England where the *Queen of Bermuda* will berth for complete refit.'

On the last trip to Bermuda, I helped Cookie pack. He was leaving the ship on his home island. He'd been such a great friend. We went on deck and paused at the gangplank to say goodbye. 'I ain't gonna sing any more, am I?' I said. 'Not without you.'

'You got fingers, ain't you?' he growled, big eyes bulging. 'More dan a whole year you been learnin' dem chords. You just need a box of your own, man.'

I shrugged. It was true.

'*So*, I'm tellin' you, you gotta get off your white ass and do what you gotta do, on your *own*. You gotta play for yourself, boy.'

'But I can't!'

'Not *now*, you dumb bastard. Tomorrow!' He grinned.

I watched him sway down the plank and tried to imagine my fingers doing what his did on those strings.

'Tomorrow,' he had said. It might just as well have been 'today'. Impossible!

The British blokes spent their last days in New York running around buying as much American gear as they could afford. A Brooks Brothers suit, plus all the trimmings, would be their passport to a hundred and one nights in the arms of the English roses who waited in bunches for someone 'hep' to come along. For me it was a time of reflection. I knew that, within days, I was going to sail away from what, up until that blinkin' notice, had been my whole life. I loved my job, my mates and my music. But I refused to believe that the happy days were over. Another adventure was out there somewhere if only I could tune my heart and look.

And then I found her. She was dark, beautifully curved and, as I caressed her shapely hips, I knew she had to be mine. I carried her into the light and whispered, to the swarthy man with the tattoos, 'How much?'

The next morning I sent a telegram to my folks: 'HOME SATURDAY STOP GROWN SIX INCHES STOP LOVE TOMMY STOP PS BOUGHT A GUITAR TODAY STOP'

Six days later the voice of the BBC announcer came over the Tannoy: the Channels began. England!

22

When I got home to London it was like the return of the Prodigal Son. To the family I had changed, of course. I was a man, tall, tanned and everything. The kids ran round me as if I was a sacred totem pole. But it was the guitar that fascinated everybody. No one had ever seen the instrument before, let alone heard it. It was such a rarity that there was only one shop south of the river that sold strings for it. They were called Cathedrals – known to me as the Death of a Thousand Cuts.

A seaman's time on the beach had no limit: you could be waiting a week or a year before the Pool notified you of a new ship, and I had to be careful with the money I'd saved. One night when I was in Tottenham Court Road I saw my first coffee bar. These were a new fad in the West End, shops with a counter and a Gaggia machine that drew youngsters to small tables and subdued lighting. The Bread Basket was down the road from the Middlesex Hospital, the local for its young nurses, who were a magnet for a sailor and his music. I sat in the corner of the bar on that first night and took out my guitar. I sang 'Lonesome Cowboy' and someone bought me a coffee. Then came 'Kaw-Liga', 'Wedding Bells', another coffee and a smile from a staff nurse – 'Nice to meet you.'

Some days into my Nirvana I met a drummer called Bobby Fizz. He told me skiffle was being played in some of the jazz clubs in London and that Lonnie Donegan had made a real success of the style.

Lonnie was a banjo-player with the Chris Barber Jazz Band. He sang American folk songs – 'Rock Island Line' was a big hit at the time. It wasn't my type of music: I found it a little pagan compared to country-and-western. But if skiffle was in, as Bobby said, then who in England could play it? There were few guitarists around.

*Playing guitar to some appreciative young fans in the backyard
of our house in Frean Street.*

It could be a way of earning a few bob, I thought, but how do I
get the jobs?

'Archer Street,' Bobby explained. 'You go to Archer Street.'

Archer Street is a little thoroughfare that runs behind the Windmill Theatre and in front of Soho. Every Monday morning musicians gathered there, holding their instrument cases as a sort of
advertisement, waiting for agents to arrive with offers of gigs. For
instance, if you were holding a saxophone case, chances were that
you'd be playing in the reed section of some band that night. So
there I stood, for four clear Mondays, until the waiting paid off.

'Guitar?' the man asked, in a North American accent. 'Can you
play it?'

His name was Jack Fallon and he was a Canadian bass-player.
He had a country group called the Sons of the Saddle, and needed
a guitarist for a show that night at the American airbase in Ruislip.

'I sing too,' I said.

'What kind of songs?'

'Hank Williams, Slim Whitman, Tennessee Ernie.'

Me and a few friends in the Bread Basket Coffee House.

'What's your name?'

'Tom Hicks.'

'Sounds like Tom Mix,' he grunted. 'Anyway, it's a fiver for the gig, but we've got to do something about that name.'

The Ruislip airbase supplied an all-whistling, all-cheering crowd of Yanks, out for a good time and ready for some home-spun country. Jack ambled to the microphone and called for order. 'Now, ladies and gentlemen, let's give a wild and wonderful welcome to the fantastic, fabulous Misterrrr . . . *CHICK HICKS!'* We swung into 'Lovesick Blues'.

> *'I gotta feelin' called the blues,*
> *Oh, Lord, since my baby said goodbye . . .'*

In spite of the dreadful stage name I'd been saddled with, everything that night was wonderful. I was on a platform bathed in lights, singing songs I loved and getting paid for it.

The two sailor Hicks – me and my brother Colin. Colin went on to join the RMS Mauretania.

Then the telegram came: I was to join the RMS *Mauretania*, sailing on the Southampton–New York run. The *Mauretania* was a great liner in the Cunard tradition. She was big and beautiful, one of the fastest ships of her generation. That meant five days to New York, two days in port, and five days home again. Sad as I was to leave Jack Fallon, I was excited to be going back to the States.

During the middle of 1955 the *Maurie* sailed into Norfolk, Virginia. In the Seamen's Mission, a poster announced the Grand Ol' Opry Traveling Show. That night I went to the local town hall. There was a small stage in the middle of the room surrounded by wooden benches. That night I saw all manner of men and women dressed in different costumes, playing different instruments, but they had this one thing in common: country music. The audience joined in every number, clapping and foot-tapping. After about an hour a boy walked on to the stage. He was about my age, six feet tall, and wore massive horn-rimmed spectacles.

He played an electric Gibson guitar and, like everybody else that night, he played country. He sang three songs but in the middle of the third, he did something that to my ears was remarkable. He changed the rhythm and what had been a forlorn someone-done-me-wrong song suddenly went into a beat and style that shook my soul. For the first time in my life, I was listening to rock-and-roll and it was being played by a fella called Buddy Holly.

> *If you knew, Peggy Sue,*
> *Then you'd know why I feel blue . . .*

Back on the *Maurie* that night, I couldn't sleep for hearing in my head the sheer thrill of the slappin' bass and the uninhibited chords. It was crude country but I loved it – and knew I could play it too. I wanted to hear more of the same, to listen and learn. On my next night in New York I heard 'Blue Suede Shoes'.

> *One for the money,*
> *Two for the show,*
> *Three to get ready*
> *Now go, cat, go . . .*

Carl Perkins recorded it on a country label and it blew my mind. Now I had to get into this music seriously. I got hold of the sheet music, and by the time I was back in England I knew the song and the chords.

The following week on my leave home, I hit the coffee bars with it. The reception was fantastic! Then the film *The Blackboard Jungle* opened – a story of wild teenagers. The soundtrack took the country by storm: 'Rock Around the Clock' by Bill Haley and the Comets.

Now everybody knew what I knew!

The image of the kids' reaction to the film was not the image a strait-laced Britain relished for its young. In some cinemas the seats were ripped out, there were fights in the streets and headlines announcing 'Rebels at the Gates'. But this revolution had other

The boys outside the 2I's coffee bar, where John Kennedy first found me.

sides: there was a new-found market among teenagers, to whom fashion and records had become all-important. Messrs Crosby, Sinatra and Laine were no longer the flavour of the decade. Now the young Yanks were on their way – Elvis Presley, Bill Haley, Pat Boone, Fats Domino and Little Richard. As each of these artists conquered America, I was on their doorstep, hearing the hits early enough to perform them in Soho before their official arrival in Britain.

On my last trip home on the *Maurie*, I was invited to a party with a shipmate called Ivan Berg. It was held on a bombsite in Waterloo, opposite the Old Vic Theatre. That February in 1956 was cold – not the kind of weather to look for a party in the Waterloo area, and all Ivan Berg knew about it was that it would take place at the Yellow Door. After half an hour we saw it, slap in the middle of the bombsite: a yellow door! No house around it, just a door, standing like a sentinel in the fog. Beyond it, amid the pile of debris, was a welcome blaze with a crowd of people laughing. The centre of their attention was a small man with a

*My first public appearance was at the Stork Club for £20 a week. I'd made a
few records for Decca, but so far that was all.*

huge hooked nose, a Beatnik beard, and a wide picture hat. He
danced around, brandishing a feather boa and a hurricane lamp,
singing a song as flat as a pancake: 'A pretty girl is like a melody . . .'

'That's my cousin,' Ivan said proudly. 'He's a printer in the East
End but he writes songs.'

The cousin finished singing and floated over to us. 'Who's the
chicken?' he asked Ivan.

'I'm Tommy Hicks, a shipmate.'

'I'm Lionel Bart, a success.' He grinned. 'I've just sold a song to
Billy Cotton. "Oh, For A Cuppa Tea, Instead Of A Cappaccini".
I got twenty-five guineas for it, *ergo* the party. The door I found!'

That night was one of those happy happenstances. I met Lionel,
who was to be the force behind my early songs, and Mike Pratt –
one day to become the original Randall in *Randall & Hopkirk
(Deceased)*. We were like spirits the three of us, Mike full of humour
and an ache to write tunes, Lionel a magician with words, and me.
After that party I decided not to go back to sea. We three swore
to become a trio: we would write and perform our own brand of
rock, and if a bit of Lionel's luck rubbed off, maybe we'd never
look back.

So, there I was at home in Frean Street, trying to explain to my
mum that I was staying ashore even though I had no work. That

was bad enough, but with my dad's experience of Soho during the war, I had to face, 'You be careful, it's a den of iniquity, that place, full of loose women!'

'And rock-and-roll,' I joked.

They didn't laugh.

By the middle of June the joke got serious. One night I was making my way home from the Bread Basket via Old Compton Street where there was a coffee bar called the Heaven and Hell. Sometimes Lionel and Mike hung out there, and I hadn't seen them for a couple of days. Opposite I saw flashing lights coming from the basement of a new bar called the 2I's. It hadn't been there a few days before so I guessed this must be its opening night. I crossed the street and tried to look down into the basement windows but all I could see was clouds of smoke. There was also music – guitar music: skiffle! Yuk!

> *I'm gonna pick, pick, pick, pick,*
> *Pick a bale of cotton*

Not the most testing of lyrics, but that was skiffle.

I went into the bar. Paul Lincoln was serving the coffee, a big ex-wrestler but a real gentle giant. He saw my guitar and guessed what I was after. 'It's down the stairs. Follow the sweat.'

The basement was jammed with teenagers, and at the back photographers were flashing away. A bloke named Wally Whyton was onstage with a group called the Vipers. He was a tall, good-looking bloke who sang calypsos. After he'd finished his set he moved back into the crowd. In the hiatus I jumped on to the stage, dragging my guitar out of its case. 'Twelve-bar blues in C,' I yelled. The band started to strum with me, but not a lot was happening. It was a bit too folksy so I called to the drummer, 'Off beats!'

He started to emphasize the second and fourth beats of the bar, the bass-player caught on and slapped his strings. The audience went quiet. This wasn't skiffle and it wasn't calypso.

> *The old-time cave-dweller lived in a cave.*
> *Here's what he did when he wanted to rave.*
> *He took a stick, and he drew on a wall,*
> *Man, how that fella had himself a ball.*
> *Rock with the caveman . . .*

It was one of Lionel's most sarcastic lyrics, the joint rocked and I did two more numbers. Then I went back up the stairs and out on to the street. As I turned into Shaftesbury Avenue, a tall well-dressed bloke I'd seen earlier was almost beside me. I was sure he was following me so I decided to take the bull by the horns. I swung round and growled, 'What's your bloody game, mate?'

The bloke laughed. 'I'm a photographer with the *Daily Sketch*,' he said. 'I saw you performing in the 2I's and I've got some great shots of you and the audience. Fleet Street hasn't got stuff like this, so I thought –'

'You thought what?'

'I thought if I get the stuff into the paper maybe I could handle your career.'

'As a photographer?'

'As an agent.'

'What d'ya know about show business?'

'About as much as you do!' He grinned. 'I'm John Kennedy.'

'I'm Tom Hicks.'

'Shit!' He laughed. 'It sounds like –'

'I know. Tom Mix.'

Twelve fags and twenty coffees later, I had a manager and a new name: Tommy Steele. If nothing else, it was better than Chick Hicks.

'The first thing we have to do is find the right presentation,' was Kennedy's opening gambit. Rock-and-roll was beating out an image of rough and rebellious kids, demanding change and being noisy about it. I didn't see any harm in that, but if Kennedy was the establishment and the establishment was the door into

With John Kennedy and Larry Parnes.

showbusiness, I would go along with the strategy. First, there would be no more coffee bars. Instead I would appear in nightclubs of pedigree, places like the Colony and the Stork Club. Every time I did, Kennedy had an 'exclusive' lined up with a national newspaper and with every 'exclusive' came a Kennedy headline: '"HE'S GREAT, GREAT, GREAT!" SAYS THE DUKE OF KENT' accompanied a picture of him leaving the Colony. A photo of young ladies queuing outside the Stork Club was captioned, 'THE COCKNEY DEBS' DELIGHT'. The debs were actually five call-girls Kennedy had hired for an hour.

The summer steamed on – 'LONDON FLOCKS TO TEENAGE SENSATION' – and because no one had done it before it seemed that every move we made was the right one.

'We need business acumen,' Kennedy announced one day. 'Someone to handle the deals.'

'What deals?' I inquired. We'd had a lot of press but to date no deals.

In late July Larry Parnes joined the clan. He was a dapper, hard-nosed businessman, and when the deals came, he was a joy to watch. Every contract he negotiated was based on two principles: what he knew they would offer and what he insisted he

My first night at the Stork Club.

would get. He never wavered: he did his figures and stuck to them, and as Kennedy was a genius with the press, so Parnes Shillings and Pence was with the business. What more could a budding rock star need?

'An agent!' they said. 'The best in town with clout and class!'

Ian Bevan was an agent unlike any depicted in the movies. He was slight, with spectacles, a three-piece suit and a rolled umbrella. I had just finished the last show at the Stork Club and was sitting on the stage, waiting for the amplifier to cool off when he appeared.

'I found the act quite wonderful,' he said. 'The sound is a trifle brash, but one must expect a certain excessive cacophony.'

I thought he was taking the piss.

'One can't enjoy the *1812* if one is gun-shy?' He smiled.

He was so nicely serious, and for the next forty-odd years, I sat and listened gratefully to him as he summed up on everything I did. He had a way of explaining things so that even when he was handing out a bollocking it sounded like a compliment with provisos.

'But you can't move forward without a record,' he went on, 'because with records you get radio, and with radio you go into homes, and in homes . . .'

There was very little pop music on television in those days. The main contact an artist had with the record-buying public was through the BBC Light Programme, and the Beeb was a pompous tight ship.

The following night Ian brought to the show someone who might have been his double. He dressed like Ian and spoke like Ian. The only difference between them was the fountain of ash that fell from his permanent cigarette on to his waistcoat. He was Hugh Mendl, the artist and repertoire manager of the Decca Record Company. 'I know absolutely nothing about these rocking songs.' He coughed. 'Up to now they're all imported and, quite frankly, I'm not sure we have the chaps to write them in this country.'

'Lionel Bart and Mike Pratt,' I ventured.

'And we have no rocking musicians,' he parried.

'I play the guitar and any other musicians just follow me. It's rhythm and blues with a bit more beat.'

There came a long pause as he gave the matter more thought. Then, with a cross between a cough and a splutter, he said, 'Yes, yes, I like it. Three o'clock Monday, Decca Studios in Hampstead. Do be on time.'

That Monday, Lionel, Mike, Hugh Mendl and I stood up on the production floor looking down into the vast recording hall of Decca studios. Big enough to house a full symphony orchestra, it made the four musicians waiting for me below look like Lowry stick men. As I hadn't formed a band yet Mendl had fixed the line-up. 'They're all jazz chaps,' he wheezed. 'Just show them the music and we'll have a little listen.'

I didn't mention that I had no music, just the two songs in my head, 'Rock Around The Town' and 'Rock With The Caveman'. I went down to the studio floor and faced the group. 'On account of I don't have no music,' I began, 'I thought mebbe I ought to play you the numbers first.'

'Just in case we ain't clairvoyant,' the sax player cracked.

'It's a sort of twelve-bar blues,' I went on.

'In sort of what key?' the bassist added.

Sod this, I thought. It's shit or bust. I dived in with both boots.

At home listening to my Ferguson Radiogram.

'It's vocal once through, then segue two choruses of sax solo, pick up vocal at the bridge, through to the coda, plus tag.'

There followed a long pause.

'Now we fuckin' know, don't we?' The drummer laughed.

Hugh Mendl loved 'Caveman'. 'It's the A side, chaps,' he cried, with a fall of soot, 'and with a miracle we can press it and release it in four weeks.'

'When can my mum hear it?' I asked.

'In four weeks,' he repeated, and saw my disappointment. 'Perhaps we might make an acetate for you,' he added. 'It's most irregular for our artists to take away demonstrations but in this case we might make an exception.'

Even then I had to wait until the next day before I got the hot-wax demo. It ran at 78 r.p.m. and lasted about eight plays before it self-destructed. In Frean Street, the family crowded round a newly acquired radiogram, which, considering it had fallen off the back of a lorry, played the record terrific. My mum thought I sounded like Danny Kaye, Darbo opted for my late uncle Alf, and my sister Sandra thought I was stuck inside the machine and screamed the place down.

'Caveman' went into the Top Twenty in its first week after release, and the music papers took notice: 'HOME GROWN ROCK OF STEELE'. Things were moving.

Family party in Frean Street.
Sandra and Roy dig my Rebel Rock

At a gathering of the clan Ian mentioned television. 'Now we go for the Top Ten!'

There was only one television show in the country that leaned towards popular music, called *Off the Record*, fronted by Jack Payne, a band-leader, in white tie and tails, who thought he was Britain's answer to Paul Whiteman. I went on the show feeling as if I'd burgled the place. Payne's introduction came as a threat. 'And now, ladies and gentlemen, we have rock-and-roll. Personally I can take it or leave it!'

That week 'Caveman' hit the Top Five.

23

In August 1956 Ian Bevan mapped out the next move: Variety. The mighty Moss Empire Theatres ruled the roost in every major city in the country, playing twice-nightly shows at six fifteen and eight thirty six days a week. In September I met the producer Harold Fielding, whom I came to know affectionately as the Guv.

'You'll top the bill, of course,' the little gentleman announced, in a high-pitched voice. He darted round a desk that resembled an aircraft carrier and emphasized his minute stature. 'Harold Fielding presents,' he squealed, 'the Dynamic Tommy Steele with the Steelmen! It will be spectacular!' He loved that word. Everything he created in his great shows started off spectacular and grew to stupendous. He was the perfect example of the blank-cheque producer. Once he got his teeth into a show the budget went out of the window. But those days were yet to come. Back in '56, he was beginning the journey from symphony-concert impresario to showbusiness proper.

On 5 November 1956 the explosions filling the grey skies over the Sunderland docks were not unlike those over London during the blitz. I was in town to fulfil my first theatrical date. The fireworks were having a dual effect: on the one hand they were a sort of welcome, on the other an ominous warning as, through the gloom and cordite, the Sunderland Empire came into view. It stood like Hatter's Castle, daring me to come closer, but above its roof an enormous poster announced, 'THE DYNAMIC TOMMY STEELE – BRITAIN'S TEENAGE IDOL – WITH THE STEELMEN.' Blimey! To this day I get a lump in my throat when I remember that nineteen-year-old kid walking, with his newly formed band, through his first stage door on to his first professional stage into the world of showbusiness and the lair of the watch committee.

The show's cast was assembled in a circle round four stern men

EMPIRE
SUNDERLAND

Booked by MOSS' EMPIRES, Ltd.   Telephone: 3274/5   Manager: JESSE J. S. CHALLONS

6.15 | Commencing **MONDAY, NOVEMBER 5th** | **8.30**
TWICE NIGHTLY

"HE'S GREAT, GREAT, GREAT!" KER ROBERTSON —DAILY SKETCH

"ROCK"

SINGING HIS BEST SELLERS
'DOOMSDAY ROCK' AND
'ROCK WITH THE CAVEMAN'

WITH DECCA'S DYNAMIC TOMMY STEELE

REG UNKNOWN TO MILLIONS
THOMPSON
★   ★
MIKE AND BERNIE WINTERS
TV's CRAZY FUNSTERS

JOSEPHINE ANNE THE CRAZY GANG'S GIRL FRIEND
THUNDERCLAP JONES
WILD WELSHMAN OF THE KEYBOARD

JOHNNIE
LAYCOCK
BLOW, MAN BLOW
★   ★
BALLET MONTMARTRE

TRIBE BROS., LTD., London & St. Albans

who were obviously not of the blood. They, I was to learn, were the watch committee: 'a murder' of local dignitaries formed to protect the morals of prospective theatregoers. Their spokesman was a fat, pompous bloke, with an Oliver Hardy tash engulfed in an oversized astrakhan coat and bowler. Condensation puffed from his mouth as he spoke in a dull monotone: 'There'll be no bloodys, no blasphemies and no bum gags,' he muttered. 'And we'd like a word with the lad with the electrical condiments.'

That was me!

'We can't have that contraption on a public forum,' he said, indicating my amplifier.

I couldn't believe my ears. 'Why not?'

'Because there are electricals coming from it into your banjo.'

'It's a guitar.'

'I don't care if it's a pookin' piccolo. It's a firetrap.'

'But it's rock-and-roll. I *sing* rock-and-roll!'

'You can sing "Rock of Ages" for all I care, but not with electricals!' he stuffed.

'It has a *sound*, mate,' I yelled. 'It has a bloody beat, too, and if I can't do it the way I do it then up yours!'

My first theatrical engagement had lasted about five minutes. I was off! Thankfully, me and the theatre manager came to a compromise. That night I made my theatrical début, appearing with my amplifier, my Steelmen *and a fireman in full uniform*, holding a smoke-blanket and a fire-bucket.

Just before the show the clan had arrived. Parnes departed to the box office to check ticket sales and Kennedy to the bar with the local press. Ian Bevan came to my dressing room as I was tuning my guitar. He handed me a leather-bound book he had written in 1952, titled *'Top of the Bill', A History of the London Palladium*. He had inscribed on the flyleaf, 'To Tommy Steele who tonight joins the "Top of the Bill" company.' Then we heard the trumpet fanfare, which was my cue to creep behind the stage curtain and plug in.

'Ladies and gentlemen, and now . . .'

I nodded nervously to the Steelmen, who managed a group wink.

'. . . the Sunderland Empire is proud to present . . .'

The fireman adjusted his kit and sat in his chair, face ashen.

'. . . Britain's teenage idol . . .'

I started to pick a rolling lick, the bass started to slap, the drums to beat.

'. . . the dynamic Tommy Steele!'

As I walked into the light, a mass scream started in the darkness of the auditorium and rolled over the footlights towards me like a great killer wave. I froze like a scared rabbit. I knew my fingers were still playing but I couldn't feel the beat, my feet were soldered to the stage. I started to sing: 'One for the money, Two for the show . . .'

Now came the clapping!

And the yelling!

And deafening screams!

The usherettes out there in the battle zone were in sheer panic, running up and down the aisles calling for quiet, flashing their torches along the rows of teenagers, who were jumping up and down like bobbins.

It was pure pandemonium.

But, strangely, within twelve bars it had melded with the music as if, for some bizarre reason, it belonged. It was an enigma.

What happened during that first performance in Sunderland has been recorded many times by others in the annals of rock history. My memory is simply, in the vernacular of Darbo, that 'Something had occurred!'

If that first show was mind-blowing for me, it was the next that defied all reason. When I came on, the roar of the crowd caused such an explosion that the stage shook beneath my feet. Twenty minutes later the curtain came down and it was like entering the calm eye of a hurricane.

Kennedy arrived first with the local critic. 'Wonderful! First class, lad,' the hack muttered. 'Never in the field of human conflict . . .'

'He's pissed!' Kennedy whispered.

Ian came with the smile that I grew to learn meant all was well!

Then Parnes appeared. 'We have trouble! Big, big trouble! They're very worried,' he puffed, pulling me into my dressing room, followed by all and sundry. 'This is very serious.'

'What is?' I asked.

'Can't you hear it?'

'Hear what?'

'The bloody crowd outside!'

Ian cocked his head towards the window. 'It's our audience going home.'

'Going home my *arse*!' Parnes exploded. 'It's a mob – listen, for God's sake!'

The four of us stood with our ears slammed against the frosted glass. Somewhere out in the November night we could hear distant chants: '*We want Tommee! We want Tommee!*'

The theatre manager entered, followed by the local bobby wearing a hangdog expression and cycle clips. 'I'm estimating some five hundred,' he mumbled, apparently quoting from a notebook, as if he was in a witness box. 'Assembled some time after ten thirty, outside the Empire Theatre stage door, November the –'

'We know the soddin' date,' Parnes fumed. 'How does he get out of here?'

'Well, you can't leave by the stage door!' the manager expostulated. 'Old Cyril's got the key and he's too frightened to come out of his cubicle.'

'How about the front of the theatre?' Ian suggested. 'Surely that's clear.'

And that was the way we went, escaping like thieves into the night. I followed the clan along the foggy streets, leaving my triumph behind me as if it were something illegitimate. My head was still buzzing and my fingers itching to play more music. I couldn't wait for tomorrow. I was in showbusiness – even though I hadn't been 'born in a trunk'!

Mike and Bernie Winters, Cockney brothers who had been around the business for a couple of years, were in the show too.

They'd watched my act and told me that because the hard spotlights pointed directly at me, my face had looked washed out. 'Makeup!' they advised.

'I can't wear that stuff!' I argued. 'That's for Richards and irons.'

But Bernie insisted I learn the art by watching him make up half of my face, then I would do the other.

That would have been fine if Lulu hadn't come into the equation. She was their dog, a mongrel, and the biggest gag in their act. Bernie would quote poetry:

> *'I am a tree that looks at God all day,*
> *A tree that lifts its arms to pray,*
> *I am a tree . . . I am a tree . . .'*

On that cue, Lulu would run onstage and chase him off to a roar of laughter. Once off stage Bernie would come back on for the applause, leaving Lulu to trot back to the dressing room. Then the boys would sing their closing number and announce the star of the show – in this case, me. All fine, but there I was sitting in their dressing room studying the half face in the mirror when the pooch arrives and comes to the canine conclusion that I'm not part of *her family*! A low growl, followed by a nip, might keep me at bay until her masters returned. So, Mike and Bernie were announcing Tommy Steele while Tommy Steele was trying to get past the Hound of the Baskervilles *with only half a boat race*! Drum roll . . . 'And now, ladies and gentlemen . . . the star of the evening . . .' *growl, growl, snap, growl* '. . . Britain's teenage sensation . . . Tommy . . .' screaming girls, throbbing band '. . . Steele!' *Growl, bark, snarl* – jump, run. I skidded centre stage and froze in the light with my half face.

During that first week the company and I had formed a wonderful relationship. Every evening after the show, with the stage door cleared, I followed them to their digs. Over cheese sandwiches and Camp coffee I sat among the other acts on the bill, Thunderclap Jones, Paul and Peta Page, Josephine Anne, and Reg Thompson – *'unknown to millions'* – listening to a thousand and

one anecdotes of showbiz folk. I was mesmerized – so much so
that I checked out of my hotel and followed my new family into
digs, for thirty bob a week, *plus use of cruet* and priceless tales.

I toured England with that first rock show for two months,
every Monday a new town. Rock-and-roll was travelling across
England like a wagon train. At each stop the locals came to share
a new world of music. It was the time of the teenager: no more
hand-me-down music from our parents – now we had choice and
spent our hard-earned money exercising it. As the weeks went by,
the shows drew adults accompanying their kids. Some came out
of curiosity and some, I guess, as security guards. Then the press
came and the radio (no TV yet!), still unsure how to receive this
music. I hit London in January 1957. The newspapers had a field
day: 'BRITAIN'S ANSWER TO ROCK INVADES' and 'LOCK UP YOUR
DAUGHTERS'. But the twelve shows played to thirty thousand
people, there was no sacking, no pillaging and no one fell apart
under the spell of that 'voodoo music'.

Then came the confidence of innocence. Kennedy had a call
from the London Coliseum. A charity had booked it for a one-
night stand but they had a problem: they'd sold out the stalls but
they couldn't get rid of the top circle. 'Perhaps Tommy Steele
could appear and we could sell tickets to teenagers?'

Ian Bevan was dead against it. 'It's a West End theatre,' he
cautioned. 'He's not ready yet!'

'It's a charity, for God's sake,' Kennedy argued. 'What's wrong
with that?'

'It's free, that's what,' said Parnes.

The ear-splitting screams that greeted me that night at the Coliseum were the beginning of a disastrous chain of events. As the
kids howled from the circle, the adults started to leave. On stage I
was singing in a daze of confusion and embarrassment. My parents
were in the audience and I could see Darbo darting up and down
the aisles, pulling people back into their seats, then more exoduses
and more embarrassment! But when the house curtain started to
come down half-way through a number, anger took over. It

Steady on, girls!

whizzed past my eyes, blocked out the auditorium, hit the stage and bounced up again into the flies. Within a few seconds it did it again! I looked to the prompt wing and saw Kennedy and Parnes wrestling with a man who was the image of Captain Mainwaring in *Dad's Army*. The object of the tussle was the curtain: each time Mainwaring wound it down, Parnes and Kennedy wound it back up. What was left of the audience was now in hysterics. The number ended and I stormed offstage towards the trio.

'I'm Sam Harbour,' Mainwaring puffed, 'the theatre manager, and I won't have barbarians on my premises.'

Then, out of the gloom, came sunshine.

After the show Lionel Bart arrived backstage. 'Meet Annette Donati.' He beamed, throwing himself on the sofa in my dressing room with the panache of an East End Oscar Wilde. 'It's a stage name, of course. She dances at the Windmill Theatre.' Her real name was Ann Donoughue and she was lovely, vivacious and mischievous. She was taking us to a party, she said, but didn't know what time it started. She hadn't heard the show because of the screams and amplifiers, and when the audience had made for the exits she'd thought I looked a bit lonely in the spotlight. On top of all that she was from Leeds, a northerner – which got right up my nose!

We escaped through a rear exit into a van Lionel had brought to smuggle me through the crowds. I sat in the back surrounded by paint tins and turpentine while people banged on the roof. Later, Annie told me that seeing me huddled there had made her want to cuddle me. 'You looked so helpless,' she said.

Eventually, we found the party venue, only to discover that the event wasn't till the next Monday. That did it for me. I gave Annie a broadside. I was tired after the fiasco at the Coliseum, and I was hungry, cold and bloody fed up with Miss Windmill.

That did it for her too! The mixture of Welsh and Irish in her brought her nose to nose with me. 'You know your trouble, don't you?' she growled. 'You're bloody spoilt! We're all cold, we're all hungry and we're all fed up!'

'And it's all because of you!' I snapped.

'No, it's not, it's all because of the party!' she said. 'If it hadn't changed its mind, we could have been having it tonight.'

Did she really say that? I couldn't argue. Instead I laughed and so did she.

Lionel shrugged, and headed for pastures greener, leaving us alone. We hit the Sabrina coffee bar in Wardour Street and stayed till morning, exchanging jokes and singing the jingles that had become popular since the recent introduction of commercial television. It's something we've done ever since.

The next of the Guv's innovations was the Tommy Steele Rock Tour, a series of one-night stands from 'coast to coast', Land's End to John o'Groats. It was nothing like an American tour because there was no proper organization: no 'roadies', no sound and lighting rigs, just me and the Steelmen turning up at a date. If I set the house stand microphone as high as my chin and gave the lighting man simple instructions – 'on and off' – it usually worked. As for security, apart from the local Lazarus on the stage door, there was none. But somehow everything worked out.

Until the Caird Hall, Dundee.

It was a great concert hall and used more for orchestral recitals than popular shows. Rock was from another planet. So, when they sold out the auditorium, some enterprising spark sold the choir seats too, on banks of platforms situated at the rear of the stage. Come the performance, I walked on and started the act oblivious of the little redhead leaving her choir seat and walk-ing across the stage, past the Steelmen and up to my back. She tapped my hip and the screams of the throng in the auditorium rose to a frenzy. I turned to the redhead, she smiled and offered me a sweet.

That did it! The audience became a heaving mass of hysteria. They'd all got sweets so they all came on stage. Sweets to the right of me, sweets to the left!

I woke up in Edinburgh. The orthopaedics specialist explained that my left arm muscles had been damaged and that I needed a course of deep massage before I could play my guitar again. There was just one obstacle to that remedy: the deep scratches on the arm had to heal first.

'I can't go on with the tour,' I said.

'Why?' Parnes asked, surprised.

'Because I can't play my instrument.'

'You can still sing, can't you?'

'Yeah, but I can't play the fuckin' guitar!'

'Sing without it.'

'It's rock-and-roll, for Christ's sake! You can't have rock-and-roll without a guitar.'

'We'll hire a guitarist.'

'This is Scotland! How about a piper?'

We argued.

I had a lot of trouble getting through to him that a country guitar player would not be available. I needed the country rhythm pumping out with those solo guitar licks that gave the music its pedigree.

I also needed a rest. My body ached and I kept falling asleep.

We cancelled the tour, I went south and shut myself up in Fortress Bermondsey. The press came in packs and the new telephone installed in our scullery rang off the hook. 'Tommy Steele Mobbed in Scotland' and 'Rock Star to Retire' the headlines declared. Every day they spouted yet another fable, and get well cards arrived in their hundreds. Plus a letter: 'You are to appear before the High Court.'

The Guv was about to sue me for non-appearance.

My mum wanted 'to go round there and give him a piece of my mind', but Darbo's main concern was 'porridge' – Cockney slang for a jail sentence. ''Ow much can they give ya?' he asked.

When Kennedy explained that it was a civil action he retorted, 'There's nuffin' civil about court cases 'specially if there's a china involved!'

At the trial the judge handed down his decision with the words, 'This boy is being handed about like a silver chalice . . .' He found against the Guv and suggested I get some rest. Maybe a chat with a psychiatrist might be of some use to my future, he added.

★

Dr Stafford Clark, the chief psychiatrist at Guy's Hospital in London's Waterloo, invited me to his home one afternoon and we chatted in the garden over a pot of tea. After a couple of hours he put his arm round my shoulders. 'What's your main worry right now?' he asked.

'To get my arm better.'

'That will happen in less than a week.' He smiled. 'What do you dream about when you nod off?'

'I can't recall.'

'But you do dream?'

'I s'pose so.'

'Anything else?'

'How d'ya mean?'

'Anything else on your mind?'

'No, not really.'

'So when all is well you'll perform again?'

The question came like a gunshot, and I went blank.

'Let's have some more cake.'

We sat among his fruit trees until late afternoon. Then I thanked his wife and left. It had been so calm and relaxed. Before, I'd had a head full of noise and confusion. As we stood at the gate I wanted to say something in farewell, something that might show him I trusted him. It was a secret I hadn't known I'd been keeping until that moment.

'They didn't let me finish,' I whispered. 'They just wanted to get on the stage and stop me.'

He linked arms with me as we went through the gate. 'No, lad, they were just a lot of youngsters with no time to think,' he said. 'If you went again tomorrow they'd apologize.'

I never saw or spoke to him again.

24

In February 1957 Hugh Mendl called me to Decca House on the Albert Embankment. I found him leaning over a gramophone, fiddling with a new needle. 'Ever heard of a chap called Guy Mitchell?' he wheezed.

I rattled off the hit list of Mitchell's country songs and said I had seen him on Broadway. 'Well, he's released a rather catchy little thing. I thought you might like to cover it for us.'

That weekend I recorded 'Singin' The Blues', which became my first number-one hit. The kids bought 100,000 copies in a week! It wasn't rock and it wasn't pop, it was pure country. And it was a great song.

Its success called for another clan gathering at Ian Bevan's office. 'Now we go for the West End,' he said.

'But we tried that at the Coliseum charity night,' Kennedy cried. 'You said it was a bad move then, what's changed your mind?'

'Circumstances. Three months ago Tommy was just a headline. Three months ago rock was just a headline. Now it's become a cult and Tommy Steele is an icon. It's a showbusiness phenomenon. A sailor goes on the stage and comes off a star! It's pure theatre and that's why we change tack.'

'In what direction?' Larry muttered.

'The Café de Paris!'

'You want me to work in a *caff*?' I choked.

'It's not a caff, it's the *Café*,' Ian explained. 'It's the epitome of London night life and the shop window for the greatest stars in the world.'

'What's the money like?' Parnes inquired.

'It's worth more than money!' Ian snapped. 'Every top theatre critic in town will see him.'

I felt the blood rush from my head. 'I don't think I can do it,' I said, remembering the Coliseum, with my mum crying and Darbo threatening to punch Kennedy's nose for sending me into the lions' den.

'If you want to stay in this business you're going to have to face the critics some day,' Ian cajoled.

'But they hate rock-and-roll!'

'They don't *know* rock-and-roll, and the first time they come face to face with it you will be singing it. They will listen and they will write, I believe, favourably.'

The following day I dined with Major Neville Willing, the manager of the Café. He stood five feet two, with a full head of blue-rinsed hair, a waxed moustache, a red velvet smoking jacket and a monocle. 'You will follow in the steps of Noël Coward and Marlene,' he cooed. 'My patrons will take you in their arms and cry, "Hosanna!"' With that he snatched the flowers from the vase on the table and tossed them into my lap, all wet and sticky.

Later that night I broke the news to my parents. My mum reacted as if I had been summoned to Buckingham Palace. 'Ooh!' she said. 'It'll be so posh. Don't forget to ring us when you've done your songs.'

'There'll be no need,' I said. 'You're both coming to the first night. That means a new evening gown for you, Mum, and a flash whistle for Dad.'

At that Darbo got off his chair without a word and went outside into the backyard. At first, as the lavatory was out there, I didn't suspect much, but I soon realized he wasn't using it – I could see the glow of his cigarette as he stood in the dark.

Something was up.

I waited till Mum had gone to bed to ask, 'What's up, Dad?'

'Nuffin'.'

'Yes, there is. What's occurred?'

'I told ya, nuffin'.'

'I'm not bloody blind, so c'mon, tell me.'

'It's this caff gaff. It gives me a turn, that's all.'

'Why?'

'It don't sound right, y'know sorta . . .'

'Omnibus?'

'Y'know, funny.'

'But it's the Café de Paris, Dad, a nightclub, a *fun* place!'

'It's a *death pit!*'

I was dumbstruck. He pulled his chair so close to mine that our knees touched. Then, with his chubby fingers holding fast to his Woodbine, he explained: 'It was during the blitz on a Saturday night late. I was working at the Nest in Soho when we heard the bang. There was no panic, it was past theatre closing and the area was empty, so everyone stayed under cover till the raid was over. Then someone remembers the caff that was in Coventry Street, in the basement of Lyons Corner House and it's Saturday night. It'll be packed!'

Fuckin' 'ell!

'We all legged it down Shaftesbury Avenue, full of smoke, and Wardour Street, full of dust, and then into Coventry Street, full of nothin' but rubble and flames. Me and Nick the Bubble followed Frankie the Iron, who played the joanna in our rubber, into the entrance to the caff and down the apples. There were already firemen, wardens and coppers down there. We just done what everybody else did, pulled away hot bricks and listened for voices. I made my way into the gents' khazi. That's when I found him, a posh gent in a tail suit. All calm he was, sittin' on the pot with his strides round his ankles. He was Hovis. I dragged him up to the street where the pavement was laid out with rows of stiff bodies all dressed to the nines. We stopped searching in the morning. Everyone was dog tired. Anyway, there wasn't any more room in the street for the dead. That's the last time I saw the caff, and with you about to work there, I sorta come over all . . .'

'Omnibus?'

'Yeah. Rum, ain't it?' he said, flicking the last of the Woodbine into the fire. It was the longest conversation I'd ever had with him.

But why had he told me the story? Because I'd insisted? Or because he meant to warn me – but, if so, about what?

I was soon to find out.

★

'Come into my parlour,' Major Willing suggested, as I descended from the street to the plush foyer of the Café. He took my hand and led me down the splendid curved staircase, which led to an intimate dance-floor surrounded by a crescent of empty dining-tables. I was there for rehearsal and the Steelmen were already on the bandstand: Alan Stuart on saxophone, Alan Weighell on bass, Dennis Price on piano and Leo Pollini on drums. 'I'll leave you to settle your feathers,' the major carolled. 'Get yourself used to the microphone and the lights, and I'll pop down later with some tea. Be good!' He disappeared, like the White Rabbit.

So there I stood, the boys behind me and the tables in front, with a cleaning lady skirting the perimeter. As we ran through the songs, the lights changed with each number, and the cleaner moved closer. More songs, more lights. Then she was in the middle of the dance-floor, the spotlights just brushing her grey hair. 'Diss lights are killink you,' she muttered, in a thick German accent. 'Only ze old people light from the back and only ze vooman haff blue. For you der must be fire, reds, pinks! I make der change *mit* your permission.'

She spoke with such authority that I could only nod. She ambled over to the lighting board and poked her fingers on the buttons. Lights flashed on and off. Then she said, 'Dass okay for now. Vee continue layder,' and left.

The major arrived with the tea-tray. 'How are things?'

'Fine,' I said, 'but the cleaner changed the lights so it got a bit hot.'

'Oh, that's Marlene,' he said. 'What Dietrich says, the major does. She's never wrong, you know.'

That week I followed in the footsteps of Marlene Dietrich, who was finishing her season. My opening night arrived, as did my parents and the clan. The major came into my dressing room minutes before I was due to go on and dropped the bombshell. 'I've put your guitar at the top of the stairs. You pick it up in the darkness, pose, then the spotlight hits you and there you are – my star! You walk down to applause and then –'

'How about the amp lead?' I asked.

'What's an amp lead?'

'It's the electric lead to my guitar. I have to plug it in.'

'Plug?' he exclaimed. 'I thought you plucked!'

It was no use explaining to him: the overture was playing and I was on. I stood at the top of the stairs in the dark, waiting for the announcement and the spotlight that would take me down to the stage and the critics. But all I could think about was getting to the bandstand, plugging in my amp lead, getting the power to my strings and starting to rock.

The announcement came: 'The Café de Paris proudly presents the dynamic Tommy . . .'

Now the spot.

'. . . Steele!'

And the explosion – bang!

Followed by complete darkness.

What with Miss Dietrich's lighting and my amplifiers, every fuse in the club had blown, leaving only the glow from the candles on the dining-tables. Memories of the Coliseum loomed.

The applause died.

The Steelmen ran out of introduction music.

The place was silent.

Darbo was right. Everything was *omnibus*!

I felt the fingerboard of the guitar and hit a chord waiting for inspiration, and that was when Hank Williams whispered in my ear. I started singing:

> '*Kaw-Liga was a wooden Indian standin' by the door*
> *He fell in love with an Indian maid over in the antique store.*'

I began to walk round the tables serenading the diners. 'Cheatin' Heart' followed, then 'Wedding Bells' and 'Lovesick Blues'. I even did a couple of Cookie's calypsos. At last the electricity came back on, the amplifiers buzzed, I plugged in, and hit them with rock: '*One o'clock, two o'clock, three o'clock, rock . . .*' The audience clapped and the joint rocked with the act I should have done before the

After Marlene Dietrich and Noël Coward and Eartha Kitt – Tommy Steele from Bermondsey at what my mum called 'that caff' . . .

blackout. The next day brought wonderful reviews – just bloody wonderful!

During my season at the Café a series of visits moved my career in a direction that went off the map of dreams. Noël Coward found 'The rhythm exhilarating and the lyrics not unlike those of a modern-day Keats! Fred Keats, my milkman!' But he really did enjoy it, and offered me a lot of encouragement. 'The theatre is calling you, dear boy.' He smiled. 'You *will* come when you're ready, won't you?'

From that time on he came to every first night I did.

My next visit was from a plump young man with glasses, not a lot older than me. He was waiting in the foyer when I arrived to get ready for a show. The major floated over to greet me with his usual flourish. 'Greetings, my prince. There's a high tea in your boudoir, a packed house in your kingdom, and Billy Bunter here giving my foyer a bad name!' With that he disappeared, leaving Bunter in shock.

'I'm Jack Good, I've come from the BBC.' He spoke like a masculine Joyce Grenfell. 'They'd rather like me to put a television series together. I said I could if it was with you. So, I've got this neat idea for a teenage beat show. I'm calling it *Six-Five Special*. It comes on at five past six on a Saturday, after the football results. Wizard prang, don't you think?'

That show was the forerunner of every pop-music show since. There was no story, just a series of current hits performed by the original artists in front of an invited crowd of teenagers who wandered round the studio, getting in the way of the cameras and causing such chaos that, in the words of the show's architect, it made for a 'wizard prang'.

Then I met Nat Cohen and Stuart Levy, partners in Anglo Amalgamated Pictures. They were quite different from that other British film mogul, J. Arthur Rank. Where Rank was C. Aubrey Smith, Cohen and Levy were Abbott and Costello. They didn't so much hold a meeting as do an act.

Cohen: 'We want to make a big musical.'

Levy: 'A small documentary!'

Cohen: 'With Technicolor, stereophonic sound.'

Levy: 'A black-and-white talkie.'

Cohen: 'With plenty of time to rehearse and prepare and shoot a masterpiece.'

Levy: 'Four weeks maximum.'

They were hardly the British answer to Hollywood's Sam Goldwyn and Jack Warner. Or were they?

There was a degree of madness about them – but you had to be mad to take the chances they took – with a little eccentricity for good measure.

Cohen: 'We want twelve great songs.'

Levy: 'Maybe six.'

Cohen: 'And we need a great script to link the tunes.'

Levy: '*Gone with the Wind* it ain't.'

So, I met up with Lionel Bart and Mike Pratt to map out some numbers, and within a month we had the score written.

'Any ideas for a script?' I asked one afternoon. 'We start shooting in a fortnight.'

'How about a story of a young sailor who takes up a guitar and makes it in rock-and-roll?' Mike joked.

And so it came to pass. *The Tommy Steele Story* had been made and released by the end of the year.

I crept on to the sound stage of my first film at Beaconsfield Pictures like a stranger in the night. The director, Gerry Bryant, was more like a poet than a showman. His long, thin, bony fingers constantly flicked through the pages of the script he clutched. When he spotted me, he asked for the silence bell to ring. 'Ladies and gentlemen,' he called, his soft voice barely reaching into the high gantry that was stuffed with electricians and huge arc-lights, 'would you take your tea break now?'

The studio fell into a mass chatter as the technicians left through the huge dock doors that slid open like giant jaws. Then we were alone, Gerry and me. He walked over to the cold black machine that dominated the centre of the stage. 'This is the camera,' he began. 'It sees all and forgets nothing. Respect it by knowing your lines and listening to everybody else's. Remember that, and you'll be friends for life.'

25

One morning in midsummer of 1957, my mum came into my bedroom as usual, smiling above a steaming cup of tea. Everything about her was warm and tender – you always knew that, whatever the day held, she would be there, protective, encouraging, full of love. God, how I miss her. 'You've got this funny thing in the post,' she said. 'It's got that mark on the envelope – y'know, the one that told people someone was killed during the war.' With that cheering thought she left me.

But the war was over: no one was getting killed any more. Whatever the letter was about, it wasn't about catastrophe.

I was wrong. It began: '. . . under section . . . of the Conscription Act of . . . you will report to the nearest recruitment office at 09:00 hours. By Order of Her Majesty's Armed Services.'

I called the War Office. 'But I've been in the navy for five years. I'm exempt from conscription!' I insisted.

'Sorry, Mr Hicks, you were in the *Merchant* Navy. It doesn't count.'

The recruiting office was full of young men in their late teens, wearing nothing but glum faces. We were about to have the dreaded medical, which would condemn us to two years of lingering death. My medic was Dr Crippen, who took an age over every prod and orifice. At last, with a final cough, I got dressed and sat outside the recruiting officer's door. He was quite friendly, considering his rank: full colonel.

'So, Hicks, what d'ya fancy?'

'Sorry?'

'Which regiment would you like to join?'

'I didn't know I had a choice.'

'Well, it might help us place you.'

I had visions of mud-holes, rats and trench mouth. 'Commando,' I muttered.

'Sorry, not on, I'm afraid.'

'Paratrooper, then.'

'Again, sorry, old chap, you have to do basic training before you can apply for Special Services. How about Signals?'

'Signals? That's all flags and pigeon shit.'

'No, no, m' lad, it's a grand outfit today. Radio, radar, Morse! It's a perfect start if you want Special Services. If I were you I'd –'

'Okay, fine, Signals it is,' I grumbled, and signed the form.

As I left the office the recruiting sergeant was waiting with a couple of grinning corporals. 'We've 'ad a bet.' He beamed. 'You took Signals, right?'

I nodded.

'I've just won 'alf a quid on you.'

'And now you're gonna tell me how,' I grunted.

'Right.' He began. 'You're Thomas Hicks, otherwise Tommy Steele, the rocker, right?'

'Right.'

'And he's a colonel in the Signals, right?'

'Right.'

'Well, we've never seen him here before, so I does a check-up and what do I find? He runs the biggest band in the British Army and he's looking for a vocalist. You've been done, my son!'

That weekend the clan met at Ian's office to discuss my call-up. Ian referred to it as an unforeseen hiatus. Larry's concern was contracts and cancellations. Kennedy sat silent but deep. The results of my medical had arrived that morning. We opened the dreaded envelope.

'God, what's a Four F?' Kennedy exclaimed.

'Low category,' Ian said.

'What's lower?'

'Death!' Parnes rapped.

'"Fallen arches,"' I read.

Long pause.

'My God, he's got flat feet.' Ian chuckled.

'Oh, no, he hasn't,' Kennedy rapped. 'You can't announce that Tommy Steele's missed National Service because of flat bloody feet. It'll ruin his image!'

We sat and argued and congratulated ourselves on our reprieve. That Sunday the *Pictorial* announced, 'TOMMY STEELE HAS BAD HEART.'

My mum had Kennedy in her kitchen over that one.

'What did you say to him?' I asked her later.

'Nuffin',' she said. 'I just give 'im a cup of tea.'

'He got off lightly, then.'

'Not really.' She grinned. 'I put senna pods in it.'

Ian Bevan read from the letter with the trace of a tear in his eye: 'By command of Her Majesty Queen Elizabeth . . .' I didn't take in the rest because my head was spinning and my heart was crashing out of my ribcage. The Royal Command Performance is the finest accolade a performer can receive and now, still only in my first year in showbusiness, I had been given the honour of appearing before my sovereign queen. I couldn't get home quick enough to tell the family.

It really was too much for my mum: it had been a tough year for her, sitting in our kitchen waiting for me to come back from 'Gawd knows where', doing 'Gawd knows what' with 'Gawd knows who'. She had never recovered from that night at the Coliseum, and what with the electric blow-out at 'the caff', court cases and constant press pressure . . . 'Now the Queen's gettin' in on the bleedin' act. Oooh, I don't know, Tommy, I really don't,' she fussed, chucking a mountain of sugar into her tea.

'But it's the Royal Command, Mum. It's a great honour!'

'Well, you'd best behave yourself!' She strode out of the kitchen, thrilled to bits but keeping it to herself.

'And mind the road.' Darbo rubbed his hands and winked one of his mischievous eyes.

*

Mum gives me a chord on the old joanna.

The following Monday I arrived at the London Palladium. It was the day of the show and I had been instructed to appear for my band call at ten a.m. I left the taxi in Regent Street and walked down the little alley at the back of Dickens and Jones, which led to Argyll Street and the theatre. As usual, she was sitting squat betwixt the shops to either side of her and, as usual, she gave out that nonchalant air of controlled greatness. She knew what she was and she knew what she had: she was the Ace Variety Venue, the epitome, the peak.

I slipped across the road in three strides, entered the theatre and walked up the marble stairs, pretty much as I had that night back in '46, full of thrill and anticipation. The foyer was empty, save for a couple of ushers polishing the brass stair rail that led to the vestibule and the Royal Box. Bloody hell! I had to stop thinking about royalty: appearing at the Palladium was bad enough. I slid past the stalls bar and into the main auditorium. Without a crowd, the seats looked like a gigantic carpet of red plush. The house lights were on, the fire curtain was up and the empty stage was dark.

Complete silence!

Blimey, it's the wrong day, I thought.

Then a crash of drums came from the depths of the orchestra pit, followed by the thrilling eruption of the full Palladium band.

I moved down the centre aisle hypnotized by the music, arrived at the pit rail and looked over the hunched shoulders of the conductor as he waved encouragement. From this distance the brass instruments deafened me and the tympani roared. I had never been so close to such a large orchestra, and the feeling was . . .

'What time will you be needing them?' a nervous little man said, emerging from the dark like a nearsighted badger.

'Needing who?' I asked.

'The band, the orchestra.'

'No, thanks, I've got my own.'

'Oh, God, that's going to be very difficult,' he mumbled, into his clipboard. 'These *Royal Variety Shows* are all the same – everyone has their own everything. Their own props, their own dancers, and now their own bands! And where do I put them? All I have is one backstage and one set of dressing rooms.'

He marched up and down, wailing to himself: 'Judy Garland, Gracie Fields, Vera Lynn all with bands, and now you, sir, and you're down for forty pieces. And where do I put them? I ask myself. And don't tell me the band room. I've got Count Basie's lot down there. It's like Rorke's Drift.'

'But I haven't got forty pieces,' I said, 'I've only got four – piano, bass, sax and drums. The Steelmen.'

The badger blinked into his notes. 'Steelmen . . . but they're with Tommy Steele.'

'That's me.'

He had a closer look, took in my jeans and denim shirt. 'You're not Mario Lanza, then?'

'No, I'm Tommy Steele. He's Mario Lanza.'

Above us in the half-light of the stage, a small stocky man stood with a huge overcoat draped over his shoulders. The great tenor's eyes flashed with confidence. He walked towards the footlights, and the backcloth rose to reveal a full string orchestra. 'This morning I rehearse. Tonight I will sing "Nessun Dorma",' he called into the auditorium.

As the orchestra began to play, a tall, elegant man joined me.

'Rehearse my aunt Sally,' he whispered. 'Not if I know Mr Lanza.'

The music continued as the maestro stalked the stage, humming to himself. My legs started to shake. Mario Lanza was up there and pretty soon it was going to be my turn. Bloody hell! I thought. I've gotta get out of here, I've gotta find the exit and –

'I'm Val Parnell,' the man at the rail whispered. 'I'm producing this show and it's wonderful to have you and your music.'

I don't know if he meant it, or if he'd guessed that the kid was about to leg it, but those words came with the timing of a Bob Hope tag-line . . . So did the finale of 'Nessun Dorma'. The aria was fast approaching its climax. Lanza was slowing from a stalk to a stand-off. He glared up at the host of spotlights, took a deep breath, and Val Parnell, the greatest of all Palladium impresarios, gripped my arm. 'Here it comes, son!' The voice of Mario Lanza rang out and I swear that every piece of glass in that theatre held on for dear life. Then it was over.

'Now you may applaud.' Lanza smiled and was gone.

That night I stood at the side of the stage and watched the 'greats' perform their miracles. One by one they walked on to applause and off to acclaim.

'And now,' the MC announced, 'representing the music of the modern era . . . Tommy Steele.'

I went on to a polite reception. My knees were like jelly and I barely made it to the centre microphone. Then the Steelmen thudded into 'Rock With The Caveman'. 'Come on, everybody, clap your hands,' I croaked.

Nothing from the stalls.

'How about you up there, then?' I yelled, pointing up to the dress circle. 'It won't hurt, honest.'

Still nothing.

Christ, I thought. The Royal Family's in the box to my left – I've had it. Today the Palladium, tomorrow the Tower.

Then she saved me. The Queen Mum saved me! That small package of dynamite leaned over the rail of the Royal Box and tapped her long white gloves together, eyeing the audience with a regal reprimand. The mob roared with laughter and joined in.

For the first time in its history the house rocked and I lived to roll another day.

That Christmas, of 1957, Freddie Carpenter came on the scene. He was the country's leading pantomime director and the man who introduced me to the musical. We were gathered in the freezing cold Royal Court Theatre in Liverpool for *Goldilocks and the Three Bears*.

'I want you to do a few dance steps in the opening number,' he said. 'I want you to play a love scene with Goldilocks in the second act. I want you to get a few laughs in the slapstick routine – and you won't need *that*.' He gestured to my guitar, which I held on to for dear life. Dances, laughs and love scenes were unknown to me, and yet there I was, the new boy in a room full of strangers. Uncomfortable was an understatement.

The choreographer was Malcolm Goddard, a bloke with the patience of Job, who introduced me to the mirrors. 'What you don't see in them, you don't have. Trust them.'

Ricki Fulton was a famous panto dame. 'Wait, wait,' was his motto. 'Get to the tag and wait for the laugh. If you rush you'll leave the audience behind, and they don't like being second.'

Goldilocks was less helpful. Before I even touched her, she announced, 'You're not supposed to put your tongue in my mouth. If you do I'm allowed to stop the rehearsal.' I thought she was joking, but in case she wasn't I kissed her for eight weeks with a mouth shut as tight as a duck's arse.

When the first night arrived I sat in my dressing room and shook like a leaf. In previous productions I had taken my opening performances with a tinge of fear, but I'd always had my rock-and-roll. Somewhere in the back of my young mind I had faith that it would protect me, but this pantomime lark! Where was my armour? All of a sudden I felt naked. I was about to charge up the hill with what? Hope and ambition? Desire and rehearsal? Shit or bust, here we go!

My first entrance came like the old 'good news, bad news' joke. The good news was that my arrival onstage was greeted with a

Tommy (Rock-with-the-Caveman) Steele.

Steele

thousand cheers. The bad news was that the cheers didn't stop. True, they sometimes weakened into a scream, sometimes even a whimper, but every word I spoke in that first scene drew a vocal reaction from the crowd. That was bad enough, but it was the looks on the other performers' faces that hurt. They were actors and dancers so they had never witnessed teenage hysteria before. They spat out their lines and glared at me, as if I was the usurper and these 'intruders' had come in with me. During the second scene, after I had told Goldilocks I loved her, the roof came off with a mass yell of 'Oh, no, you don't!'

That was it.

I'd had enough.

I walked up to the footlights like an angry young bear. 'Look, there's people acting up here!' I roared.

The place went into a sort of silent limbo.

'So do me a favour and shut your gobs!'

If the press liked the show, they *loved* the ad-lib. The headlines in the Lancashire papers heralded it as if I'd quoted from some tablet of stone: 'Tommy Tells 'Em to Shut Your Gobs!'

But it worked. Apart from the odd relapse, the kids had got the message. One cheer when he comes on, then you wait three hours for the end to cheer again.

For me, that show was a joy and a revelation: every time I went onstage, I fell deeper under the spell of showbusiness.

Then came that matinée.

Even today, fifty years on, whenever I visit Liverpool, someone reminds me of it.

The show started like any other. The overture played and I went on, greeted by the solitary cheer – and what sounded like hundreds of pages being turned in hundreds of hidden books. I let the moment pass and began my first speech. 'Hi, everybody, my name's Tommy and –'

'And I'm lost!' yelled a thousand voices.

Something strange was happening but I didn't have time to find out what.

I continued: 'If anyone can help me I'd –'

'Be much obliged,' the voices roared.

There was another rustle.

At the end of the scene I couldn't wait to get off. I rushed to the prompt corner and the stage manager. 'What's going on?' I gasped.

He sat with his head in his hands. 'I don't believe it, I just don't believe it. It's a bloody rag!'

'What's a *rag*?' I cried.

'Students having a bit of fun.'

The theatre manager crashed through the pass door leading from the auditorium to the backstage. He was sweating like a pig. 'They've bought out the top circle and they've got copies of the script,' he moaned. 'Every time someone gets to a joke they shout the tag.'

'But they can't do that, can they?' I asked.

'They're Liverpool college students. They can do anything they like, it's a –'

'I know, it's a fuckin' rag!' I muttered.

'A lot of the children out there are getting very upset and confused.'

Another raucous shout came as another gag hit the deck.

'Put the auditorium lights on,' I said, and strode on to the stage. The lights came up as I hit front and centre. I glared up to the gods, and an ocean of laughing faces looked back, bringing me to the boil. 'Look, you lot,' I called, 'you're spoiling the show and frightening the children, so put a sock in it.'

This brought a chorus of mocking song: '*He never felt more like singin' the blues.*'

'All right, all right!' I shouted. 'You're all supposed to be educated so here's a bit of plain English. One more mouthful and I'm bringing the curtain down and cancelling the show.'

With that I nodded to the company standing in the wings. Then, with the auditorium lights dimming, we carried on. But as the next gag began, the tag-line rang out, and the curtain went down.

The show was cancelled but the drama was only just beginning.

First, a few punch-ups in the foyer: there were fathers among
the audience, and a bunch of so-called intellectuals had spoiled
the kids' afternoon and were begging for a smack. Then came the
fourth estate: they chased the student ringleaders all over the city
until they got their names and photos.

Then came the headlines, the local press, national news, radio
interviews, and the declaration. First it was word of mouth, and
then the papers alleged that the gentle folk of Liverpool had issued
an edict: any student seen wearing a college scarf in the streets or
hostelries would receive the wages of sin. The point was taken. The
streets lost their 'learned presence' for as long as the pantomime was
playing and beyond. It had been an unforgivable act of hooli-
ganism, for no other reason than 'Let's have a bit of a rag.'

26

In the summer of 1958, with the success of *The Tommy Steele Story*, I heard that I had fans outside Great Britain. The clan decided that, as an international artist, I needed to go abroad. My first port of call was Scandinavia. First, the inhabitants saw *The Tommy Steele Story*, then the Steelmen and I gave a *live* concert. During the tour the local press held a popularity poll, which, I am told, is still referred to as the Last of the Viking Wars. The question posed was 'Who is the greatest, Elvis or Tommy?' Apparently the streets outside the newspaper offices were mobbed with hundreds of good-natured aficionados, chanting the name of their idol, but it was all good fun and better still when the count came in: I won!

My second trip was to Moscow, and it turned into a clandestine spy story. It came about with an inquiry from the Soviet Embassy in London: would Tommy Steele consider joining a cultural visit to Russia representing the youth of Great Britain?

'For how much?' Parnes asked.

'We ought to pay them,' Kennedy said. 'It's a natural for a publicity picture – "Tommy Steele Rocks in Red Square." It'll go all over the world.'

The Russian ambassador was a charming man, wearing the regulation wing collar and striped trousers; his face was pure Cossack. 'We Russians would be very happy for you to come and join us,' he said.

I didn't much fancy the 'join us' bit but maybe I'd lost something in the translation. The world at that time was in the middle of a war so cold that it was near freezing point, Stalin still almost warm in his grave, the Korean War barely over, and China girding its loins. The invitation from the Reds came out of the blue.

Moscow was worse than I had expected. I'd thought England was losing the peace with food shortages and untouched bombsites,

Me on set during filming of The Tommy Steele Story.

but post-war Moscow looked like it was still recovering from
Napoleon. The people moved bleakly across a cold landscape.
Our personal guide and interpreter, Boris Plakov, was regulation
serious. A great bear of a man with bushy black eyebrows and a
rough swagger, his interest in my guitar and Kennedy's camera
took up most of our first meeting. 'We do not do performance,'
he remarked, when he saw me tuning the instrument.

'It's for the photo –' I began, but Kennedy interrupted me.

'Tuning,' he snapped. 'He has to keep it tuned.'

Now Boris took up the Kennedy camera. 'Is this German?'

Kennedy shrugged. 'I've no idea, I just point the thing and
press.'

Just an innocent conversation you might have thought, except

Tommy or Elvis?

that Kennedy had lied. He was a first-class photographer and the Rolleiflex was a professional piece of equipment. He'd never pointed and pressed in his life, so why say so?

'We do not do performance,' Boris repeated, indicating the guitar again. 'And no photographs. Culture Office has all you need.' He lumbered out.

'I don't trust the bloke,' Kennedy whispered, as if the room was bugged.

'Why? He's Boris the guide.'

'Nope, he's Boris the Bolshevik and he's bloody nosy.'

'So he's nosy, so what?'

'So the photo, that's what! We're here to get that shot of you in Red Square, and the sooner we get it the better. C'mon!'

We went out of the hotel and headed for the dramatic domes of the Kremlin, Kennedy with the Rolleiflex, me with the guitar. Red Square was vast, and hordes of people were walking across its well-worn cobblestones, but there was no hubbub, no small-talk, just a mass of figures.

Performing in Red Square.

'Do it now,' Kennedy muttered, whipping out his camera.

I tore the guitar out of its case and swung it on.

'Sing!'

'Sing what?'

'Any soddin' thing. Make a crowd!'

So I sang: ' "I never felt more like singin' the blues . . ." '

The reaction of the people in the immediate area was not as expected. Instead of gathering round a busker, they scattered as if I'd tossed a hand grenade, but Kennedy kept clicking. 'Keep going, keep going!' I finished 'Singin' the Blues' and started 'Hound Dog'.

Now people were coming closer and eventually I had a ring round me. Kennedy kept clicking.

The long black government car skidded alongside us, spilling out Boris with thunder in his eyes. He bundled us into the back and his giant hands tore the Rolleiflex from Kennedy's neck and snapped it open, exposing the film to the light. Kennedy sat sheepish and repentant. Then it was my turn. 'I confiscate guitar too!' he roared. 'No performance. No roll-and-rock. This is Russia!' Back at the hotel he left us in our room.

In the street below, the long black government car was parked with Boris in the back. And there it waited till nightfall and the banquet. This was the big event of the visit: all the representatives of the western arts were assembled before Comrade Mikoyan, the Soviet cultural secretary. He was a cold, stiff man. All evening he sat at the top table with a blank stare, as if contemplating his next chess move. After the main course I was summoned to his side. 'The minister would like to drink toast with Mr Stalin,' his interpreter announced. 'Steel' in Russian is 'Stalin'. Mikoyan pulled himself out of his chair and the enormous hall fell silent. The only sound was the click of the microphone as it was placed under our noses.

'I drink to the youth of our two countries. May there never be war in our time.'

There now followed a series of jousts that I cannot explain. Maybe I was angry about the Red Square incident, or maybe this starchy politico was getting to me, but my reaction was, to say the least, impertinent. I put my glass down. 'I refuse to drink to the youth of our two countries with the word "war" in the toast.'

The hall rattled as various translators passed on the news.

Mikoyan gave the moment a little more thought, and then he replied: 'I drink to the youth of our two countries. May there always be peace.'

I put my glass down again. 'No. That suggests there *might* be war.'

He gave a gesture of annoyance and muttered to the interpreter who explained, 'The minister says for you to make the toast.'

'I drink to the youth of our two countries,' I began, 'and the best of British luck.'

'*Niet!*' Mikoyan yelled. Then, in perfect English: 'Why should the British have all the luck?'

The next day, as we boarded the plane for home, Boris gave me back my guitar with a Russian doll for my mother. Kennedy only got his camera.

'You did great at the banquet last night,' Kennedy said, snapping on his seat-belt. 'The press will have a field day.'

'I'm sorry you didn't get the Red Square picture,' I said, as the plane climbed into the sky.

Kennedy felt down the front of his trousers towards the crotch and pulled out a roll of film. 'The things I do for Kodak,' he said.

The crafty sod had swapped the film at the square before Boris the Bolshevik had even got out of his car. We had triumphed, after all.

With the success of Scandinavia and Russia, and of my career so far, the clan and I accepted the offer of a tour to South Africa without fear. We were on a roll. The pioneer train was rolling on, and the very idea of circling the wagons was unthinkable. The attack came at dawn on the morning that the *Winchester Castle* docked in Cape Town, with me on board full of the joys of touring.

The day before we made port, the ship had picked up South African Radio. Every hour on the hour the announcer was counting down to its arrival with me and the Steelmen, so we were all excited. The first disappointment was the reception at the docks: three girls and a dog waving from the room of a warehouse. The second was an officious-looking civilian, accompanied by two stern policemen: 'Pretoria has barred you from the capital,' he said, in a guttural Afrikaner accent. 'Your music is considered decadent and unfit for the young of this country. Therefore you are advised to stay onboard this vessel until it returns to the UK.'

Kennedy and Parnes went berserk. There was no way we were going to kowtow to such a suggestion – we hadn't come all this way to be warned off by some jumped-up Pretorian boor.

The official shrugged and left us with the two coppers.

'Do not enter the precincts of Cape Town,' one barked. 'If you do I am ordered to recall your escort. What happens then is your own responsibility.'

With that they left, followed defiantly, an hour later, by us, bag and baggage. Kennedy, Parnes and I got into the first open limousine, the Steelmen into the second, and then, with police outriders front and back, we set off for Cape Town. We drove through the beautiful countryside beneath the hot sun. Then, as we neared the top of a rise, the police outriders stopped, the limousines stopped and everything was quiet, except for the buzz of a distant swarm of locusts. Then, in a cloud of dust, the outriders vanished. Now there was just us and the locusts.

Our driver was Sam, a bundle of nerves. He drove the limousine as if we had nitro-glycerine in the boot.

'I don't see why we need an escort anyway,' Kennedy mused, 'unless the Zulus are back on the warpath.'

'It ain't the Zulus you got worries about,' Sam remarked, as he crunched another gear. I saw the look on his face in the rear-view mirror. 'What do you mean, Sam?' I asked.

'You'll see.'

The distant roofs of the town came closer. So did the sound of the locusts, but with each passing minute the sound changed from a buzz, to a hiss, then a hum, and finally a throb. As we turned a corner, it culminated in a cheer, a great, fantastic, frightening cheer! It was later estimated that over a hundred thousand people were in the streets of Cape Town that day, and us without a copper in sight! Parnes gave a gasp, Kennedy a whistle and Sam almost gave birth. 'What I'm gonna do, boss?'

'You gonna keep going,' I said. 'If we stop we've had it!'

I knew from experience that if you kept on the move, crowds tended to stand and watch you. But if you stopped or turned, it was a sign of weakness and you were done for. So, we ran the gauntlet and, apart from the odd daredevil jumping on the bumpers, we made it to the steps of the hotel in one piece. The manager was waiting, his head soaked with sweat.

'Please,' he begged, 'don't come in. I retire this year and it would ruin my reputation.'

Parnes and Kennedy pushed us all past him and entered the foyer. There, a policeman was waiting. 'If this establishment doesn't want your custom, it doesn't have to have it,' he informed us. 'So, you'd better get back in your car and tell your *kaffir* to take you somewhere else – like England!'

So that was that. No room at the inn.

'Well, I don't fancy looking for digs followed by that lot,' I said, as the crowds surged closer to the hotel entrance.

So we had an extraordinary general meeting. We would wait until dark, leave the hotel by the rear exit and go back to the ship. Night fell. The crowds dispersed. Sam picked us up in the alleyway behind the hotel and drove us out of the precincts and back to the docks.

But not to the ship. That wasn't going to happen.

I had a show to do the following night and I wasn't about to turn tail and run. But where could we lie low? I'd docked in enough ports to know that there were always rooms to be had when sailors were around, so we roamed the wharves looking for 'ladies of the night' and the 'Street of a Thousand Hopefuls'. The Steelmen found it a big joke, Kennedy found it sexually arousing, and Parnes felt the shame was worth it to get the show on. As for me, I just wanted to go to bed and concentrate on what I would do tomorrow, if I ever got on to that stage.

The next day Sam arrived at our chosen bordello with Parnes and Kennedy, who had earlier gone undercover to see the hall we were to play that night. 'It's sold out.' Parnes smiled, like a cat with the cream. 'It's going to be great.'

'Tell him about the placards,' Kennedy muttered.

'Oh, there were just a few people outside . . .' Parnes trailed off.

'What kind of placards?' I asked.

'Oh, you know, pieces of board with writing on them.'

'What do they bloody say?'

' "Down with Steele" and "Death to Rock-and-Roll." '

That night, as the hour of the performance neared, Sam slowed at the corner opposite the hall. We could see the placards were still there, carried by a dozen or so adult white males in smart tuxedos with bright red carnations in the buttonholes. We found out later they were local professionals, doctors, lawyers, architects, with wives and children safe at home – until the coming of Beelzebub.

In the auditorium, the Dapper Dozen were slap in the middle of the front row, placards on their laps, arms folded. There wasn't a blink from them during the numbers, and as each song ended they lifted their placards like prophets of doom rather than applauding. But the rest of the audience that night was as enthusiastic as the crowds in the street the day before.

And that was how the tour went on. Durban and Johannesburg had their memorable moments, the last being after my final show. Sam picked us up at the stage door, we stacked our gear in the limousine and settled down for the trip to the docks and home. 'I like you to come say hello to my family,' he said. 'It's on the way, boss, no trouble, eh?'

Half an hour later we arrived in the middle of a clump of what seemed like cowsheds, with the soft glow of oil lamps coming from inside. Sam left the limo and padded towards a huge two-storey wooden building. It was about two in the morning. 'Are you sure they're awake?' I whispered.

'Oh, day awake, boss. C'mon,' he called, and pushed open the double doors of the building. There, in the light of a hundred lanterns, sat a thousand people with million-kilowatt smiles. Suddenly the place exploded into song and rhythm that stay, indelible, in my mind. Was it rehearsed? I couldn't say. Was it coincidence that such a large body played and sang in perfect harmony without losing a beat? Don't ask me!

All I know is that I wish I had a bit of it in my armoury. That night, during the height of apartheid, South African blacks gave me the concert I wasn't allowed to give them, and I'll be for ever grateful.

I got back to England in time to move my family into our new home. It was a lovely residence on the brow of a hill in Catford, a suburb of London. On that first day my brothers and sister chased all over the place, choosing their bedrooms and dragging the dog round the backyard, which had grass instead of Frean Street's mould and trees instead of railway arches. But it was the bathroom that had Darbo entranced. 'It's amazing,' he muttered. 'An inside khazi and a barf you don't 'ang on the rory.' He'd never had such a thing before, so he was going in and out of it as if he'd had a sudden attack of dysentery. My mum kept brewing tea and taking the tray into different rooms. I wondered how she would handle such a change in her life, but the delight on her face and the kiss she gave me in her new kitchen told me I had nothing to worry about.

27

I was contracted to Cohen and Levy for one more picture. I had been a fan of Mark Twain's *The Prince and the Pauper* since I was a kid, so I mapped out a modern version called *The Duke Wore Jeans*. In the retelling of the tale I would play both parts, the Duke and the Young Lad, who, as the Duke's double, would take his place at Court. It wasn't only a chance to act a bit, it was also an opportunity to kick around new musical ideas. I wanted to act a good part and sing show numbers. The love song 'Princess' was great, so were 'What Do You Do' and 'It's All Happening' but one number in particular proved Lionel Bart's talent as a wordsmith. The song was called 'Our Family Tree'. It's a musical soliloquy, telling the story of a noble family's famous forefathers. It was a bastard to sing but I relished it:

> *My great-great-great-grandfather*
> *Came over with a conqueror name of Bill.*
> *He pinched a bow and arrer*
> *From an arrer-seller's barrer,*
> *Shot 'Arold in the eye on 'Astings 'Ill.*
> *What a guy, if looks could kill . . .*

During the shoot of the film, Lionel told me he was writing a musical called *Petticoat Lane* and would I star in it? Then he played the opening number, 'Consider Yourself'. I turned it down!

It was in 1958 that my theatrical mentor Harold Fielding offered me my West End début in his production of Rodgers and Hammerstein's pantomime *Cinderella* to be staged at the Coliseum. I was to play Buttons – not only a great part but an opportunity to sing show tunes. The Guv was very excited about getting the rights to the score and presenting the most lavish spectacle ever seen on the West End stage. He had other plans for me too: 'I want you to go to New York,' he enthused. 'I've arranged for you to visit Chappell's Music Publishing, where they've assembled some extra Rodgers and Hammerstein material. Go over the songs and, if they suit, they're in the show.'

The following week I was there.

New York was busy and bad-tempered. The traffic along Broadway was stuck, horns blared and taxi-drivers yelled at each other in typical New Yorker style. I was already fifteen minutes late and I knew that my meeting at Chappell's was at least four more blocks away so I paid off the cab and legged it. At the entrance to the building a giant of a man was waiting for me. 'So you're the late Mr Steele.' He scowled. Everything about him was enormous: he was six feet plus with shoulders to match, a huge head, and his face was a mass of cracks and crevices. I followed him into the lift. 'You're a singer,' he growled. 'Tell me this, what's more important, the music or the lyrics?'

The question came out of the blue. I shrugged.

'The lyrics,' he answered himself. 'The words are the reason to sing the song in the first place.'

'Yeah, you gotta know what the song's about,' I ventured hopefully.

The lift came to a stop; the giant lumbered out and indicated a corridor. 'It's the second office on the left,' he muttered, and disappeared in the opposite direction.

I knocked on the door and a voice called me in. As I entered, a kindly-looking man was standing by an upright piano. He hobbled towards me on a walking-cane. 'I'm Richard Rodgers, and just in case Oscar got to you first, music is the food of love, the lyrics come second.'

As promised, the Guv had assembled a show of shows, with spectacular sets and costumes by Loudon Sainthill, three revolving stages, an orchestra of forty, a cast of seventy and Oscar Hammerstein. He huddled in the front stalls of the Coliseum every day at rehearsal, picking up on any deviation from his lyrics, in particular in a song of mine, 'A Very Special Day'. One line read, 'her far from flimsy fancy négligé'. I had trouble separating each word because of the music's tempo and it came out as 'her faar frrom fancy gobbledegook'. One fateful day he crossed the vast Coliseum stage in two strides of his seven-league boots, towered above me and thundered, 'You must enunciate each of my words. I trust my knowledge of English grammar affords me that consideration.'

'It docs,' I snapped back. ' "There ain't nuttin' like a dame"!' All went quiet. He pulled his great form up to its full height and bellowed, '*Touché*, Mr Steele.'

Some years later I heard Mrs Hammerstein on a radio talk show. The interviewer mentioned that Jerome Kern had written 'Old Man River'. The lady corrected him: 'My husband wrote "Old Man River",' she said. 'Mr Kern wrote da da dah dah . . .'

On the first day of the pantomime I walked back on to that Coliseum stage with Oscar Hammerstein. Sam 'Mainwaring' Harbour scuttled up from the auditorium to greet Oscar like Uriah Heep. 'Welcome to the finest stage in Europe,' he mumbled – ever so 'umble. 'I'm sure you'll do it proud.'

'And when we're finished with it, you can stick it up your arse!' I said.

That was the first time I saw Oscar smile.

Cinderella has so many fantastic memories for me. A great score, a magnificent orchestra, spectacular sets and . . . Kenneth Williams. He was truly remarkable as an Ugly Sister – not the usual male comic in outrageous makeup, but a reckless spoilt woman, with a bitter façade and hilarious repartee. Onstage he amused; in real life he shocked. One day we were walking down St Martin's Lane when he stopped suddenly, waited for me to go on ahead, then picked up the tails of his overcoat, draped them over his forearms, like a crinoline, and screamed at me, 'Don't walk away, you beast. I'm carrying your child and I'm destitute.'

That was in 1958.

The crowds didn't know him from any other poor soul and I felt a right berk. You couldn't trust him, but you couldn't resist his company.

'We've been invited for lunch at Annie's,' I announced to him one day. 'Now, for Christ's sake, don't swear,' I warned him. 'I don't want her embarrassed.'

His reaction was endearing. 'Tommy, the invitation is quite charming, as I will be. Thank you both.'

So, there we were, sitting quietly in Annie's little kitchen in Great Newport Street. She brought the lamb chops to the table and, apropos nothing, Kenny exclaimed, 'And his cock was *enormous*!'

The chops hit the deck!

Kenny and I hit the street!

He laughed his head off and I swore I'd never trust him again.

The same year brought the musical *Expresso Bongo* to the West End. It was a blatant send-up of my career to date, and instead of accepting it as a compliment I reacted to it like a spoilt child. I told the author, Wolf Mankowitz, that I considered it insulting and libellous. He just laughed and invited me to sue him, adding, 'It'll be good for business!'

The show was a brilliant piece of modern theatre with Paul Scofield playing a Kennedy-type manager and James Kenney portraying the boy, Bongo. Annie was dancing and understudying Millicent Martin, the leading lady. The second time I saw it Annie was playing the lead. She was nervous because she had to kiss Scofield in the second act. The closer the scene came the paler she got. Then it arrived, low lights, seductive music. She was standing downstage in a black négligé. He was approaching her, hunger in his eyes. The music built: I could see her tiny frame stiffen as the predator prepared to pounce. Then, in a crescendo, he snatched her into his arms and . . . pecked her on the cheek. A very kind man, Paul Scofield.

It was during the run of *Bongo* that Annie and I got engaged. It wasn't the wonderful moment it should have been, no press announcement, no party, no photo opportunity, just two kids confessing their love for each other in the secret garden of Kennedy's worst fears. He was paranoid that if the media got hold of the story my career as a rock singer would end. And, for a while, Annie and I had to believe him.

In 1959 I made another film, *Tommy the Toreador*, a musical set in Spain. Lionel Bart, Mike Pratt and I followed the pattern of *The Duke Wore Jeans*, presenting a score of tunes and lyrics that joined the plot without stopping it in its tracks. 'Little White Bull' was one of these, and if ever a song helped make a new career it was that one.

> *Once upon a time there was a Little White Bull,*
> *Very sad because he was a Little White Bull.*
> *All the black bulls called him a coward,*
> *Just 'cos he was white,*
> *Only black bulls go to the bullring*
> *Only black bulls fight!*

Children loved it, so parents brought them to my rock shows just to hear it. It was like Walt Disney said, 'Make things for the young and the adults will come along.' Nothing warms the soul more than the laughter of children.

The director of the film, John Paddy Carstairs, was a chubby, jovial bunch of energy. He was well known in the industry as a competent handler of comedy; he was also a best-selling novelist, a fabulous painter and a whirling dervish. A conversation with him was like playing a pinball machine: as he spoke, his round frame bounced from one side of the room to the other with sheer enthusiasm. During the twelve weeks of filming in Spain, his direction was always precise and without fuss. But, strangely, every evening after a hard slog under the sun, he vanished – no communal dinner, no post-mortem drink, he just thanked everybody and disappeared. Late one night I was roaming the corridors of our hotel when I passed his suite. Light came from under the door, I could see his shadow passing to and fro – it was pure Brontë. Somewhere beyond the portal a dark secret was living a life of turmoil. It wasn't till the picture ended that I heard he had finished a book and painted three canvases during the shoot, but only once did I see him drained of energy.

We were shooting deep in the countryside near Seville when we heard a volley of gunfire. All of a sudden a crowd of local farmers brandishing shotguns surrounded us. They were seriously angry – and not acting! Their leader rattled off a long speech in Spanish at Pepe, our assistant director. Paddy bounced over and offered his hand to the man, but Pepe pulled him away and called to me: 'They want to speak to *el inglés*,' he said.

'Who's that?' I asked.

'You.'

'Me!'

'They think you're an English bullfighter, a man of honour, and they rely on you to settle their grievance.'

'What grievance?'

'It's the food scraps from the location caterers. They say we're giving them to the dogs. They say if you have food to throw away you should give it to the children of the village.'

Paddy waded in again, beaming. 'Of course, if we have offended –'

The farmer pushed him away and growled at me.

'He says to tell *el inglés* that if it happens again they will shoot the dogs,' Pepe explained.

Paddy couldn't operate – he felt so guilty. These were poor folk and he had insulted them. We hardly got any work done for the rest of the day. But the next morning he reappeared ready to film 'Little White Bull'. 'I've got a better idea for shooting the number than we rehearsed,' he said. 'Instead of you doing it alone you sing it to a crowd of kids.'

'Kids?'

'Yeah, about fifty of 'em!'

'But we're in the middle of nowhere! Where are you going to find fifty kids?'

He grinned, his face like a red balloon.

Just before shooting they arrived: farm carts packed full of kids from the *pueblos*, all cheeky little rascals with grubby faces rushing away from their proud parents to hit the set with screams of excitement.

The cameraman called, 'Turning.'

The soundman called, 'Playback.'

Paddy yelled, 'Action,' and we began.

'"Once upon a time there was a Little White Bull . . ."'

During that week of filming, they crowded round the location caterer, as he unloaded a ton and a half of hamburgers into them. Paddy had found a way to forgive himself, the farmers were content and *el inglés* took all the credit.

Paddy wanted a large colourful vista to showcase the film's bullfight finale, and the script called for me to walk in the Parade of the Toreadors, surrounded by matadors, picadors and bandoleros, with yelling crowds in the background and brass bands playing a cross between Reveille and a lament. 'What better way to show it than to put you in a real procession, at a real *corrida*!' Paddy exclaimed, giving his impression of Cecil B. de Mille.

So I went backstage at the Plaza de Toros to wait in the damp sand for the action. It was like that scene from *Spartacus* when the two gladiators sat in the holding cage, watching through the slats in its sides. Bright sunlight flashing, onlookers chatting and death waiting in the wings, all in the name of entertainment. My only concern was my costume and makeup, but the minds of the three real matadors were on more serious things. They knelt in their corners, praying to small saintly effigies that they might seize the day from the Reaper. They were, like me, in their mid-twenties, their faces white, contrasting sharply with their sleek black hair, their eyes blank, no longer mirrors for their souls. And all the while, close by in their dark corrals, the giant angry black bulls roaring, snorting and pawing the sand with their hoofs. They could smell their tormentors and craved revenge. Suddenly a bell tinkled and a priest appeared. He fell to his knees before the gigantic closed doors that led to the ring and the trio of matadors followed, spreading their arms like angel wings. Outside in the arena the drums rolled, the crowds' chatter became a rising cheer, and the priest scampered back into the shadows, the sand rising in the wake of his cassock. The parade lined up, trumpets blared, the great doors opened and we walked into the burning sun.

A host of first nights lay ahead in my career, each with its own worry and fear, but how could they compare to that afternoon in the sun? For the matador it was the moment of truth, life or death; for me, at least 'dying' could only happen on stage.

28

After we'd finished shooting *Tommy the Toreador* it was good to be home with Annie, my family, and my latest record in the hit parade. It was quite a surprise too, because 'Nairobi' was a novelty tune. I had not made it with any hope of big sales: I just felt that instead of *sending* an audience it might *amuse* it. And because of its success I went on to make more records like it. Songs like 'Hiawatha', 'I Puts The Lightie On', 'Wot A Mouth' and, of course, 'Little White Bull'. I put them into my act, too, and got laughs. So much so that I started adding more funny bits, not jokes, just amusing things to bring a giggle. The laughter was like a drug – such a change from screams. But with the laughs came the illusion that I was a comedian.

Later that year when I turned up in Coventry for the *Birthday Show*, I asked the director if I could do some gags in the opening sequence. 'You'd better ask Jimmy,' he replied.

Jimmy James was the finest comedian I have ever seen. He worked front and centre with two stooges. Now, three men talking to each other for twenty minutes may not sound entertaining but, believe me, the theatre shook with laughter at their madcap routine of words. So there I was, in the presence of the great Jimmy James, a man with the looks of an ancient basset hound.

'So, you want laffs. Do you have any jokes?' he chortled, in a dour northern accent.

'No. I thought you might give me some.'

'Okay, here's what you do. I come on and you say, "What did you have for breakfast this morning?" I say, "Haddie." You say, "Finnan?" I say, "No, it was a big piece." We wait for the laff, then exit stage right.'

We ran the routine for a week of rehearsal. At the dress rehearsal,

Always the joker.

the orchestra played, the company made their opening entrances and I came on from stage left, to speak to the great man, centre stage. 'What did you have for breakfast this morning?'

'Cornflakes!' he said, and walked off, leaving me standing there like a rabbit transfixed.

During the teabreak he came to my dressing room. 'Never ask a comic for a laff, son,' he said. 'If you want jokes you get your own and, remember, comedy is the second oldest profession, which, like the first, is being ruined by amateurs.'

Later that evening he brought me a handful of dog-eared pages. 'It's a set of cross-overs.' He smiled. 'Y'know, a-funny-thing-happened-on-the-way-to-the-theatre stuff. I used 'em in the thirties. We'll put them in on opening night, all right?'

One evening after the show I was leaving the stage door late when two girls came out of the shadows. 'What time d'ya call this?' one shouted. 'We've been waiting ages.' She continued berating me as she shoved a cigarette packet and a blunt eyebrow pencil into my hand. 'You'd better sign this.'

I signed and handed it back.

'How am I supposed to read that?' she screeched. 'You'd better do it again,' and pushed it back in my face.

'Don't be so bloody rude,' I said. 'Shove off home.'

'Oh, yeah?' the other girl taunted. 'Well, don't you forget we made you and we can break you!'

Then they were gone, leaving me in a state of shock: they had been insulting – but they were right. My records were selling to an ever-changing teenage market, and every recording success was built on numbers. How many records had I sold today and how many would I sell tomorrow? I didn't want the mathematics of pop. I wanted the majesty of the theatre and I wanted the thrill of it for ever. I was still a newcomer in a business that was built on experience, and if I wanted my peers to believe in my ambitions, and if I wanted to be an entertainer, I would have to show them I was serious.

That night, on my walk back to the hotel, I made the biggest decision of my career.

No more rock records. No more rock.

I knew it was now or never.

Now I would be free to tell the world that I loved Ann Donoughue. I had loved her for three years, she loved me, and we were to be married soon.

Kennedy had blocked our togetherness at every opportunity because he'd never liked the idea of admitting to my fans that I had one special girl. On the other hand Parnes had always said that true love was worth a thousand sighs. But he, too, was a money man and this would not sit well in his pocket.

I arrived at Annie's flat early the following Sunday morning. We sat in her tiny kitchen and went over the events that had taken place outside the Coventry stage door. To me it had been pretty much my road to Damascus; to her, it was not so much prophetic as disappointing. 'Are you sure you aren't just hurt by a couple of silly kids?' she said. 'Maybe you're overreacting . . . Perhaps in time you'll get over it.' But I knew in my heart that my angel had opened another door and I had to go through it.

That afternoon we went home to Catford for Sunday lunch and a family sit–down. There we were: Mum and Dad sitting close enough to cuddle, Sandra on Annie's lap, Colin and Roy playing with the dog, not wanting to be part of something so serious, and me pouring out my heart. Eventually I finished. Now they knew how I felt – but did they understand?

'Oooh, I say,' Mum began. 'They really upset you, didn't they?'

'It's not that, Mum,' I explained. 'It told me –'

'It told you what you already knew,' Dad interrupted. 'Always the sign of a good tip. Mind you,' he added, 'it ain't always wise to bet against the favourite.' He fished for a fag and tweaked Mum's cheek.

I could see she was worried. Here we all were, living in a wonderful new world, something we couldn't have expected in our wildest dreams, and now I seemed to be inviting Fate to come and take it all away. But I knew my mum: if she thought for one moment that I was making a mistake she would find a way to tell me. A word, a look, a shrug. She just smiled at Annie. 'He's got that look in his eye.' She sighed. 'You'll get used to it, love.'

I made the vital telephone calls.

That night I sat with Darbo in the kitchen, listening to cars arriving, doors slamming, the bell ringing, and Mum leading muffled voices into the front room. Then she came to us, her face red with excitement and trepidation. 'They're all here, son. Parnes, Kennedy, Ian Bevan, Harold Fielding, and the man from Decca! They know something's up. I think you'd better go in.'

I made for the front room, my heart beating out of my sweater. I could hear them whispering on the other side of the door. Then, just as I reached for the knob, something pulled me back.

It was Darbo, eyes dancin'. 'Good luck, son,' he whispered.

As I took his outstretched hand I felt the warm half-crown slip into my sweaty palm – and once more I knew that my coming back was more important than my going. I turned the knob and went in.

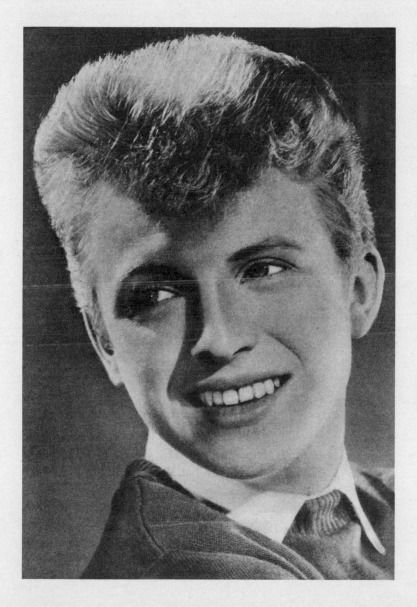

Acknowledgements

The author and publisher wish to thank all copyright-holders for permission to reproduce their work, and the institutions and individuals who helped with the research and supply of materials.

Picture sources

All photographs by Charles Hewitt for *Picture Post* © Getty Images pp. 251 and 288 reproduced by permission of Tommy Steele

Text sources

'Peggy Sue'   Words and music by Allison Petty & Holly © 1957 MPL Communications Inc. Peermusic (UK) Ltd, London. Used by permission

'Sugarbush'   Words and music by Josef Marais © Copyright 1942 & 1952 G. Schirmer Incorporated, USA. G. Schirmer Limited/ Campbell Connelly & Company Limited. Used by permission of Music Sales Limited. All Rights Reserved. International Copyright Secured

'Blue Suede Shoes'   © Carl Perkins Music Inc. (Administered by Wren Music, A Division of MPL Communications Ltd)

'Matilda'   Words and Music by Norman Span © 1957 Colgems-EMI Music Inc/Pickwick Music Corp, USA. Reproduced by permission of EMI Music Publishing Ltd, London WC2H 0QY

He just wanted a decent book to read ...

Not too much to ask, is it? It was in 1935 when Allen Lane, Managing Director of Bodley Head Publishers, stood on a platform at Exeter railway station looking for something good to read on his journey back to London. His choice was limited to popular magazines and poor-quality paperbacks – the same choice faced every day by the vast majority of readers, few of whom could afford hardbacks. Lane's disappointment and subsequent anger at the range of books generally available led him to found a company – and change the world.

'We believed in the existence in this country of a vast reading public for intelligent books at a low price, and staked everything on it'
Sir Allen Lane, 1902–1970, founder of Penguin Books

The quality paperback had arrived – and not just in bookshops. Lane was adamant that his Penguins should appear in chain stores and tobacconists, and should cost no more than a packet of cigarettes.

Reading habits (and cigarette prices) have changed since 1935, but Penguin still believes in publishing the best books for everybody to enjoy. We still believe that good design costs no more than bad design, and we still believe that quality books published passionately and responsibly make the world a better place.

So wherever you see the little bird – whether it's on a piece of prize-winning literary fiction or a celebrity autobiography, political tour de force or historical masterpiece, a serial-killer thriller, reference book, world classic or a piece of pure escapism – you can bet that it represents the very best that the genre has to offer.

Whatever you like to read – trust Penguin.